Workshop on Computational Approaches to Deception Detection 2012

AA005478

Held at the 13th Conference of the European Chapter of the Association for Computational Linguistics (EACL 2012)

Avignon, France
23-27 April 2012

ISBN: 978-1-62276-473-0

Printed from e-media with permission by:

Curran Associates, Inc.
57 Morehouse Lane
Red Hook, NY 12571

CURRAN ASSOCIATES INC. proceedings.com

Some format issues inherent in the e-media version may also appear in this print version.

Printed by Curran Associates, Inc. (2013)

For permission requests, please contact the Association for Computational Linguistics at the address below.

Association for Computational Linguistics
209 N. Eighth Street
Stroudsburg, Pennsylvania 18360

Phone: 1-570-476-8006
Fax: 1-570-476-0860

acl@aclweb.org

Additional copies of this publication are available from:

Curran Associates, Inc.
57 Morehouse Lane
Red Hook, NY 12571 USA
Phone: 845-758-0400
Fax: 845-758-2634
Email: curran@proceedings.com
Web: www.proceedings.com

Introduction

Welcome to the EACL-2012 Workshop on Computational Approaches to Deception Detection. In organizing the workshop, we hope that it will allow us to review the foundations of this relatively new subfield with computational linguistics and encourage more work in the area.

For much of the twentieth century, the fields of psychology and criminal justice have studied the behaviors that might be associated, directly or indirectly, with deception. Three types of behavior have been examined: facial expressions and body movements; vocal behaviors, including prosodic features; and verbal behaviors, including the words and structures that might correlate with deception.

Now is a good time to review the NLP approaches that have been tried, and to consider the foundations and trends, both theoretical and applied, that will enable us to move forward productively. Several areas of natural language processing are ripe to address the vocal and verbal features that might be associated with deception and new approaches may well combine information from all three modalities. A spate of recent NLP papers on the classification of narratives as truthful or deceptive suggests that the field is ready to open up to this promising area. We see some trends in deception research, expressed in the current collection of papers by descriptions of stylometric techniques, sensor technologies, machine learning approaches and models of data collection and processing.

We are pleased at the interest in the workshop represented by the 14 high quality submissions we received. The committee accepted 9 as papers, 3 as posters, and two as demos. Among these are papers that will help us define the parameters of the field, build collections to test approaches, and create novel applications. We are especially pleased by the presence of cross-linguistic studies and the prospect of future work that extends deception research to a range of cross-cultural and cross-linguistic contexts.

We would like to thank EACL for its endorsement of the workshop. We would also like to thank the EACL workshop co-chairs, Kristiina Jokinen and Alessandro Moschitti, for their support. Most of all, we would like to thank our enthusiastic program committee members for their timely and thoughtful review comments. Without them, this workshop on Computational Approaches to Deception Detection could not be implemented successfully.

Organizers:

Eileen Fitzpatrick, Montclair State University
Joan Bachenko, Linguistech Consortium
Tommaso Fornaciari, University of Trento

Program Committee:

Claire Cardie, Cornell University
Rajarathnam Chandramouli, Stevens Institute of Technology
Jeffrey F. Cohn, University of Pittsburgh
Carole Chaski, Institute for Linguistic Evidence
Jeffrey Hancock, Cornell University
Julia Hirschberg, Columbia University
Thomas O. Meservy, University of Arizona
Rada Mihalcea, University of North Texas
Kevin Moffitt, Rutgers Business School
Isabel Picornell, Aston University and QED Ltd.
Massimo Poesio, Univesrity of Essex and University of Trento
Victoria Rubin, University of Western Ontario
Eugene Santos, Dartmouth University
Carlo Strapparava, Fondazione Bruno Kessler (FBK)
Koduvayur Subbalakshmi, Stevens Institute of Technology
Douglas Twitchell, Illinois State University
Scott Weems, Center for Advanced Study of Language, University of Maryland

Invited Speaker:

Daniel Baxter, U.S. Department of Defense

Table of Contents

Linguistic Cues to Deception Assessed by Computer Programs: A Meta-Analysis
Valerie Hauch, Iris Blandón-Gitlin, Jaume Masip and Siegfried Ludwig Sporer 1

"I Don't Know Where He is Not": Does Deception Research yet Offer a Basis for Deception Detectives?
Anna Vartapetiance and Lee Gillam 5

Seeing through Deception: A Computational Approach to Deceit Detection in Written Communication
Ángela Almela, Rafael Valencia-García and Pascual Cantos 15

In Search of a Gold Standard in Studies of Deception
Stephanie Gokhman, Jeff Hancock, Poornima Prabhu, Myle Ott and Claire Cardie 23

Building a Data Collection for Deception Research
Eileen Fitzpatrick and Joan Bachenko 31

On the Use of Homogenous Sets of Subjects in Deceptive Language Analysis
Tommaso Fornaciari and Massimo Poesio 39

Invited Talk: *Current and Future Needs for Deception Detection in a Government Screening Environment*
Daniel Baxter 48

The Voice and Eye Gaze Behavior of an Imposter: Automated Interviewing and Detection for Rapid Screening at the Border
Aaron Elkins, Douglas Derrick and Monica Gariup 49

Let's Lie Together: Co-Presence Effects on Children's Deceptive Skills
Marc Swerts 55

Argument Formation in the Reasoning Process: Toward a Generic Model of Deception Detection
Deqing Li and Eugene Santos 63

Pastiche Detection Based on Stopword Rankings. Exposing Impersonators of a Romanian Writer
Liviu P. Dinu, Vlad Niculae and Maria-Octavia Sulea 72

Making the Subjective Objective? Computer-Assisted Quantification of Qualitative Content Cues to Deception
Siegfried Ludwig Sporer 78

Modelling Fixated Discourse in Chats with Cyberpedophiles
Dasha Bogdanova, Paolo Rosso and Thamar Solorio 86

Detecting Stylistic Deception
Patrick Juola 91

Identification of Truth and Deception in Text: Application of Vector Space Model to Rhetorical Structure Theory
Victoria L. Rubin and Tatiana Vashchilko 97

Workshop Program

Monday, April 23, 2012

Session W3: (9:00) Session 1

Linguistic Cues to Deception Assessed by Computer Programs: A Meta-Analysis
Valerie Hauch, Iris Blandón-Gitlin, Jaume Masip and Siegfried Ludwig Sporer

"I Don't Know Where He is Not": Does Deception Research yet Offer a Basis for Deception Detectives?
Anna Vartapetiance and Lee Gillam

Seeing through Deception: A Computational Approach to Deceit Detection in Written Communication
Ángela Almela, Rafael Valencia-García and Pascual Cantos

Session W3: (11:00) Session 2

In Search of a Gold Standard in Studies of Deception
Stephanie Gokhman, Jeff Hancock, Poornima Prabhu, Myle Ott and Claire Cardie

Building a Data Collection for Deception Research
Eileen Fitzpatrick and Joan Bachenko

On the Use of Homogenous Sets of Subjects in Deceptive Language Analysis
Tommaso Fornaciari and Massimo Poesio

Session W3: (14:00) Session 3

Invited Talk: *Current and Future Needs for Deception Detection in a Government Screening Environment*
Daniel Baxter

The Voice and Eye Gaze Behavior of an Imposter: Automated Interviewing and Detection for Rapid Screening at the Border
Aaron Elkins, Douglas Derrick and Monica Gariup

Monday, April 23, 2012 (continued)

Session W3: (15:30) Session 4: Posters

Let's Lie Together: Co-Presence Effects on Children's Deceptive Skills
Marc Swerts

Argument Formation in the Reasoning Process: Toward a Generic Model of Deception Detection
Deqing Li and Eugene Santos

Pastiche Detection Based on Stopword Rankings. Exposing Impersonators of a Romanian Writer
Liviu P. Dinu, Vlad Niculae and Maria-Octavia Sulea

Making the Subjective Objective? Computer-Assisted Quantification of Qualitative Content Cues to Deception
Siegfried Ludwig Sporer

Modelling Fixated Discourse in Chats with Cyberpedophiles
Dasha Bogdanova, Paolo Rosso and Thamar Solorio

Session W3: (16:30) Session 5

Detecting Stylistic Deception
Patrick Juola

Identification of Truth and Deception in Text: Application of Vector Space Model to Rhetorical Structure Theory
Victoria L. Rubin and Tatiana Vashchilko

Linguistic Cues to Deception Assessed by Computer Programs: A Meta-Analysis

Valerie Hauch,
Justus-Liebig-University of Giessen, Germany
Valerie.Hauch@psychol.uni-giessen.de

Iris Blandón-Gitlin,
California State University, Fullerton, USA
iblandon-gitlin@.fullerton.edu

Jaume Masip, &
University of Salamanca, Spain
jmasip@usal.es

Siegfried L. Sporer
Justus-Liebig-University of Giessen, Germany
Sporer@psychol.uni-giessen.de

Abstract

Research syntheses suggest that verbal cues are more diagnostic of deception than other cues. Recently, to avoid human judgmental biases, researchers have sought to find faster and more reliable methods to perform automatic content analyses of statements. However, diversity of methods and inconsistent findings do not present a clear picture of effectiveness. We integrate and statistically synthesize this literature. Our meta-analyses revealed small, but significant effect-sizes on some linguistic categories. Liars use fewer exclusive words, self- and other-references, fewer time-related, but more space-related, negative and positive emotion words, and more motion verbs or negations than truth-tellers.

1. Introduction

Meta-analytic findings indicate that human judges are just slightly better than chance at discriminating between truths and lies (Bond, & DePaulo, 2006). Likewise, meta-analyses of training programs designed to teach lie detection have shown a small to medium effect size in improving judges' detection accuracy (e.g., Hauch, Sporer, Michael, & Meissner, 2010). Together, these findings suggest that there is a great need to better understand factors involved in deception and find ways to improve its detection. Attempts at these tasks have led researchers to use computer programs to analyze linguistic markers in truthful and deceptive statements. A number of verbal cues have been shown to differ in lies and truths (DePaulo, Lindsay, Malone, Muhlenbruck, Charlton, & Cooper, 2003; Sporer, 2004, Vrij, 2008), and teaching content cues has shown to improve detection more effectively than teaching nonverbal or paraverbal cues (Hauch et al., 2010).

The automatization of lie detection is appealing for at least two reasons. First, such systems can be considered more objective than human judges who are prone to biases (Levine, Park, & McCornack, 1999). Second, online judgments of various deception cues from videos or transcripts can tax the cognitive capacity of judges and lead to time delays and errors. Researchers have used different computer programs for the evaluation of the truth status. Computers can quickly analyze large amounts of text and provide more reliable data. Moreover, the linguistic categories evaluated across studies have varied. In some cases, the direction of the effect for the same linguistic categories has been opposite across studies, or opposite to theoretically-based predictions.

These methodological differences and inconsistencies in findings calls for a quantitative analysis and integration of findings. This is the goal of the present meta-analytic review.

2. Method

After a thorough literature search (*Social Sciences Citation Index*, *PsycInfo*, *Dissertation Abstracts*, *Google Scholar*, and cited reference searches), a large number (k = 84) of published

Proceedings of the EACL 2012 Workshop on Computational Approaches to Deception Detection, pages 1–4,
Avignon, France, April 23 - 27 2012. ©2012 Association for Computational Linguistics

and unpublished studies were located. Studies were only included into the meta-analysis if they meet several inclusion criteria.

2.1 Inclusion Criteria

- Use of computer-based method/program to analyze transcripts in terms of specific linguistic categories;
- Datasets of transcripts (from spoken or written language) which include deceptive and truthful accounts;
- Independence of datasets;
- Specific linguistic categories applied to predict truth status;
- Sufficient statistical data (means and standard deviation separately for lies and truths) to calculate effect sizes (Cohen's d) for specific categories;
- Sources written in English, Spanish, or German.

2.2 Exclusion Criteria

- Psychophysiological methods or use of subjective ratings;
- Ground truth of real statements only established from verdicts or media commentaries (or not established);
- Only computer-analysed linguistic variable is "word count".

Thirteen studies using the Linguistic Inquiry Word Count (LIWC) program (Newman, Pennebaker, Berry, & Richards, 2003) met the inclusion criteria. The initial statistical synopsis of these LIWC studies is presented below. The conference presentation will additionally include the meta-analysis of all other studies meeting the inclusion criteria ($k = 16$) using different computer programs (e.g., General Architecture for Text Extraction (GATE), Agent99-Analyzer, CohMetrix).

2.3 Independent Variables Coded

(a) number of senders, (b) number of linguistic categories used, (c) medium used by senders to provide accounts, (d) type of and valence of the event, (e) senders' motivation, (f) senders' preparation, (g) theory motivating the selection of categories, and (h) predictions for specific categories.

2.4 Dependent Variables Coded

(a) Effect sizes for each category in discriminating between truths and lies, (b) logistic regression or multiple discriminant analysis results for truths, lies, and overall classifications, and (c) reliability of each category.

2.5 Effect Size Measure

In order to compare the results from different studies, we computed the standardized mean difference as an effect size, which is referred to as Cohen's d (1988). Formula for computation of Cohen's d and for the entire meta-analytic procedure can be found in Cooper, Hedges, and Borenstein (2009), Hedges and Olkin (1985), or Lipsey and Wilson (2001). Cohen (1988) cautiously classified the effect size d into three categories of magnitude, with $d = .20$ defined as small, $d = .50$ defined as medium and $d = .80$ defined as large effect sizes. If a specific linguistic cue was more often used during deception than in a true story, d becomes a negative sign. In case a linguistic cue occurred more often during a true than a deceptive story, d becomes a positive value.

3. Results and Discussion

3.1 Descriptive Analyses

Results of $k = 13$ LIWC studies (from 9 sources; $k = 5$ published and $k = 4$ unpublished) revealed that most of the studies ($k = 11$) examined English transcripts, and two either Spanish or Dutch transcripts. In sum, 1143 transcripts were analyzed with a mean of 111 per study, which were given (handwritten or typed ($k = 5$), audiotaped or videotaped ($k = 6$) by 697 individuals. Senders' task was to lie or tell the truth about different topics, and in 38.46% of cases the story's valence was negative. Senders were slightly motivated in 60% of the studies, either receiving a small amount of money or a short verbal instruction.

Before analyzing the transcripts, they were corrected for errors (according to the manual) in 9 studies, whereas the remaining 4 did not report on that. From 68 default linguistic LIWC-categories, on average, 42 dimensions ($k = 10$) were analyzed at times with respect to a theoretical background (e.g., cognitive or emotional approaches, Reality Monitoring). Other categories were excluded due to a low base rate or due to nonsignificant findings.

3.2 Meta-analytic results

Effect sizes with negative signs indicate that liars used the linguistic categories at a higher rate. At this point, 15 categories were chosen with at least $k = 5$ each. Liars tend to use more words expressing negative emotions ($d = -0.111$, $p = .041$, $k = 13$,) and positive emotions ($d = -0.201$, $p = .030$, $k = 5$), more emotional words (Figure 1, $d = -0.187$, $p = .046$, $k = 5$), more motion verbs ($d = -0.141$, $p = .011$, $k = 12$), and more negation words ($d = -0.188$, $p = .010$, $k = 4$).

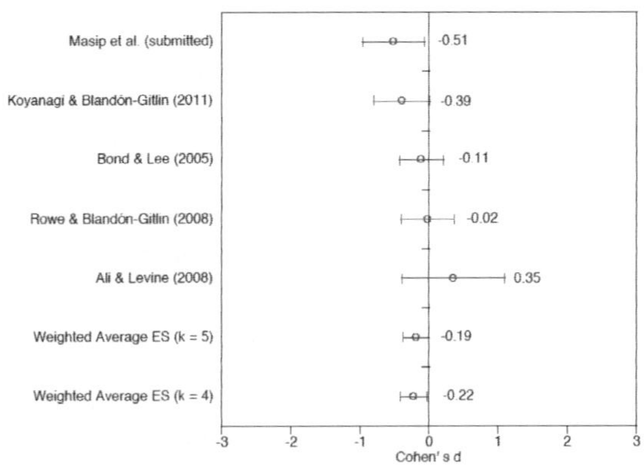

Figure 1. Distribution of Individual Effect Sizes for Emotion Words.

In contrast, truth-tellers make more use of self-references than liars ($d = 0.123$, $p = .044$, $k = 10$), other-references ($d = 0.138$, $p = .019$, $k = 10$), exclusive words (Figure 2, $d = 0.360$, $p = .000$, $k = 12$), slightly more tentative words ($d = 0.172$, $p = .071$, $k = 4$) or time-related words ($d = 0.177$, $p = .057$, $k = 5$) than liars.

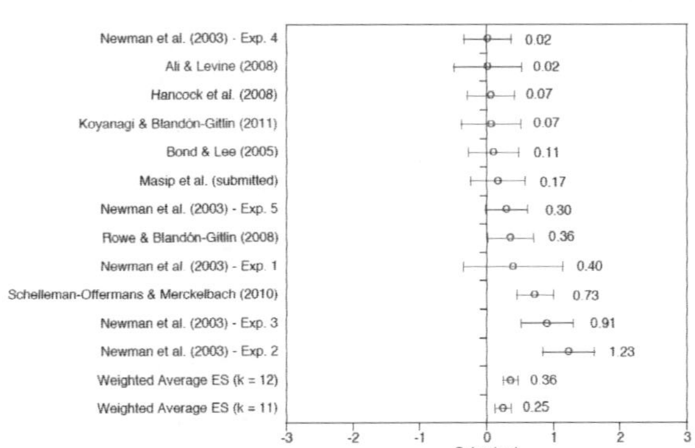

Figure 2. Distribution of Individual Effect Sizes for Exclusive Words.

No significant differences between liars and truth-tellers emerged for word count (Figure 3), the use of sensual and perceptual words, cognitive mechanisms or certainty words.

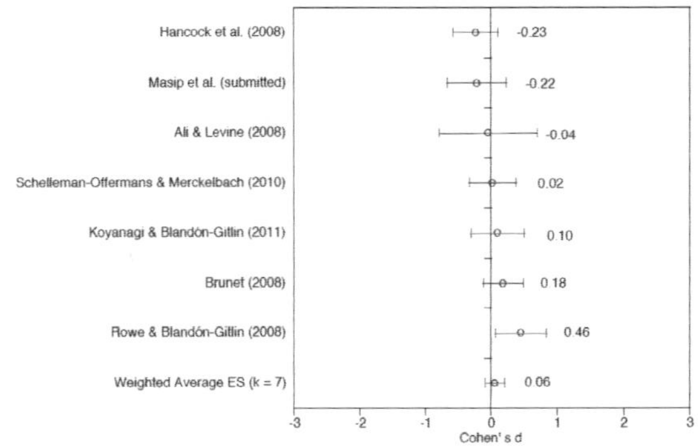

Figure 3. Distribution of Individual Effect Sizes for Word Count.

Although we found significant differences for some categories, we have to be aware of their general small magnitude (mean of all unweighted and absolute *d*s = 0.122, mean of all weighted and absolute *d*s = 0.137) and the small numbers of studies within each meta-analysis.

While some linguistic categories included in LIWC studies do not appear to have empirical precedence (e.g., motion verbs), others do have support from cognitive and emotional theoretical approaches (Bond & Lee, 2005). It has been proposed that truth-tellers make more self-references because they are more likely than liars to associate themselves with the communication. Similarly, whereas truth-tellers are believed to use more exclusive words, signaling more complex explanations of what occurred, liars are believed to engage less in such explanations. Time, affect, space-related, and sensory words are features in accounts based on experienced events as predicted by the Reality Monitoring framework (Mitchell & Johnson, 2000; Sporer, 2004). Negative emotion words are predicted to be higher in deceptive than true statements due to guilt or anxiety associated with the act of deception (Vrij, 2008). These predictions were partially supported by the current meta-analysis.

Further meta-analyses with other computer programs (e.g., Fuller, Biros, Burgoon, Adkins, & Twitchell, 2006; Humpherys, Moffitt, Burns, Burgoon, & Felix, 2011; Zhou, Burgoon, Nunamaker, & Twitchell, 2004) and theoretically driven moderator analyses (e.g., difference between children and adults, the effect of senders' motivation or preparation) will elucidate the linguistic pattern of truth-telling versus lying under specific conditions.

4. References

References marked with an asterisk are included in the meta-analysis.

*Ali, M. & Levine, T. (2008). The language of truthful and deceptive denials and confessions. *Communication Reports, 21,* 82–91.

Bond, C. F., & DePaulo, B. M. (2006). Accuracy of deception judgments. *Personality and Social Psychology Review, 10,* 214-234.

*Bond, G. D., & Lee, A. Y. (2005). Language of lies in prison: Linguistic classification of prisoners' truthful and deceptive natural language. *Applied Cognitive Psychology, 19,* 313-329.

*Brunet, M. K. (2009). *Why bullying victims are not believed: Differentiating between children's true and fabricated reports of stressful and non-stressful events* (Unpublished master's thesis). University of Toronto, Toronto.

Cohen, J. (1988). *Statistical power analysis for the behavioural sciences* (2nd ed.). Hillsdale, NJ: Erlbaum.

Cooper, H., Hedges, L. V., & Valentine, J. C. (Eds.) (2009). *The handbook of research synthesis and meta-analysis* (2nd ed.). New York: Russell Sage Foundation.

DePaulo, B. M., Lindsay, J. J., Malone, B. E., Muhlenbruck, L., Charlton, K., & Cooper, H. (2003). Cues to deception. *Psychological Bulletin, 129,* 74-118.

*Fuller, C., Biros, D. P., Burgoon, J. K., Adkins, M. Twitchell, D. P. (2006). *An analysis of text-based deception detection tools,* Proceedings of the 12th Americas Conference on Information Systems, Acapulco, Mexico.

*Hancock, J. T., Curry, L. E., Goorha, S., & Woodworth, M. (2008). On lying and being lied to: A linguistic analysis of deception in computer-mediated communication. *Discourse Processes, 45,* 1-23.

Hauch, V., Sporer, S. L., Michael, S. W., & Meissner, C. A. (2010, June). *Does training improve detection of deception?* A meta-analysis. Paper presented at the 20th Conference of the European Association of Psychology and Law, Gothenburg, Sweden.

Hedges, L. V., & Olkin, I. (1985). *Statistical methods for meta-analysis.* New York: Academic Press.

*Humpherys, S. L., Moffitt, K. C., Burns, M. B., Burgoon, J. K., Felix, W. F. (2011). Identification of fraudulent financial statements using linguistic credibility analysis. *Decision Support Systems, 50,* 585–594.

*Koyanagi, J. & Blandón-Gitlin, I. (2011, March). *Analysis of Children's Deception with the Linguistic Inquiry and Word Count Approach.* Poster session presented at the 4th International Congress on Psychology and Law / 2011 Annual Meeting of the American Psychology-Law Society, Miami, Florida.

Levine, T. R., Park, H. S., & McCornack, S. A. (1999). Accuracy in detecting truths and lies: Documenting the "veracity effect". *Communication Monographs, 66,* 125-144.

Lipsey, M. W., & Wilson, D. B. (2001). *Practical meta-analysis.* Thousand Oaks: Sage Publications.

*Masip, J., Bethencourt, M., Lucas, G., Sánchez-San Segundo, M., & Herrero, C. (2011). Deception detection from written accounts. *Scandinavian Journal of Psychology.*

Meissner, C. A. & Kassin, S. M. (2002). "He's guilty!": Investigator bias in judgments of truth and deception. *Law and Human Behavior, 26,* 469-480.

Mitchell, K. J., & Johnson, M. K. (2000). Source monitoring: Attributing mental experiences. In E. Tulving, & F. I. M. Craik (Eds.), *The Oxford Handbook of Memory* (pp. 179-195). New York: Oxford University Press.

*Newman, M. L., Pennebaker, J. W., Berry, D. S., & Richards, J. M. (2003). Lying words: Predicting deception from linguistic styles. *Personality and Social Psychology Bulletin, 29,* 665–675.

*Rowe, K. & Blandón-Gitlin, I. (2008, March). *Discriminating true, suggested, and fabricated statements with the Linguistic Inquiry and Word Count approach.* Poster session presented at the Annual Meeting of the American Psychology-Law Society, Jacksonville, Florida.

*Schelleman-Offermans, K., & Merckelbach, H. (2010). Fantasy proneness as a confounder of verbal lie detection tools. *Journal of Investigative Psychology and Offender Profiling, 7,* 247-260.

Sporer, S. L. (2004). Reality monitoring and the detection of deception. In P.-A. Granhag & L. Stromwall (Eds.), *Deception detection in forensic contexts* (pp. 64-102). Cambridge University Press.

Vrij, A. (2008). *Detecting lies and deceit: Pitfalls and opportunities.* Chichester, England: Wiley.

*Zhou, L., Burgoon, J. K., Nunamaker, J. F., & Twitchell, D. (2004). Automating linguistics-based cues for detecting deception in text-based asynchronous computer-mediated communication. *Group Decision and Negotiation, 13,* 81-106.

"I Don't Know Where He is Not": Does Deception Research yet offer a basis for Deception Detectives?

Anna Vartapetiance
Department of Computing
Faculty of Engineering & Physical Sciences
University of Surrey
a.vartapetiance@surrey.ac.uk

Lee Gillam
Department of Computing
Faculty of Engineering & Physical Sciences
University of Surrey
l.gillam@surrey.ac.uk

Abstract

Suppose we wanted to create an intelligent machine that somehow drew its intelligence from large collections of text, possibly involving the processing of collections available on the Web such as Wikipedia. Does past research in deception offer a sufficiently robust basis upon which we might develop a means to filter out texts that are deceptive, either partially or entirely? Could we identify, for example, any deliberately deceptive edits to Wikipedia without consulting the edit history? In this paper, we offer a critical review of deception research. We suggest that there are a range of inconsistencies, contradictions, and other difficulties in recent deception research, and identify how we might begin to address deception research in a more systematic manner.

1 Introduction

Deception exists in various forms, and there can be acceptance in society of deceits of various kinds - typically geared towards personal gain (self-deception) or protection from harm. Often termed "white lies", these differ significantly from those likely to be of a more harmful nature ("black lies") – and here we would include the misrepresentation *of* science and the misrepresentation *as* science; the latter is prevalent in, for example, the advertising of cosmetic products. It remains difficult to discern, however, whether the portrayal by an apparently trusted media outlet of a reported survey of 200 students' responses to a question of whether they thought they had hallucinated after drinking coffee fits the former or the latter when characterized by the BBC as "'Visions link' to coffee intake". Could we rely on existing deception research to enable us to distinguish amongst the presentation of such things on the Web?

In this paper, we present a critical review of deception research, seeking to answer the questions outlined above. We first explain our preferred definition of deception, to disentangle deceptions from lies, and then clarify the impact that selection of a specific medium (text) has on the likely nature of deception. We then review the features that researchers tend to focus on as "cues" that might be used for detecting deception, focus these down to a set as may be detectable in text, and then demonstrate that in treatments of such cues by leading deception researchers there are various inconsistencies, contradictions, and other difficulties. We further consider how we might begin to address these difficulties, such that a more systematic approach might emerge from this research, and what future work might emerge.

2 Defining Deception

To understand deception, it is important to establish what we mean by it. Out of various definitions for deception, (e.g. Masip, Garrido & Herrero, 2004; Hall & Pritchard, 1996; Russow, 1986), we settle on Mahon (2007):

> *"To intentionally cause another person to have or continue to have a false belief that is truly believed to be false by the person intentionally causing the false belief by bringing about evidence on the basis of which*

Proceedings of the EACL 2012 Workshop on Computational Approaches to Deception Detection, pages 5–14,
Avignon, France, April 23 - 27 2012. ©2012 Association for Computational Linguistics

the other person has or continues to have that false belief."

This particular definition leads with intent, which offers contrast with unintended actions as might lead to deception, and also allows us to distinguish from the ill-informed (e.g. believing the Earth is flat, the centre of the Universe, and so on). This also covers a deception occurring through a variety of actions or inactions. Some researchers equate lies with deceptions and have a tendency to use both terms interchangeably (Ekman; 1985; Vrij, 2000); we consider lies to be a specialized subgroup of deception and again highlight Mahon (2008):

> *"... to make a believed-false statement with the intention that that statement be believed to be true".*

Hence, lies have an essentially narrow scope to specific false statements. For example, deliberately pointing the wrong way without saying which way to go would be a deception, but only becomes a lie through a speech act. Being "very economical in his information" and hence concealing the truth leads to a deception but not a lie.

Given these differences between deception and lies, it then becomes interesting to see how actions and statements can be constructed in order to bring about such "false beliefs".

3 Structure and Media

Just like any other human interaction, deceptive behaviour can be divided into two main groups: planned and unplanned. In planned interactions, people have time to think, reflect and compare situations with past experiences. They know or have time to consider knowing the person who they interact with (DePaulo, 2003). In unplanned interactions, people are not necessarily aware of actions that will happen which might need to be controlled. They are not fully aware of the person they will interact with and cannot guarantee the outcomes. Planned deceits should be harder to detect simply because the deceivers have time to rehearse their words and behaviours in order to present the impression of being truthful, or at least being more compelling.

Moreover, the choice of medium for communication can force the type of interaction. Based on Hancock, Thom-Santelli & Ritchie, 2004), deceptiveness in media relates to three main elements:

- **Synchronicity:** to what extent the medium provides real-time communication.
- **Distribution:** whether the people who are communicating are in the same physical location or not.
- **Recordability:** to what extent the medium is automatically recordable.

By knowing these, it is possible to argue that synchronicity and unplanned interactions are directly related, so media that are synchronous should be avoided for planned deceits as they give opportunity to discuss whilst deceivers might need time to rehearse their answers so will prefer asynchronous communication – for example, email.

If we focus on running text as the medium for deception, then while synchronicity and distribution are variable, recordability is certain. This will mean that most of the deceits can be planned well in advance, which could well make their detection somewhat more challenging. On the other hand, social media tends to assume greater degrees of synchronicity and a notionally lower distribution, so deceptions in social media may be more prevalent, not least because there can be less opportunity for planning. The next question, then, is what might be detectable. This brings us to the notion of deception "cues".

4 Deception Detection Cues

Possibilities of being able to formulate human deception processes have encouraged experts in many fields such as psychology, sociology, criminology, philosophy and anthropology to study such behaviour and look for cues as might indicate it. Researchers have shown that telling a lie or being engaged in deceptive behaviour is mentally, emotionally and physically more challenging than being truthful (Miller & Stiff, 1993; Zuckerman et al., 1981; Vrij, Edward, & Bull, 2001). It is emotionally challenging because deceivers might experience Fear and Threat (of being caught), Guilt and Shame (of deceiving someone and of having their trust questioned) or even Duping Delight (joy of deceiving someone). It is mentally challenging as deceivers need to create a story that is believable and consistent and try to remember what they are saying just in case they are questioned later (Miller & Stiff, 1993; Vrij, 2000; Zuckerman et al., 1981; Cody, Marston & Foster, 1984; Vrij, Edward & Bull, 2001). It is physically challenging as deceivers usually attempt to control the physical signs of their deceptive behaviour (Buller & Burgoon 1996; Vrij & Mann, 2004). These attempts can give away a deception or a lie as it is not easy to hide nervousness and fear/guilt, remember lies in detail, and try to manage all of these to make an honest impression at the same time. These will result in behaviours which would be different from truthful actions, giving *Cues of Deception*.

In principle, almost any aspect of human existence that is involved in any action and behaviour may be carrying a cue to flag up deception; that can be eye movement, choice of words, arm positions or motions, and much more. One or many of these may be involved in a single communication, but some will be more specific to certain types of communication. For example, body language and eye movements are mainly considered in synchronous, non-distributed communication, while the structure of the sentence will be more apparent in recordable, distributed communication such as IMs and emails. Such cues can be readily grouped by the *3Vs*:

Visual (Non-verbal): any physical behaviour; reactions, movements, etc in three main groups of Body Acts, Postures and Face.

Vocal: elements that accompany verbal communication with two main features involved: Nature of voice (e.g. Tone/ Tension, Pitch) and Rhythm (e.g. number and the length of pauses).

Verbal: anything said or written (e.g. wording and structure).

However, it is important to note that the physical signs, the visual and vocal, cannot entirely be trusted since specific conditions may lead to similar effects. In certain circumstances, people will be naturally nervous or may feel fear simply because of a situation. For example, in an interview, and in particular in interviews with law enforcement officers, a cue to deception may be out of the normal for *that* interaction, whilst all parts of the interaction could indicate deception in contrast to everyday interactions (Navarro, 2008).

With our interest in detecting deception in text, we focus towards Verbal and in particular Written. Here, the deceiver must make words and patterns of those words do the work, and there is some expectation that this leads to different word usage and language patterns from those that might be considered, somehow, normal.

5 Verbal Deception Detection Cues

Three main types can be defined for verbal deception:

- **Spoken** (e.g. face-to-face, audio and video recordings)
- **Written** (e.g. blogs, emails, testimonies, academic articles)
- **Transcripts of spoken** (phonetic transcription, orthographic transcription)

However, recordings of speech will retain vocal elements which may offer cues, and transcripts may offer surrogates for pauses and retain the speech disfluencies ("ums", "ahs", "like", and so on). Written text, then, is possibly hardest to treat as the visual and vocal cues are missing in contrast to spoken and transcripts (Gupta & Skillicorn, 2006). Interestingly, this suggests that Web content could offer ready source material but with the significant challenge in terms of detecting deception in it as the deceiving authors of written content will have the opportunity to plan.

Many researchers have investigated the lexical, syntactic, and meta-content features of verbal deception, classifying pattern changes into three main dimensions: (1) Quantity; (2) Quality; and (3) Overall impression. *Quantity* changes relate to the number of words being used. *Quality* change focuses on the difference between the word choices but still on a quantitative basis. However, *Overall Impression* is based on human judgment from deceivers' verbalizations including such elements as friendliness, sounding helpful, serious, uncertain, and so on (DePaulo et al. 2003). We discard these cues due to reasons of subjective interpretation - judges (detectors) would need to be trained, and while something seems believable and helpful to one, it may not appear the same to others, and exploring inter-annotator agreement would become a distraction. We focus only on existing measurable cues that should be independent of a judge's training and so could be used by both humans and machines.

For Quantity and Quality measurements there are various hypotheses, different lists of cues, and even different expected changes. We have focussed more on studies where ideas have gained traction through adoption (citation and derivative exploration) by others. For example, Pennebaker's research has been adapted based on its style (word-by-word), accuracy and flexibility for both written and spoken text (e.g. Toma &

Hancock, 2010; Little & Skillicorn, 2008; Gupta and Skillicorn, 2006; Newman et al. 2003).

5.1 Generalized Cues

DePaulo et al. (2003) developed a list of 158 visual, verbal and vocal deception cues, extracted from an analysis of 116 research papers between 1920 and 2001. From this list, we consider just 25 cues to relate to verbal and to be measurable, and these relate to just 10 research papers over that period. The cues include: Response length, Talking time, Cognitive complexity, Unique words, Generalising terms, Self-references, Mutual and group and other references, Word and phrase repetitions, Negative statements and complaints, and Extreme descriptions. As we will show, research since 2001 picks up on several of these cues, and we have been able to use DePaulo's coding system to cross-reference subsequent papers for our own purposes.

5.2 Frequency-based Cues

A number of researchers appear to make use of Pennebaker's Linguistic Inquiry and Word Count (LIWC) system to support their experiments and claims (e.g. Gupta & Skillicorn, 2006; Hancock et al., 2004; Keila & Skillicorn, 2005a, b, c). They mention that the cues defining deception according to Pennebaker involve:

Self-references: Using first-person singular (e.g. me, I and my) shows speaker ownership of a specific statement or event. This offers a link between the reality and the speaker, and as deceivers haven't experienced that link they will reduce the use of self-references.

Negative words: Emotions such as guilt, shame and fear may be attributed to the deceivers' discomfort (DePaulo et al., 2003) and the effect of negative emotions on the pattern of language is believed to lead to an increase in the use of negative words.

Cognitive complexity: As suggested earlier, cognitive complexity increases while deceiving. These effects become apparent in statements in various ways, which directly affects the structure of the text by changes in two main categories. **(a)** Exclusive words: Statements grounded in reality are more likely to highlight the details, including what happened and related reactions. Deceivers, lacking these details, use fewer exclusive words such as except, but, without and exclude. **(b)** Motion/action verbs: A decrease in exclusive words can result in an increase in action verbs (e.g. go, lead, walk) while trying to sound more assuring and convince others to take actions based on their words. Moreover, cognitively, it is easier to use simple and concrete actions in stating false stories compared to fake evaluations and retaining details.

However, we have so far found little evidence that Pennebaker has proposed cues for deception except for one research paper by Newman, Pennebaker, Bery & Richards (Newman et al., 2003). In that paper, the authors discuss cues previously offered by others (that relate to categories in LIWC) along with the reduction in the number of 3rd person pronouns, which contradicts previous studies such as Knapp et al., (1974). Subsequent authors have referenced such articles ambiguously, which may give the impression that LIWC itself offers the answer, for example, Hancock et al., (2004):

> *"[LIWC] was used to create empirically derived statistical profiles of deceptive and truthful communications (Pennebaker et al., 2003),..."*

and Gupta & Skillicorn (2006):

> *"Pennebaker et al. have constructed a model (LIWC) (Newman et al., 2003; Pennebaker, Francis & Booth, 2001) for deception based on the frequencies of various classes of words."*

Whilst LIWC can offer analysis of data, when it comes to understanding the behaviours of cues as might indicate deception by "increase" or "decrease" in frequency, there is no clear baseline. So, to be able to detect any deception, work would first need to be done in order to (1) establish the frequency ranges for different elements within a specific collection, (2) set thresholds of deception per-collection and per cue, and then (3) manually verify those above and below the deception threshold. Relationship to some collection-specific average is unlikely to readily produce appropriate results.

5.3 Category-based Cues

Burgoon and colleagues have categorized deception cues. However, Burgoon and other researchers have, without much explanation that we can find, varied the number of categories and also reported cues in different categories in different research papers (Burgoon & Qin, 2006; Qin et al. 2005; Qin, Burgoon & Nunamaker,

2004; Zhou et al. 2004; Zhou, Burgoon & Twitchell, 2003; Zhou et al. 2003; Burgoon et al. 2003). Indeed, they appear to add, delete, or otherwise emphasise different cues throughout their work. Neither the cues nor the threshold related to their deceptiveness appear stable. A set of cues that have been moved around categories is represented by Black cells in Table 1. Table 1 also shows, in gray, certain inconsistencies amongst these researchers: in Zhou et al. (2004), the number of words, sentences and the emotiveness index show an increase in cases of deception, but in Burgoon et al. (2003) and Zhou et al. (2003) all three are shown to decrease.

Burgoon and colleagues are not alone in offering a categorization; Pennebakers' LIWC categories would be related, modulo terminological and category variation. However, indications of expected values for such cues remain elusive and we only have information that some may rise whilst others may fall.

Cues	(1)		(2)		(3)		(4)		(5)	
Word	**	Q	+**	Q	+**	Q	-**	Q	-**	Q
Sentence	**	Q	+**	Q	+**	Q	-**	Q	-**	Q
Modifiers	-**	U	+**	U	**	Q	**	Q	--	--
First-person singular	--	--	-**	V	+**	V	-**	V	--	--
2nd person pronouns	--	--	-**	U	**	V	--	--	--	--
3rd person pronouns	--	--					**	V	--	--
Temporal details	**	S	+**	S	--	--	-**	S	--	--
Spatial details	**	S			--	--			--	--
Perceptual information	--	--	+**	S	--	--	-**	S	--	--
Affective terms	**	A	--	--	--	--	--	--	-**	S
Positive	--	--	+**	S	+**	A	-**	S	--	--
Negative	--	--	+**	S	+**	A	+**	S	--	--
Emotiveness index	--	--	+**	E	--	--	+**	E	-**	S
Lexical diversity	-**	D	-**	D	-**	D	-**	D	--	--
Redundancy	-**	D	-**	D	**	D	+**	D	--	--
Passive voice	**	V	+ **	V	**	V	+ **	V	--	--
Modal verbs	-**	U	+**	U	**	V	+**	V	--	--
Uncertainty	+***	--	-**	U	**	V	+**	V	--	--
Objectification	--	--	-**	V	+**	V	**	V	--	--
Typo errors	-***	--	+**	I	+**	I	+**	I	--	--

Quantity = Q; Complexity = C; Specificity = S; Affect = A; Activation /Expressiveness = E; Diversity = D; Verbal non-immediacy = V; Informality = I; Uncertainty = U; Vocabulary Complexity = VC; Grammatical Complexity = GC;
(1) Qin et al. 2005 (2) Zhou et al. 2004 (3) Zhou, Burgoon & Twitchell, 2003 (4) Zhou et al. 2003 (5) Burgoon et al. 2003
Gray= inconsistency in expected results; in Black= inconsistency in categories
[**] included, [***] mentioned but not highlighted

Table 1: Contradictions in Cues and Expectation

5.4 Evaluating the Cues

Despite commonalities in what can be and is being studied amongst DePaulo, Pennebaker and Burgoon, it is apparent that there is not yet a clear set of cues with predefined expected values that could be used for detecting verbal deception. However, without clear descriptions of how to interpret results it is also possible that results could have been misreported. To address this, we undertook a number of small experiments – mainly geared around repetition of previous reported experiments – to try to understand the behaviour of deception cues.

Our experiments involve analysis of the BBC article "'Visions link' to coffee intake" mentioned previously (BBC, 2009) with cues identified by Pennebaker, Mehl, and Niederhoffer, 2003), tests on academic work (we used 100 scientific abstracts[1], which we have no reason to believe are deceptive), and attempting to repeat an analysis of the Enron email corpus including the emails of the executives (Keila, and Skillicorn, 2005a, b, c). The latter of these is made all the more difficult by offering three differing numbers of emails for the analysis without

[1] MuchMore Springer Bilingual Corpus, Available at: http://muchmore.dfki.de/resources1.htm

details of how to obtain such a number from the full collection. Unfortunately, experiments all tended to support the idea that it would be hard to detect deception "in the wild" reliably, in part because deceptive texts may "hide" amongst non-deceptive. We can see how this might happen with a simple experiment using the online version of LIWC. We use the 7 LIWC categories, scaled by the maximum of each, for the 100 texts from the MuchMore Springer corpus. We then select the closest matching text (Nearest) from the first 10 to the coffee article (Coffee), and note that values for 5 of these 7 are already close together with differences for social words and cognitive words more marked, but still well within the ranges. A broad grain such as this is unlikely to be revealing.

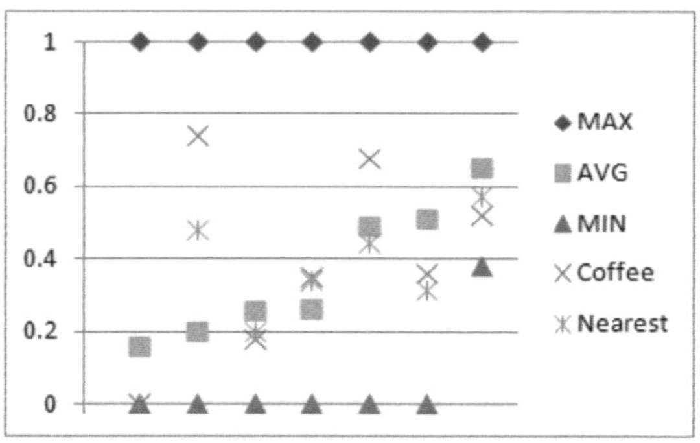

Figure 1: How a deceptive article might hide amongst scientific articles

6 Readability and Deception

Given variation in cues and expectations of values for those cues, a question arises of whether it is possible to provide some common, relatively well understood, and static baseline from which it would be possible to consider the variations in the values. Interestingly, various cues used in relation to deception also feature in Readability research, so might Readability scores offer such a baseline for comparison? Daft and Lengel (1984) argue that more ambiguous texts are more likely to contain deception, and such a claim has been supported in relation to fraudulent financial reports that contained more complex words, while truthful reports attained scores indicating better readability (Moffit and Burns 2009).

Historically, readability measures have been used to indicate the proportion of the population that would be able to understand a given text, but it has become apparent that word familiarity, cognitive load/complexity, cohesion, and other features of text contribute to its readability (Newbold and Gillam, 2010, Gray and Leary, 1935) and are also features considered in deception research.

Given the apparent overlap, we consider whether we might use readability measures to point more reliably to deceptive texts. Table 2 shows the cues covered by Gray and Leary (1935) for readability which are *also* studied as verbal cues for deception, along with expected direction of change in relation to readability and to deception (direction for the latter as suggested in e.g. Burgoon et al., 2003; Qin, Burgoon & Nunamaker, 2004)[2]. Not only is there an overlap with readability, but there seems to be a clear suggestion that more difficult texts are more likely to be deceptive.

Could such a clear relationship hold in practice? What would happen with articles such as "'Visions link' to coffee intake" or the 100 scientific abstracts? Scientific texts, and texts offering a misrepresentation *of* or *as* science, will probably both contain Big words, likely Nouns, may contain Rare words in contrast to general language, and possibly have relatively complex sentences. The writing style is also likely to impact on pronoun count. So systematic differences amongst such values might offer an indication of deception.

Cues	**R**	**D**
Big words	-	+
Nouns	- *	+
Verbs	*	+
Rare words	-	+
Sentence complexity	-	-
Number of first person pronouns	+	-
Number of second person pronouns	+	-
Number of third person pronouns	+	-
Average syllables per word and sentence	-	+
* may vary depending of the structure of the sentence and the words before and after them		

Table 2: Readability features and their relationship to Deception

Also, the online version of LIWC has a category for Big words (those with more than 6 letters). The values from this follow a similar pattern to that of Grade level for readability. For

[2] There are contradictions for expectancy rate for these cues so chosen expectations might conflict with other theories.

Coffee against 10 Springer articles, dividing Big word by Grade level provides the lowest value for the Coffee article. So, it is possible – indicatively, but not conclusively - that the ratio of Big words to Grade level could offer an indication.

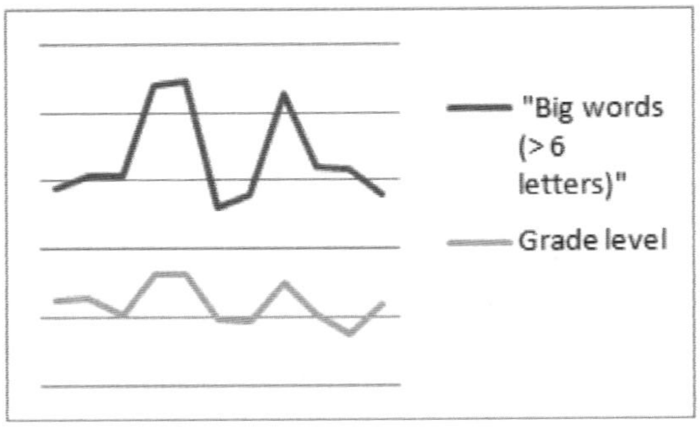

Figure 2: How Big words and Grade level tend towards indicating each other.

To explore how such a relationship might hold in practice, we consider a small experiment comparing essentially the same core content, but which results in different readability scores. A document that has been (supposedly equivalently) translated several times, albeit with particular variations, offers such a basis, and a good example of this is the Bible. We selected the Gospel of John (because it contains first person pronouns) from the following four Bibles[3];

- New International Version (NIV)
- New King James Bible (NKJB)
- King James Bible (KJM) and
- New America Standard Bible (NASB)

We are not suggesting here that the Gospel of John is general representative for the English language, nor that it should be seen to be deceptive per se, but as translations from a single source it should help to demonstrate any effect.

We choose four Pennebaker categories for our comparison. Since we have yet to find complete lists in Pennebaker's research, and since Newman et al. (2003) does not offer up full lists of words, we make use of the list of 86 words cited by Little & Skillicorn (2008) as being from Pennebaker. If all versions of the Gospel of John essentially contain the same content, and if we can use these categories for ranking purposes, we might expect to either see equal ranks for all four cases or to have the old versions (KJM and NASB) flagged up with higher ranks of deceptiveness.

Table 3 shows the scores for First Person (FP), Negative Words (NW), Exclusive Words (EW) and Motion Verbs (MV) as well as Grade Level and Reading ease score which shows, in terms of readability, NIV and NKJB are the better.

	FP	NW	EW	MV	Grade Level	Reading ease[4]
NIV	1.96	0.24	0.53	0.47	6.48	78.11
NKJB	3.44	0.12	1.00	0.48	7.24	77.21
KJB	2.29	0.28	0.69	0.37	7.78	74.48
NASB	2.04	0.23	0.65	0.44	8.38	73.88
Newman et al. (2003): Light Gray Little and Skillicorn (2008): Dark Gray						

Table 3: Variables for Deception and Readability for Gospel of John in 4 Bibles

For Newman et al. (2003), the deceptive text will have:

- Decreased frequency of first person singular pronouns ➔ NIV
- Increased frequency of negative emotion words ➔ KJB
- Decreased frequency of exclusive words ➔NIV
- Increased frequency of action verbs ➔NKJB, NIV

On the other hand, Little and Skillicorn (2008) expect a deceptive text should show:

- Increased frequency of first person singular pronouns ➔ NKJB
- Increased frequency of negative emotion words ➔ KJB
- Increased frequency of exclusive words ➔NKJB
- Increased frequency of action verbs ➔NKJB, NIV

Interestingly, these results suggest that the New International Version (NIV) and New King James Bible (NKJB) score higher on deception despite both having higher readability values. These results contradict what we would expect in relation to readability, further underlining the

[3]Accessed from link below for stability in structure and sentencing http://www.biblegateway.com

[4] Readability values from: http://www.online-utility.org/english/readability_test_and_improve.jsp

difficulty in relying entirely on the existing literature and leading us to question whether even readability offers gain at this grain.

7 Further critique

Analysis and experiments presented above suggest that difficulties emerge from present considerations of cues of deception – at least in relation to verbal deception. However, it is unclear whether this is a consequence of how the cues are being treated, or whether there are other biases which have a telling effect. In much of this research, conclusions have tended to be drawn on specific datasets, many of which are not readily available for inspection or use in repeat experiments by others.

The datasets were usually collected in one of three ways:

Role Playing: some are asked to deceive others (e.g. Hancock et al., 2005; Burgoon et al., 2003; Qin et al., 2005; Qin, Burgoon & Nunamaker, 2004).

Diary Keeping: individuals are asked to document their own interactions (e.g. DePaulo et al., 1996; Hancock et al., 2009; Hancock, Thom-Santelli and Ritchie, 2004). In this type of study, participants take time to document, once per day, their lies and to self score them based on dimensions such as seriousness, feelings while lying, and fear of getting caught.

Obtained as-is: (e.g. Keila, and Skillicorn, 2005a, b, c). Most such studies adopt Pennebaker's approach. This means that any classificatory thresholds have to be manually set and evaluated, via the means of the Human Eyeball.

All three approaches suffer from potential experimental effects. For the first two, it would be important to control for the *Hawthorne effect* which highlights that "observation and studies can change the behaviour of the participants" regardless of whether they should have really changed anything specifically in diary based studies (Franke, 1978; Jones, 1992). We believe during such studies peoples' behaviours might change, intentionally or otherwise. This might be because they become more cautious about perceptions of them by the researchers, want to avoid fear, shame, and so on, or feel uncomfortable with undertaking or documenting such an act. Indeed, the researchers may even be being deceived about the deceptions by the subjects. The third approach leaves the decision regarding actual deceptiveness of the text or statement open to the possibility that the researcher has been "primed by expectations". (Doyen et al., 2012).

8 Conclusion and Future Work

This paper has outlined a critical review of previous research in deception detection in order to assess whether it is possible to create deception detection. On present evidence, whilst there may be various important findings, there are too many areas open to question to believe that such a system could readily be constructed.

We still believe that previous deception detection research has a significant role to play, but many of the difficulties outlined in this paper need to be addressed first. Essentially, this requires a more systematic approach towards both datasets and treatment of cues. The public availability of deception-bearing texts covering different text types and genres would offer an ideal basis for such an approach, and a similar rigour in identifying cues tested, following DePaulo, would be highly beneficial. From this, it may be possible to identify specific cues as worth study in certain genres, whilst of little interest in others – irrespective of their relative frequency of use.

In absence of this, in our own near-future work we intend to explore the extent to which deception cues have also featured in tasks of plagiarism detection. Here, the datasets of PAN, and in particular as relates to authorship attribution and intrinsic plagiarism detection are of interest. Since the act of plagiarism is a deliberate attempt to deceive, such collections – albeit of a synthetic nature - offer us ready grounds for repeatable explorations and might lead to further insights into the general nature of the cues themselves.

9 References

BBC, (2009). Visions link' to coffee intake. *BBC News*. Retrieved 10.0d.2011 from http://news.bbc.co.uk/1/hi/health/7827761.stm

Buller, D.B. and Burgoon, J.K. (1996). Interpersonal Deception Theory. *Communication Theory*, 6, 203-242.

Burgoon, J.K., Blair, J.P., Qin, T., & Nunamaker, J.F., Jr. (2003). Detecting Deception through Linguistic Analysis. *Proceedings of First NSF/NIJ Symposium on Intelligence and Security Informatics (ISI)*, June 2-3, 2003, Tucson, AZ, 91-101.

Burgoon, J.K. & Qin, T. (2006). The Dynamic Nature of Deceptive Verbal Communication. *Journal of Language and Social Psychology*, 25(1), 76-96.

Cody, M.J., Marston, P.J., & Foster, M. (1984). Deception: Paralinguistic and Verbal Leakage. In Bostrom, R.N. and Westley, B.H. (Eds.). *Communication Yearbook 8*. Beverly Hills: Sage. 464-490.

Daft, R.L. & Lengel, R.H. (1984), Information Richness: a New Approach to Managerial Behavior and Organizational Design. In Cummings, L.L. and Staw, B.M. (Eds.). *Research in organizational behaviour*. 6, Homewood, IL: JAI Press, 191-233.

DePaulo, B.M., Lindsay, J.J., Malone, B.E., Muhlenbruck, L., Charlton, K., & Cooper, H. (2003). Cues to Deception. *Psychological Bulletin*, *129*(1), 74-118.

Doyen S , Klein O , Pichon C-L, & Cleeremans A , (2012) Behavioral Priming: It's All in the Mind, but Whose Mind? PLoS ONE 7(1): e29081. doi:10.1371/journal.pone.0029081

Ekman, P. (1985). Telling lies, Clues to Deceit in the Marketplace, Politics, and Marriage. New York: W.W. Norton & Company.

Franke R.C. & Kaul J.D. (1978). The Hawthorne Experiments: First Statistical Interpretation. *American Sociological Review*, 43(5), 623-643.

Gray, W.S. & Leary, B (1935). *What Makes a Book Readable*. Chicago: Chicago University Press.

Gupta, S. & Skillicorn, D. (2006). Improving a Textual Deception Detection Model, *Proceedings of the 2006 Conference of the Center for Advanced Studies on Collaborative Research,* October 16-19, 2006, Toronto, Canada, 1-4.

Hall, H. V. & Pritchard, D.A. (1996). Detecting Malingering and Deception. Forensic Distortion Analysis (FDA). Boca Raton, FL: St. Lucie Press.

Hall, H. V. & Pritchard, D.A. (1996). Detecting Malingering and Deception. Forensic Distortion Analysis (FDA). Boca Raton, FL: St. Lucie Press.

Hancock, J.T., Birnholtz, J., Bazarova, N., Guillory, J., Amos, B., & Perlin, J. (2009). Butler Lies: Awareness, Deception and Design. *Proceedings of the ACM Conference on Human Factors in Computing Systems (CHI 2009).*

Hancock, J.T., Curry, L., Goorha, S. & Woodworth, M.T. (2004). Lies in Conversation: An Examination of Deception Using Automated Linguistic Analysis. *Proceedings of Annual Conference of the Cognitive Science Society,* 26, 534-540.

Hancock, J. T., Curry, L., Goorha, S., & Woodworth, M.T. (2005). Automated linguistic analysis of deceptive and truthful synchronous computer-mediated communication. *Proceedings of the 38th Annual Hawaii International Conference on System Sciences (HICSS-38)*, Los Alamitos, CA: IEEE Press.

Hancock, J.T., Thom-Santelli, J. & Ritchie, T. (2004). Deception and Design: The Impact of Communication Technology on Lying Behaviour. *Proceedings of the Conference on Human Factors in Computing Systems (ACM SIGCHI)*, 129-134.

Jones S.R (1992). Was There a Hawthorne Effect? *American Journal of Sociology*, 98(3), 451-468.

Keila, P.S. & Skillicorn, D.B. (2005a). Detecting Unusual and Deceptive Communication in Email. *Centers for Advanced Studies Conference*, 17-20.

Keila, P.S. & Skillicorn, D.B. (2005b). Detecting unusual email communication. *Proceedings of the 2005 Conference of the Centre for Advanced Studies on Collaborative Research*, 117-125.

Keila, P.S. & Skillicorn, D.B. (2005c). Structure in the Enron Email Dataset. *Computational and Mathematical Organization Theory*, 11(3), 183-199.

Knapp, M.L., Hart, R.P. & Dennis, H.S. (1974). An exploration of deception as a communication construct. *Human Communication Research*, 1, 15-29.

Little, A. & Skillicorn, B. (2008). Detecting Deception in Testimony. *Proceeding of IEEE International Conference of Intelligence and Security Informatics (ISI 2008)*, June 17 - 20, 2008, Taipei, Taiwan, 13-18.

Mahon, J.E. (2007). A Definition of Deceiving. *International Journal of Applied Philosophy, 21,* 181-194.

Mahon, J. E. (2008). Two Definitions of Lying. *International Journal of Applied Philosophy, 22*(2), 211-230.

Moffitt, K. and Burns, M.B. (2009). What Does that Mean? Investigating Obfuscation and Readability Cues as Indicators of Deception in Fraudulent Financial Reports. Proceedings of Americas Confernece on Information Systems (AMCIS 2009) , 399.

Masip, J., Garrido, E. & Herrero, C. (2004).Defining Deception*, Anales de Psicologia*, *20*(1), 147-171.

Miller, G.R. & Stiff, J.B. (1993). *Deceptive Communication*. Newbury Park, CA: Sage.

Navarro, J. (2008). "What Every BODY is Saying: An Ex-FBI Agent's Guide to Speed-Reading People." New York. Harper-Collins.

Newbold, N. & Gillam, L. (2010). The Linguistics of Readability: The Next Step for Word Processing. *Workshop on Computational Linguistics and Writing: Writing Processes and Authoring Aids (CLandW 2010)*. June 6, 2010, Los Angles, 65-72.

Newman, M.L., Pennebaker, J.W., Berry, D.S. & Richards, J.M. (2003). Lying Words: Predicting Deception from Linguistic Styles, *Personality and Social Psychology Bulletin*, 29(5), 665-675.

PAN, (2011), PAN 2011 Lab Uncovering Plagiarism, Authorship and Social Software Misuse, September 19- 22, 2011, Amsterdam.

Pennebaker, J.W., Francis M.E. & Booth, R.J. (2001) *Linguistic inquiry and word count (LIWC)*. Erlbaum Publishers.

Pennebaker, J.W., Mehl, M. & Niederhoffer, K. (2003). Psychological Aspects of Natural Language Use: Our Words, Our Selves. *Annual Review of Psychology*, 54(1), 547-577.

Qin, T., Burgoon, J.K. & Nunamaker, J.F., Jr. (2004). An Exploratory Study on Promising Cues in Deception Detection and Application of Decision Trees. *Proceedings of the 37th Hawaii International Conference on System Sciences*, January 5-8, 2004, Waikoloa, HI, 23-32.

Qin, T., Burgoon, J. K., Blair, J. P., & Nunamaker, J. F. (2005). Modality Effects in Deception Detection and Applications in Automatic-Deception-Detection. *Proceedings of the 38th Annual Hawaii International Conference on System Sciences*, 23-23.

Tausczik, Y.R. & Pennebaker, J.W. (2010). The Psychological Meaning of Words: LIWC and Computerized Text Analysis Methods. *Journal of Language and Social Psychology*, 29, 24-54.

Vrij, A. (2000), *Detecting Lies and Deceit: The Psychology of Lying and its Implications for Professional Practice*. Chichester: John Wiley and Sons.

Vrij, A., Edward, K. & Bull, R. (2001). Stereotypical Verbal and Nonverbal Responses while Deceiving Others. *Personality and Social Psychology Bulletin, 27*, 899-909.

Vrij, A., & Mann, S. (2004). Detecting Deception: The Benefit of Looking at a Combination of Behavioral, Auditory and Speech Content Related Cues in a Systematic Manner. *Group Decision and Negotiation (special deception issue),* 13, 61-79.

Zhou, L., Burgoon, J. K., & Twitchell, D. P. (2003). A longitudinal analysis of language behavior of deception in e-mail. *Proceedings of Intelligence and Security Informatics, 2665,* 102-110.

Zhou, L., Burgoon, J. K. Zhang, D. & Nunamaker, J. F., Jr. (2004). Language Dominance in Interpersonal Deception in Computer-Mediated Communication, *Computers in Human Behavior*, 20(3), 381-402.

Zhou, L., Twitchell, D.P., Tiantian, Q., Burgoon, J.K. & Nunamaker, J.F., Jr. (2003). An Exploratory Study into Deception Detection in Text-Based Computer-Mediated Communication. *Proceedings of the 36th Annual Hawaii International Conference on System Sciences*, January 6-9, 2010, Waikoloa, HI, 10-19.

Zuckerman, M, DePaulo, B.M. & Rosenthal, R. (1981). Verbal and Nonverbal Communication of Deception, In Berkowitz, L.(Ed.). *Advances in Experimental Social Psychology, 14*, 1-59.

Seeing through deception: A computational approach to deceit detection in written communication

Ángela Almela
English Department
Universidad de Murcia
30071 Murcia (Spain)
angelalm@um.es

Rafael Valencia-García
Faculty of Computer Science
Universidad de Murcia
30071 Espinardo, Murcia (Spain)
valencia@um.es

Pascual Cantos
English Department
Universidad de Murcia
30071 Murcia (Spain)
pcantos@um.es

Abstract

The present paper addresses the question of the nature of deception language. Specifically, the main aim of this piece of research is the exploration of deceit in Spanish written communication. We have designed an automatic classifier based on Support Vector Machines (SVM) for the identification of deception in an *ad hoc* opinion corpus. In order to test the effectiveness of the LIWC2001 categories in Spanish, we have drawn a comparison with a Bag-of-Words (BoW) model. The results indicate that the classification of the texts is more successful by means of our initial set of variables than with the latter system. These findings are potentially applicable to areas such as forensic linguistics and opinion mining, where extensive research on languages other than English is needed.

1 Introduction

Deception has been studied from the perspective of several disciplines, namely psychology, linguistics, psychiatry, and philosophy (Granhag & Strömwall, 2004). The active role played by deception in the context of human communication stirs up researchers' interest. Indeed, DePaulo et al. (1996) report that people tell an average of one to two lies a day, either through spoken or written language. More recently, researchers in the field of opinion mining have become increasingly concerned with the detection of the truth condition of the opinions passed on the Internet (Ott et al., 2011). This issue is particularly challenging, since the researcher is provided with no information apart from the written language itself.

Within this framework, the present study attempts to explore deception cues in written language in Spanish, which is something of a novelty. The remainder of this paper is organized as follows: in Section 2, related work on the topic is summarized; in Section 3, we explain our methodology for analyzing data; in Section 4, the evaluation framework and experimental results are presented and discussed; Section 5 presents the results from a Bag-of-Words model as a basis for comparison; finally, in Section 6 some conclusions and directions for further research are advanced.

2 Related Work

There are verbal cues to deception which form part of existing verbal lie detection tools used by professional lie catchers and scholars (Vrij, 2010). Automated linguistic techniques have been used to examine the linguistic profiles of deceptive language in English. Most commonly, researchers have used the classes of words defined in the Linguistic Inquiry and Word Count or LIWC (Pennebaker et al., 2001), which is a text analysis program that counts words in psychologically meaningful categories. It includes about 2,200 words and word stems grouped into 72 categories relevant to psychological processes. It has been used to study issues like personality (Mairesse et al., 2007), psychological adjustment (Alpers et al., 2005), social judgments (Leshed et al., 2007), tutoring dynamics (Cade et al., 2010), and mental health (Rude et al., 2004). The validation of the lexicon contained in its dictionary has been performed by means of a comparison of human ratings of a large number of written texts to the rating obtained through their LIWC-based analyses.

LIWC was firstly used by Pennebaker's group for a number of studies on the language of deception, being the results published in Newman et al. (2003). For their purposes, they

Proceedings of the EACL 2012 Workshop on Computational Approaches to Deception Detection, pages 15–22,
Avignon, France, April 23 - 27 2012.

collected a corpus with true and false statements through five different studies. In the first three tests, the participants expressed their true opinions on abortion, as well as the opposite of their point of view. The first study dealt with oral language, hence the videotaping of the opinions, whereas in the second and the third ones the participants were respectively asked to type and handwrite their views. In the fourth study, the subjects orally expressed true and false feelings about friends, and the fifth one involved a mock crime in which the participants had to deny any responsibility for a fictional theft. The texts were analyzed using the 29 variables of LIWC selected by the authors. Of the 72 categories considered by the program, they excluded the categories reflecting essay content, any linguistic variable used at low rates, and those unique to one form of communication (spoken vs. written language). The values for these 29 variables were standardized by converting the percentages to z scores so as to enable comparisons across studies with different subject matters and modes of communication. For predicting deception, a logistic regression was trained on four of the five subcorpora and tested on the fifth, which entails a fivefold cross-validation. The authors obtained a correct classification of liars and truth-tellers at a rate of 67% when the topic was constant and a rate of 61% overall. However, in two of the five studies, the performances were not better than chance. Finally, the variables that were significant predictors in at least two studies were used to evaluate simultaneously the five tests, namely self-reference terms, references to others, exclusive words, negative emotion elements and motion words. The reason for the poor performance in some of the studies may lie with the mixing of modes of communication, since, as stated by Picornell (2011), the verbal cues to deception in oral communication do not translate across into written deception and *vice versa*.

From this study, LIWC has been used in the forensic field mainly for the investigation of deception in spoken language. There are some early studies in this line which are concerned with the usefulness of this software application as compared to Reality Monitoring technique (RM). First, Bond and Lee (2005) applied LIWC to random samples from a corpus comprising lie and truth oral statements by sixty-four prisoners, only taking into consideration the variables selected by Newman et al. (2003) for the global evaluation. Overall, the results show that deceivers score significantly lower than truth-tellers as regards sensory details, but outstandingly higher for spatial aspects. The latter finding goes against previous research in RM theory; such is the case of Newman et al. (2003), where these categories did not produce significant results. Apart from this difference, both studies share common ground: despite considering RM theory, the authors did not perform manual RM coding on their data. Thus, they do not draw a direct comparison between the effectiveness of automatic RM coding through LIWC software and manual RM coding.

This gap in research was plugged by Vrij et al. (2007). Their hypothesis predicts that LIWC coding is less successful than manual RM coding in discriminating between deceivers and truth-tellers. In order to test this theory, they collected a corpus of oral interviews of 120 undergraduate students. Half the participants were given the role of deceivers, having to lie about a staged event, whereas the remainder had to tell the truth about the action. The analysis revealed that RM distinguished between truth-tellers and deceivers better than Criteria-Based Content Analysis. In addition, manual RM coding offered more verbal cues to deception than automatic coding of the RM criteria. There is a second experiment in this study assessing the effects of three police interview styles on the ability to detect deception, but the results will not be presented here because the subject lies outside the scope of this work.

More recently, Fornaciari & Poesio (2011) conducted a study on a corpus of transcriptions of oral court testimonies. This work presents two main novelties: first, the object of study is a sample of spontaneously produced language instead of statements uttered *ad hoc* or laboratory-controlled; moreover, it deals with a language other than English, namely Italian. The authors continue Newman et al.'s (2003) idea of a method for classifying texts according to their truth condition instead of simply studying the language in descriptive terms, their analysis unit being the utterance instead of the text. Their ultimate aim is a comparison between the efficiency of the content-related features of LIWC and surface-related features, including the frequency and use of function words or of certain n-grams of words or parts-of-speech. They used five kinds of vectors, taking the best features from their experiment, from Newman et al. (2003), and all LIWC categories. The latter results in slightly better performance than the former, but they do not obtain a statistically significant difference.

LIWC has been also used for the investigation of deception in written language. Curiously enough, research in this line has been approached by computational linguists and not from the perspective of the forensic science. First, Mihalcea & Strapparava (2009) used LIWC for *post hoc* analysis, measuring several language dimensions on a corpus of 100 false and true opinions on three controversial topics – the design of the questionnaire is indeed similar to Newman et al.'s (2003). As a preliminary experiment, they used two ML classifiers: Naïve Bayes and Support Vector Machines, using word frequencies for the training of both algorithms, similar to a Bag-of-Words model. They achieved an average classification performance of 70%, which is significantly higher than the 50% baseline. On the basis of this information, they calculate a dominance score associated with a given word class inside the collection of deceptive texts as a measure of saliency. Then, they compute word coverage, which is the weight of the linguistic item in the corpora. Thus, they identify some distinctive characteristics of deceptive texts, but purely in descriptive terms.

In this strand of research, Ott et al. (2011) used the same two ML classifiers. For their training, apart from comparing lexically–based deception classifiers to a random guess baseline, the authors additionally evaluated and compared two other computational approaches: genre identification through the frequency distribution of part-of-speech (POS) tags, and a text categorization approach which allows them to model both content and context with n-gram features. Their ultimate aim is deceptive opinion spam, which is qualitatively different from deceptive language itself. Findings reveal that n-gram-based text categorization is the best detection approach; however, a combination of LIWC features and n-gram features perform marginally better.

These studies deal with written language as used in an asynchronous means of communication. In contrast, Hancock and his group explore deceptive language in synchronous computer-mediated communication (CMC), in which all participants are online at the same time (Bishop, 2009). Specifically, they use chat rooms. In their first study using LIWC, Hancock et al. (2004) explored differences between the sender's and the receiver's linguistic style across truthful and deceptive communication. For the analysis, they selected the variables deemed relevant to the hypotheses, namely word counts, pronouns, emotion words, sense terms, exclusive words, negations, and question frequency. Results showed that, overall, when participants told lies, they used more words, a larger amount of references to others, and more sense terms. Hancock et al. (2008) reported rather similar results from a comparable experiment. Apart from this, they introduced the element of motivation, and observed that motivated liars tended to avoid causal terms, while unmotivated liars increased their use of negations.

All these studies coincide in their exploration of a set of variables, but none of them take LIWC features as a whole for the automatic classification of both sublanguages on written statements. Furthermore, researchers usually take the language of deception as a whole, ignoring the particular features which may distinguish a speaker from the others, assuming that everybody lies similarly. Instead of comparing each individual sample of deceptive language to its corresponding control text, the whole set of statements labelled as "false" is contrasted with the set comprising "true" statements. This idiolectal comparison certainly permeates the practitioner lore within the forensic context, hence its interest for computational approaches to deception detection. It is worth noticing that the main disadvantage of a corpus of "authentic" language is precisely the difficulty to obtain a control sample of language in which the same speaker tells the truth for the sake of comparison.

3 Methodology

A framework based on a classifier using a Support Vector Machine (SVM) has been developed in order to detect deception in our opinion corpus. SVM have been applied successfully in many text classification tasks due to their main advantages: first, they are robust in high dimensional spaces; second, any feature is relevant; third, they are robust when there is a sparse set of samples; finally, most text categorization problems are linearly separable (Saleh et al., 2011).

We have used LIWC to obtain the values for the categories for the subsequent training of the abovementioned classifier. This software application provides an efficient method for studying the emotional, cognitive, and structural components contained in language on a word by word basis (Pennebaker et al., 2001). The LIWC internal dictionary comprises 2,300 words and word stems classified in four broad dimensions: standard linguistic processes, psychological processes, relativity, and personal concerns. Each word or word stem defines one or more of the 72 default word categories. The selection of words attached to language categories in LIWC has been made after hundreds of studies on psychological behaviour (Tausczik & Pennebaker, 2010). Within the first dimension, linguistic processes, most categories involve function words and grammatical information. Thus, the selection of words is straightforward; such is the case of the category of articles, which is made up of nine words in Spanish: *el, la, los, las, un, uno, una, unos,* and *unas*. Similarly, the third dimension, relativity, comprises a category concerning time which is clear-cut: past, present and future tense verbs. Within the same dimension, that is also the case of the category space, in which spatial prepositions and adverbs have been included. On the other hand, the remaining two dimensions are more subjective, especially those denoting emotional processes within the second dimension. These categories indeed demanded human judges to make the lexical selection. For all subjective categories, an initial list of word candidates was compiled from dictionaries and thesauruses, being subsequently rated by groups of three judges working independently. Finally, the fourth dimension involves word categories related to personal concerns intrinsic to the human condition. As mentioned above, this dimension has been often excluded in deception detection studies, on the basis that it is too content-dependent (Hancock et al., 2004, 2008; Newman et al., 2003).

Table 1 provides an illustrative summary of the list of the dictionary categories –a comprehensive account is included in Pennebaker et al. (2001:17-21), and the equivalences in Spanish can be found in Ramírez-Esparza et al. (2007:37-39).

We implemented our experiments using the Weka library (Bouckaert et al., 2010). We applied a linear SVM with the default configuration set by the tool. In order to train the classifier, the corpus is divided into true and false samples. For their analysis, we have considered the attributes of each dimension of LIWC previously described.

I. Standard linguistic dimension	**II. Psycholog. processes**	**III. Relativity**	**IV. Personal concerns**
Total pronouns	Causation	Space	Job or work
% words captured by the dictionary	Affective or emotional processes	Inclusive	Physical states and functions
% words longer than six letters	Negative emotions	Exclusive	Religion
Word Count	Cognitive processes	Time	Money and financial issues
First-person singular	Positive emotions	Motion verbs	Leisure activity

Table 1: Summary of the variables used in LIWC2001

Several classifiers have been obtained by using the categories of each dimension. For each classifier a tenfold cross-validation has been done and all sets have an equal distribution between true and false statements.

4 Evaluation framework and results

To study the distinction between true and deceptive statements, a corpus with explicit labelling of the truth condition associated with each statement was required. For this purpose, the design of the questionnaire for the compilation of the corpus was similar to that used by Mihalcea and Strapparava (2009). Data were produced by 100 participants, all of them native speakers of Peninsular or European Spanish. We focused on three different topics: opinions on homosexual adoption, opinions on bullfighting, and feelings about one's best friend. A similar corpus was used in (Almela, 2011), where a pilot study on the discriminatory power of lexical choice was conducted. The corpus used included a further data set, comprising opinions on a good teacher. However, it was disregarded in the present paper, since the statements were shorter and false and true opinions were not so effectively differentiated.

As mentioned above, since it was not spontaneously produced language, it was deemed necessary to minimize the effect of the observer's paradox (Labov, 1972) by not explaining the ultimate aim of the research to the participants. Furthermore, they were told that they had to make sure that they were able to convince their partners on the topics that they were lying about, so as to have them highly motivated, like in Hancock et al. (2008).

For the first two topics (homosexual adoption and bullfighting), we provided instructions that asked the contributors to imagine that they were taking part in a debate, and had 10-15 minutes available to express their opinion about the topic. First, they were asked to prepare a brief speech expressing their true opinion on the topic. Next, they were asked to prepare a second brief speech expressing the opposite of their opinion, thus lying about their true beliefs about the topic. In both cases, the guidelines asked for at least 5 sentences and as many details as possible. For the other topic, the contributors were asked to think about their best friend, including facts and anecdotes considered relevant for their relationship. Thus, in this case, they were asked to tell the truth about how they felt. Next, they were asked to think about a person they could not stand, and describe it as if s/he were their best friend. In this second case, they had to lie about their feelings towards these people. As before, in both cases the instructions asked for at least 5 detailed sentences.

We collected 100 true and 100 false statements for each topic, with an average of 80 words per statement. We made a manual verification of the quality of the contributions. With three exceptions, all the other entries were found to be of good quality. Each sample was entered into a separate text file, and misspellings were corrected. Each of the 600 text files was analyzed using LIWC to create the samples for the classifier. It is worth noting that the version used was LIWC2001, since this is the one which has been fully validated for Spanish across several psycholinguistics studies (Ramírez-Esparza et al., 2007). The whole LIWC output was taken for the experiment, except for two categories classified as experimental dimensions (Pennebaker et al., 2001): nonfluencies (e.g. *er, hm, umm*) and fillers (e.g. *blah, Imean, youknow*), since they are exclusive to spoken language. The remaining experimental dimension, swear words, has been included for our purposes in the first dimension, linguistic processes, since this is the case for the subsequent version of this software application.

The results from the ML experiment are shown in Table 2. In the first column, the number of LIWC dimensions used for each classifier is indicated. For example, 1_2_3_4 indicates that all the dimensions have been used in the experiment, and 1_2 indicates that only the categories of dimensions 1 and 2 have been used to train the classifier. The scores shown in the table stand for the F-measure, the weighted harmonic mean of precision and recall.

	Homos. adoption	**Bullfight.**	**Best friend**	**Total**
1	0.638	0.679	0.763	0.683
1_2	0.709	0.655	0.83	0.736
1_2_3	0.698	0.669	0.835	0.726
1_2_3_4	0.718	0.66	0.845	0.734
1_2_4	0.728	0.63	0.83	0.728
1_3	0.64	0.68	0.82	0.701
1_3_4	0.657	0.643	0.815	0.698
1_4	0.631	0.651	0.738	0.661
2	0.678	0.624	0.78	0.702
2_3	0.724	0.619	0.81	0.723
2_3_4	0.724	0.609	0.81	0.716
2_4	0.703	0.59	0.78	0.706
3	0.62	0.62	0.695	0.616
3_4	0.611	0.595	0.684	0.654
4	0.506	0.525	0.639	0.561

Table 2: Results from the experiment

Findings reveal that the dimension which performs overall best irrespective of topic is the second one, psychological processes (70.2%). This is in line with Newman et al.'s (2003) study, where belief-oriented vocabulary, such as *think*, is more frequently encountered in truthful statements, since the presence of real facts does not require truth-related words for emphasis. As regards dominant words in deceptive texts, previous research highlights words related to certainty, probably due to the speaker's need to explicitly use truth-related words as a means to conceal the lies (Bond & Lee, 2005; Mihalcea & Strapparava, 2009). Furthermore, according to Burgoon et al. (2003), other feature associated with deception is the high frequency of words denoting negative emotions. All these categories are included in the second dimension, and their discriminant potential in deception detection is indeed confirmed in our classification experiment.

The first dimension shows a relatively high performance (68.3%). It is natural that it should be so, bearing in mind the considerable potential of function words, which constitutes a substantial part of standard linguistic dimensions. The prime importance of these grammatical elements has been widely explored, not only in computational linguistics, but also in psychology. As Chung and Pennebaker (2007:344) have it, these words "can provide powerful insight into the human psyche". Variations in their usage has been associated to sex, age, mental disorders such as depression, status, and deception.

On the contrary, and as could be expected from previous research (Newman et al., 2003; Fornaciari & Poesio, 2011), the fourth dimension is the least discriminant on its own. The reason may lie with the weak link of the topics involved in the questionnaire with the content of the personal concerns categories. However, there is not much difference with the third one, relativity –just 0.055 points in the total score.

As shown in Table 2, when the classifier is trained with certain combinations of dimensions, its performance improves noticeably. This finding is supported by Vrij's words: "a verbal cue uniquely related to deception, akin to Pinocchio's growing nose, does not exist. However, some verbal cues can be viewed as weak diagnostic indicators of deceit" (2010:103). In this way, it seems clear that a combination of lexical features is more effective than isolated categories. The grouping of the first two dimensions is remarkably successful (73.6%). Nevertheless, the addition of the other two dimensions to this blend is counterproductive, since it makes the score worse instead of improving it, probably due to their production of noise. No doubt that the factor loadings of the four dimensions play a considerable part in here. Overall, considering the total column, it seems as if the fourth LIWC dimension is the one cutting off the discrimination power.

Furthermore, it is worth noting that the results from the classification with these dimensions are strongly dependent on the topics of each subcorpus. The topics dealt with in our experiment show that the interaction of LIWC dimensions 1_2_4 (72.8%) and 2_3 (72.4%) discriminates better true-false statements related to homosexuality adoption; similarly, the dimension selection of LIWC's 1_2_3 (83.5%) and 1_2_3_4 (84.5%) perform very positively regarding the topics related to the best friend. On the opposite scale, we get that true-false statements on bullfighting (1_3: 68%) are more difficult to tell apart by means of LIWC dimensions. A plausible explanation emerges here: when speakers refer to their best friend, they are likelier to be emotionally involved in the experiment; they are not just telling an opinion on a topic which is alien to them, but relating their personal experience with a dear friend and lying about a person they really dislike. This personal involvement is probably reflected on the linguistic expression of deception.

5 Comparison with a Bag-of-Words model

In this section we will present the results from a Bag-of-Words (BoW) representation to provide a basis for comparison with our methodology. In this model, a text is represented as an unordered collection of words, disregarding any linguistic factor such as grammar, semantics or syntax (Lewis, 1998). It has been successfully applied to a wide variety of NLP tasks such as document classification (Joachims, 1998), spam filtering (Provost, 1999), and opinion mining (Dave et al., 2003). However, its basis is not too sophisticated, hence the average scores obtained through this method in terms of precision and recall. Table 3 shows the F-measure scores obtained with this model.

Homosexual adoption	**Bullfighting**	**Best friend**	**Total**
0.654	0.622	0.715	0.648

Table 3: Results from the BoW model

Curiously enough, despite the simplicity of the method, in the first two topics the F-measure scores are better than the ones obtained from 6 LIWC dimension combinations (see Table 2). When it comes to the third topic, the number is reduced to three combinations. It is worth noting that, although the scores in this topic are good with this simple model (71.5%), a difference of 13 points is observed in the application of our methodology to this subcorpus.

By means of the comparison, it is confirmed that the third and the fourth dimensions, both on their own and combined, perform worse than the BoW model, irrespective of the topic involved. However, as regards the total results, the only two scores which are worse than BoW's are derived from the application of these two dimensions on their own. Specifically, there is a difference of 8.8 points between the best total result from our experiment (73.6%), obtained by means of the combination of the two first dimensions, and the total result from BoW (64.8%). This means that, in general terms, the classification by means of our variables is more successful than with the BoW model.

6 Conclusions and further research

In the present paper we have showed the high performance of an automatic classifier for deception detection in Spanish written texts, using LIWC psycholinguistic categories for its training. Through an experiment conducted on three data sets, we have checked the discriminatory power of the variables as to their truth condition, being the two first dimensions, linguistic and psychological processes, the most relevant ones.

For future research in this line, we will undertake a contrastive study of the present results and the application of the same methodology to an English corpus, in order to identify possible structural and lexical differences between the linguistic expression of deceit in both languages.

Acknowledgements

This work has been supported by the Spanish Government through project SeCloud (TIN2010-18650). Ángela Almela is supported by Fundación Séneca scholarship 12406/FPI/09.

References

Ángela Almela. 2011. Can lexical choice betray a liar? Paper presented at the *I Symposium on the Sociology of Words*, University of Murcia, Spain.

Georg W. Alpers, Andrew Winzelberg, Catherine Classen, Heidi Roberts, Parvati Dev, Cheryl Koopman, and Barr Taylor. 2005. Evaluation of computerized text analysis in an Internet breast cancer support group. *Computers in Human Behavior*, 21, 361-376.

Jonathan Bishop. 2009. Enhancing the understanding of genres of web-based communities: The role of the ecological cognition framework. *International Journal of Web-Based Communities*, 5(1), 4-17.

Gary D. Bond and Adrienne Y. Lee. 2005. Language of lies in prison: Linguistic classification of prisoners' truthful and deceptive natural language. *Applied Cognitive Psychology*, 19, 313-329.

Remco R. Bouckaert, Eibe Frank, Mark A. Hall, Geoffrey Holmes, Bernhard Pfahringer, Peter Reutemann, and Ian H. Witten. 2010. WEKA-experiences with a java open-source project. *Journal of Machine Learning Research*, 11:2533-2541.

Judee K. Burgoon, J. P. Blair, Tiantian Qin, and Jay F. Nunamaker. 2003. Detecting deception through linguistic analysis. *Intelligence and Security Informatics*, 2665, 91–101.

Whitney L. Cade, Blair A. Lehman, and Andrew Olney. 2010. An exploration of off topic conversation. In *Human Language Technologies: The 2010 Annual Conference of the North American Chapter of the Association for Computational Linguistics*, 669-672. Association for Computational Linguistics.

Cindy Chung and James W. Pennebaker. 2007. The psychological functions of function words. In K. Fiedler (Ed.), *Social Communication*, 343–359. New York: Psychology Press.

Malcolm Coulthard. 2004. Author identification, idiolect, and linguistic uniqueness. *Applied Linguistics*, 25(4):431-447.

Kushal Dave, Steve Lawrence, and David M. Pennock. 2003. Mining the peanut gallery: opinion extraction and semantic classification of product reviews. In *Proceedings of the 12th international conference on World Wide Web (WWW '03)*. ACM, New York, NY, USA, 519-528.

Bella M. DePaulo, Deborah A. Kashy, Susan E. Kirkendol, Melissa M. Wyer, and Jennifer A. Epstein. 1996. Lying in everyday life. *Journal of Personality and Social Psychology*, 70: 979-995.

Tommaso Fornaciari and Massimo Poesio. 2011. Lexical vs. Surface Features in Deceptive Language Analysis. In Wyner, A. and Branting, K. *Proceedings of the ICAIL 2011 Workshop Applying Human Language Technology to the Law*.

Pär A. Granhag and Leif A. Strömwall. 2004. *The detection of deception in forensic contexts*. Cambridge, UK: Cambridge University Press.

Jeffrey T. Hancock, Lauren E. Curry, Saurabh Goorha, and Michael T. Woodworth. 2004. Lies in conversation: an examination of deception using automated linguistic analysis. *Annual Conference of the Cognitive Science Society*. Taylor and Francis Group, Psychology Press, Mahwah, NJ.

Jeffrey T. Hancock, Lauren E. Curry, Saurabh Goorha, S. & Michael T. Woodworth. 2008. On lying and being lied to: A linguistic analysis of deception in computer-mediated communication. *Discourse Processes*, 45, 1-23.

Thorsten Joachims. 1998. Text categorization with support vector machines: learning with many relevant features. *ECML-98*, 137-142.

William Labov. 1972. *Sociolinguistic Patterns*. Oxford, UK: Blackwell.

Gilly Leshed, Jeffrey T. Hancock, Dan Cosley, Poppy L. McLeod, and Geri Gay. 2007. Feedback for guiding reflection on teamwork practices. In *Proceedings of the GROUP'07 conference on supporting group work*, 217-220. New York: Association for Computing Machinery Press.

David D. Lewis. 1998. Naive (Bayes) at Forty: The Independence Assumption in Information Retrieval. In *Proceedings of ECML-98, 10th European Conference on Machine Learning*, Springer Verlag, Heidelberg, Germany.

François Mairesse, Marilyn A. Walker, Matthias Mehl, and Roger K. Moore. 2007. Using linguistic cues for the automatic recognition of personality in conversation and text. *Journal of Artificial Intelligence Research*, 30(1), 457-500.

Rada Mihalcea and Carlo Strapparava. 2009. The Lie Detector: Explorations in the Automatic Recognition of Deceptive Language. In *Proceedings of the Association for Computational Linguistics (ACL-IJCNLP 2009)*, Singapore, 309-312.

Matthew L. Newman, James W. Pennebaker, Diane S. Berry, and Jane M. Richards. 2003. Lying words: Predicting deception from linguistic styles. *Personality and Social Psychology Bulletin*, 29: 665-675.

Myle Ott, Yejin Choi, Claire Cardie, and Jeffrey T. Hancock. 2011. Finding deceptive opinion spam by any stretch of the imagination. In *Proceedings of ACL*, 309-319.

James W. Pennebaker, Martha E. Francis, and Roger J. Booth. 2001. *Linguistic Inquiry and Word Count.* Erlbaum Publishers, Mahwah, NJ.

James W. Pennebaker, Cindy K. Chung, Molly Ireland, Amy L. Gonzales, and Roger J. Booth, R. J. 2007. *The development and psychometric properties of LIWC2007*. LIWC.net, Austin, TX.

Isabel Picornell. 2011. The Rake's Progress: Mapping deception in written witness statements. Paper presented at the *International Association of Forensic Linguists Tenth Biennial Conference*, Aston University, Birmingham, United Kingdom.

Jefferson Provost. 1999. Naive-bayes vs. rule-learning in classifcation of email. *Technical Report AI-TR-99-284*, University of Texas at Austin, Artificial Intelligence Lab.

Nairán Ramírez-Esparza, James W. Pennebaker, and Florencia A. García. 2007. La psicología del uso de las palabras: Un programa de computadora que analiza textos en español [The psychology of word use: A computer program that analyzes texts in Spanish]. *Revista Mexicana de Psicología*, 24, 85-99.

Stephanie S. Rude, Eva-Maria Gortner, and James W. Pennebaker. 2004. Language use of depressed and depression-vulnerable college students. *Cognition and Emotion*, 18, 1121-1133.

Mohammed Rushdi-Saleh, Maria Teresa Martín-Valdivia, Arturo Montejo Ráez, and Luis Alfonso Ureña López. 2011. Experiments with SVM to classify opinions in different domains. *Expert Systems with Applications,* 38(12):14799-14804.

Yla R. Tausczik and James W. Pennebaker. 2010. The psychological meaning of words: LIWC and computerized text analysis methods. *Journal of Language and Social Psychology*, 29, 24-54.

Aldert Vrij. 2010. *Detecting lies and deceit: Pitfalls and opportunities.* 2nd edition. John Wiley and Sons, Chischester, UK.

Aldert Vrij, Samantha Mann, Susanne Kristen, and Ronald P. Fisher. 2007. Cues to deception and ability to detect lies as a function of police interview styles. *Law and human behavior*, 31(5), 499-518.

In Search of a Gold Standard in Studies of Deception

Stephanie Gokhman[1], **Jeff Hancock**[1,3], **Poornima Prabhu**[2], **Myle Ott**[2], **Claire Cardie**[2,3]
Departments of Communication[1], Computer Science[2], and Information Science[3]
Cornell University, Ithaca, NY 14853
{sbg94,jth34,pmp67,mao37,ctc9}@cornell.edu

Abstract

In this study, we explore several popular techniques for obtaining corpora for deception research. Through a survey of traditional as well as non-gold standard creation approaches, we identify advantages and limitations of these techniques for web-based deception detection and offer crowdsourcing as a novel avenue toward achieving a gold standard corpus. Through an in-depth case study of online hotel reviews, we demonstrate the implementation of this crowdsourcing technique and illustrate its applicability to a broad array of online reviews.

1 Introduction

Leading deception researchers have recently argued that verbal cues are the most promising indicators for detecting deception (Vrij, 2008) while lamenting the fact that the majority of previous research has focused on nonverbal cues. At the same time, increasing amounts of language are being digitized and stored on computers and the Internet — from email, Twitter and online dating profiles to legal testimony and corporate communication. With the recent advances in natural language processing that have enhanced our ability to analyze language, researchers now have an opportunity to similarly advance our understanding of deception.

One of the crucial components of this enterprise, as recognized by the call for papers for the present workshop, is the need to develop corpora for developing and testing models of deception. To date there has not been any systematic approach for corpus creation within the deception field. In the present study, we first provide an overview of traditional approaches for this task (Section 2) and discuss recent deception detection methods that rely on non-gold standard corpora (Section 3). Section 4 introduces novel approaches for corpus creation that employ crowdsourcing and argues that these have several advantages over traditional and non-gold standard approaches. Finally, we describe an in-depth case study of how these techniques can be implemented to study deceptive online hotel reviews (Section 5).

2 Traditional Approaches

The deception literature involves a number of widely used traditional methods for gathering deceptive and truthful statements. We classify these according to whether they are *sanctioned*, in which the experimenter supplies instructions to individuals to lie or not lie, or *unsanctioned* approaches, in which the participant lies of his or her own accord.

2.1 Sanctioned Deception

The vast majority of studies examining deception employ some form of the sanctioned lie method. A common example is recruiting participants for a study on deception and randomly assigning them to a lie or truth condition. A classic example of this kind of procedure is the original study by Ekman and Friesen (1969), in which nurses were required to watch pleasant or highly disturbing movie clips. The nurses were instructed to indicate that they were watching a pleasing movie, which required the nurses watching the disturbing clips to lie about their current emotional state.

In another example, Newman et. al. (2003) ask

Proceedings of the EACL 2012 Workshop on Computational Approaches to Deception Detection, pages 23–30,
Avignon, France, April 23 - 27 2012.

participants about their beliefs concerning a given topic, such as abortion, and then instruct participants to convince a partner that they hold the opposite belief.

Another form of sanctioned deception is to instruct participants to engage in some form of mock crime and then ask them to lie about it. For example, in one study (Porter and Yuille, 1996), participants were asked to take an item, such as a wallet, from a room and then lie about it afterwards. The mock crime approach improves the ecological validity of the deception, and makes it the case that the person actually did in fact act a certain way that they then must deny.

2.1.1 Advantages and Limitations

The advantages are obvious for these sanctioned lie approaches. The researcher has large degrees of experimental control over what the participant lies about and when, which allows for careful comparison across the deceptive and nondeceptive accounts. Another advantage is the relative ease of instructing participants to lie vs. trying to identify actual (but unknown) lies in a dialogue.

The limitations for this approach, however, are also obvious. In asking participants to lie, the researcher is essentially giving permission to the person to lie. This should affect the participant's behavior as the lie is being conducted at the behest of a power figure, essentially acting out their deception. Indeed, a number of scholars have pointed out this problem (Frank and Ekman, 1997), and have suggested that unless high stakes are employed the paradigm produces data that does not replicate any typical lying situation. *High stakes* refers to the potential for punishment if the lie is detected or reward if the lie goes undetected. Perhaps because of the difficulty in creating high-stakes deception scenarios, to date there are few corpora involving high-stakes lies.

2.2 Unsanctioned Deception

Unsanctioned lies are those that are told without any explicit instruction or permission from the researcher. These kinds of lies have been collected in a number of ways.

2.2.1 Diary studies and surveys

Two related methods for collecting information about unsanctioned lies are diary studies and survey studies. In diary studies participants are asked on an ongoing basis (e.g., every night) to recall lies that they told over a given period (e.g., a day, a week) (DePaulo et al., 1996; Hancock et al., 2004). Similarly, recent studies have asked participants in national surveys how often they have lied in the last 24 hours (Serota et al., 2010).

One important feature of these approaches is that the lies have already taken place, and thus they do not share the same limitations as sanctioned lies. There are several drawbacks, however, especially given the current goal to collect deception corpora. First, both diary studies and survey approaches require self-reported recall of deception. Several biases are likely to affect the results, including under-reporting of deception in order to reduce embarrassment and difficult-to-remember deceptions that have occurred over the time period. More importantly, this kind of approach does not lend itself to collecting the actual language of the lie, for incorporation into a corpus: people have a poor memory for conversation recall (Stafford and Sharkey, 1987).

2.2.2 Retrospective Identification

One method for getting around the memory limitations for natural discourse is to record the discourse and ask participants to later identify any deceptions in their discourse. For instance, one study (Feldman and Happ, 2002) asked participants to meet another individual and talk for ten minutes. After the discussion, participants were asked to examine the videotape of the discussion and indicated any times in which they were deceptive. More recently, others have used the retrospective identification technique on mediated communication, such as SMS, which produces an automatic record of the conversation that can be reviewed for deception (Hancock, 2009). Because this approach preserves a record that the participant can use to identify the deception, this technique can generate data for linguistic analysis. However, an important limitation, as with the diary and survey data, is that the researcher must assume that the participant is being truthful about their deception reporting.

2.2.3 Cheating Procedures

The last form of unsanctioned lying involves incentivizing participants to first cheat on a task and to then lie when asked about the cheating behavior. Levine et al. (2010) have recently used this approach, which involved students performing a trivia quiz. During the quiz, an opportunity to cheat arises where some of the students will take the opportunity. At this point, they have not yet lied, but, after the quiz is over, all students are asked whether they cheated by an interviewer who does not know if they cheated or not. While most of the cheaters admit to cheating, a small fraction of the cheaters deny cheating. This subset of cheating denials represents real deception.

The advantages to this approach are threefold: (1) the deception is unsanctioned, (2) it does not involve self-report, and (3) the deceptions have objective ground-truth. Unfortunately, these kinds of experiments are extremely effort-intensive given the number of deceptions produced. Only a tiny fraction of the participants typically end up cheating and subsequently lying about the cheating.

2.2.4 Limitations

While these techniques have been useful in many psychology experiments, in which assessing deception detection has been the priority rather than corpus creation, they are not very feasible when considering obtaining corpora for large-scale settings, e.g., the web. Furthermore, the techniques are limited in the kinds of contexts that can be created. For instance, in many cases, e.g., deliberate posting of fake online reviews, subjects can be both highly incentivized to lie and highly concerned with getting caught. One could imagine surveying hotel owners as to whether they have ever posted a fake review—but it would seem unlikely that any owner would ever admit to having done so.

3 Non-gold Standard Approaches

Recently, alternative approaches have emerged to study deception in the absence of gold standard deceptive data. These approaches can typically be broken up into three distinct types. In Section 3.1, we discuss approaches to deception corpus creation that rely on the *manual annotation* of deceptive instances in the data. In Section 3.2, we discuss approaches that rely on *heuristic methods* for deriving approximate, but non-gold standard deception labels. In Section 3.3, we discuss a recent approach that uses assumptions about the effects of deception to identify examples of deception in the data. We will refer to the latter as the *unlabeled* approach to deception corpus creation.

3.1 Manual Annotations of Deception

In Section 2.2, we discussed diary and self-report methods of obtaining gold standard labels of deception. Recently, work studying deceptive (fake) online reviews has suggested using manual annotations of deception, given by third-party human judges.

Lim et al. (2010) study deceptive product reviews found on Amazon.com. They develop a sophisticated software interface for manually labeling reviews as deceptive or truthful. The interface allows annotators to view all of each user's reviews, ranked according to dimensions potentially of importance to identifying deception, e.g., whether the review is duplicated, whether the reviewer has authored many reviews in a single day with identical high or low ratings, etc.

Wu et al. (2010a) also study deceptive online reviews of TripAdvisor hotels, manually labeling a set of reviews according to "suspiciousness." This manually labeled dataset is then used to validate eight proposed characteristics of deceptive hotels. The proposed characteristics include features based on the number of reviews written, e.g., by first-time reviewers, as well as the review ratings, especially as they compare to other ratings of the same hotel.

Li et al. (2011) study deceptive product reviews found on Epinions.com. Based on user-provided helpfulness ratings, they first draw a subsample of reviews such that the majority are considered to be unhelpful. They then manually label this subsample according to whether or not each review seems to be fake.

3.1.1 Limitations

Manual annotation of deception is problematic for a number of reasons. First, many of the same challenges that face manual annotation efforts in other domains also applies to annotations of deception. For example, manual annotations can be expensive to obtain, especially in large-scale settings, e.g., the web.

Most seriously however, is that human ability to detect deception is notoriously poor (Bond and DePaulo, 2006). Indeed, recent studies have confirmed that human agreement and deception detection performance is often no better than chance (Ott et al., 2011); this is especially the case when considering the overtrusting nature of most human judges, a phenomenon referred to in the psychological deception literature as a truth bias (Vrij, 2008).

3.2 Heuristically Labeled

Work by Jindal and Liu (2008) studying the characteristics of untruthful (deceptive) Amazon.com reviews, has instead developed an approach for *heuristically* assigning approximate labels of deceptiveness, based on a set of assumptions specific to their domain. In particular, after removing certain types of irrelevant "reviews," e.g., questions, advertisements, etc., they determine whether each review has been duplicated, i.e., whether the review's text heavily overlaps with the text of other reviews in the same corpus. Then, they simply label all discovered duplicate reviews as untruthful.

Heuristic labeling approaches do not produce a true gold-standard corpus, but for some domains may offer an acceptable approximation. However, as with other non-gold standard approaches, certain behaviors might have other causes, e.g., duplication could be accidental, and just because something is duplicated does not make the original (first) post deceptive. Indeed, in cases where the original review is truthful, its duplication is not a good example of deceptive reviews written from scratch.

3.3 Unlabeled

Rather than develop heuristic labeling approaches, Wu et al. (2010b) propose a novel strategy for evaluating hypotheses about deceptive hotel reviews found on TripAdvisor.com, based on distortions of popularity rankings. Specifically, they test the *Proportion of Positive Singletons* and *Concentration of Positive Singletons* hypotheses of Wu et al. (2010a) (Section 3.1), but instead of using manually-derived labels they evaluate their hypotheses by the corresponding (distortion) effect they have on the hotel rankings.

Unlabeled approaches rely on assumptions about the effects of the deception. For example, the approach utilized by Wu et al. (2010b) observing distortion effects on hotel rankings, relies on the assumption that the goal of deceivers in the online hotel review setting is to increase a hotel's ranking. And while this may be true for positive hotel reviews, it is likely to be very *untrue* for fake negative reviews intended to defame a competitor. Indeed, great care must be taken in making such assumptions in unlabeled approaches to studies of deception.

4 Crowdsourcing Approaches

As with traditional sanctioned deception approaches (see Section 2.1), one way of obtaining gold standard labels is to simply create gold standard deceptive content. Crowdsourcing platforms are a particularly compelling space to produce such deceptive content: they connect people who request the completion of small tasks with workers who will carry out the tasks. Crowdsourcing platforms that solicit small copywriting tasks include Clickworker, Amazon's Mechanical Turk, Fiverr, and Worth1000. Craigslist, while not a crowdsourcing platform, also promotes similar solicitations for writing. In the case of fake online reviews (see Section 5), and by leveraging platforms such as Mechanical Turk, we can often generate gold standard deceptive content in contexts very similar to those observed in practice.

Mihalcea and Strapparava (2009) were among the first to use Mechanical Turk to collect deceptive and truthful opinions — personal stances on issues such as abortion and the death penalty. In particular, for a given topic, they solicited one truthful and one deceptive stance from each Mechanical Turk participant.

Ott et al. (2011) have also used Mechanical Turk to produce gold standard deceptive content. In particular, they use Mechanical Turk to generate a dataset of 400 *positive* (5-star), gold standard deceptive hotel reviews. These were combined with 400 (positive) *truthful* reviews covering the same set of hotels and used to train a learning-based classifier that could distinguish deceptive vs. truthful positive reviews at 90% accuracy levels. The truthful reviews were mined directly from a well-known hotel review site. The Ott et al. (2011) approach for collecting the gold standard deceptive reviews is the subject of the case study below.

5 Case Study: Crowdsourcing Deceptive Reviews

To illustrate in more detail how crowdsourcing techniques can be implemented to create gold standard data sets for the study of deception, we draw from the Ott et al. (2011) approach that crowdsources the collection of **deceptive positive hotel reviews** using Mechanical Turk. The key assumptions of the approach are as follows:

- We desire a **balanced data set**, i.e., equal numbers of truthful and deceptive reviews. This is so that statistical analyses of the data set won't be biased towards either type of review.

- The truthful and deceptive reviews should **cover the same set of entities**. If the two sets of reviews cover different entities (e.g., different hotels), then the language that distinguishes truthful from deceptive reviews might be attributed to the differing entities under discussion rather than to the legitimacy of the review.

- The resulting data set should be of a **reasonable size**. Ott et al. (2011) found that a dataset of 800 total reviews (400 truthful, 400 deceptive) was adequate for their goal of training a learning-based classifier.

- The truthful and deceptive reviews should **exhibit the same valence, i.e., sentiment**. If the truthful reviews gathered from the online site are *positive* reviews, the deceptive reviews should be positive as well.

- More generally, the **deceptive reviews should be generated under the same basic guidelines as governs the generation of truthful reviews**. E.g., they should have the same length constraints, the same quality constraints, etc.

Step 1: Identify the set of entities to be covered in the *truthful* reviews. In order to define a set of desirable reviews, a master database, provided by the review site itself, is mined to identify the most commented (most popular) entities. These are a good source of *truthful* reviews. In particular, previous work has hypothesized that popular offerings are less likely to be targeted by spam (Jindal and Liu, 2008), and therefore reviews for those entities are less likely to be deceptive—enabling those reviews to later comprise the truthful review corpus. The review site database typically divides the entity set into subcategories that differ across contexts: in the case of hotel reviews the subcategories might refer to cities, or in the case of doctor reviews subcategories might refer to specialties. To ensure that enough reviews of the entity can be collected, it may be important to select subcategories that themselves are popular. The study of Ott et al. (2011), for example, focused on reviews of hotels in Chicago, IL, gathering positive (i.e., 5-star) reviews for the 20 most popular hotels.

Step 2: Develop the crowdsourcing prompt. Once a set of entities has been identified for the deceptive reviews (Step 1), the prompt for Mechanical Turk is developed. This begins with a survey of other solicitations for reviews within the same subcategory through searching Mechanical Turk, Craigslist, and other online resources. Using those solicitations as reference, a scenario can then be developed that will be used in the prompt to achieve the appropriate (in our case, *positive*) valence. The result is a prompt that mimics the vocabulary and tone that "Turkers" (i.e., the workers on Mechanical Turk) may find familiar and desirable.

For example, the prompt of Ott et al. (2011) read: *Imagine you work for the marketing department of a hotel. Your boss asks you to write a fake review for the hotel (as if you were a customer) to be posted on a travel review website.* ***The review needs to sound realistic and portray the hotel in a positive light.*** *Look at their website if you are not familiar with the hotel.* (A link to the website was provided.)

Step 3: Attach appropriate warnings to the crowdsource solicitation. It is important that warnings are attached to the solicitation to avoid gathering (and paying for) reviews that would invalidate the review set for the research. For example, because each review should be written by a different person, the warning might disallow coders from performing multiple reviews; forbid any form of plagiarism; require that reviews be "on topic," coherent, etc. Finally, the prompt may inform the Turker that this exercise is for academic purposes only and will not be posted online, however, if such a notice is presented before the review is written and submitted, the resulting lie may be overly sanctioned.

Step 4: Incorporate into the solicitation a means for gathering additional data. Append to the end of the solicitation some mechanism (e.g., Mechanical Turk allows for a series of radio buttons) to input basic information about age, gender, or education of the coder. This allows for post-hoc understanding of the demographic of the participating Turkers. Ott et al. (2011) also supply a space for comments by the workers, with an added incentive of a potential bonus for particularly helpful comments. Ott et al. (2011) found this last step critical to the iterative process for providing insights from coders on inconsistencies, technical difficulties, and other unforeseen problems that arise in the piloting phase.

Step 5: Gather the deceptive reviews in batches. The solicitation is then published in a small pilot test batch. In Ott et al. (2011), each pilot requested ten (10) reviews from unique workers. Once the pilot run is complete, the results are evaluated, with particular attention to the comments, and is then iterated upon in small batches of 10 until there are no technical complaints and the results are of desired experiment quality.

Once this quality is achieved, the solicitation is then published as a full run, generating 400 reviews by unique workers. The results are manually evaluated and cleaned to ensure all reviews are valid, then filtered for plagiarism. The resulting set of gold standard online deceptive spam is then used to train the algorithm for deceptive positive reviews.

5.1 Handling Plagiarism

One of the main challenges facing crowdsourced deceptive content is identifying plagiarism. For example, when a worker on Mechanical Turk is asked to write a deceptive hotel review, that worker may copy an available review from various sources on the Internet (e.g., TripAdvisor). These plagiarized reviews lead to flaws in our gold standard. Hence there arises a need to detect such reviews and separate them from the entire review set.

One way to address this challenge is to do a manual check of the reviews, one-by-one, using online plagiarism detection web services, e.g., plagiarisma.net or searchenginereports.net. The manual process is taxing, especially when there are reviews in large numbers (as large as 400) to be processed. This illustrates a need to have a tool which automates the detection of plagiarized content in Turker submissions. There are several plagiarism detection softwares which are widely available in the market. Most of them maintain a database of content against which to check for plagiarism. The input content is checked against these databases and the content is stored in the same database at the end of the process. Such tools are an appropriate fit for detecting plagiarized content in term papers, course assignments, journals etc. However, online reviews define a separate need which checks for plagiarism against the content available on the web. Hence the available software offerings are not adequate.

We implemented a command line tool using the Yahoo! BOSS API, which is used to query sentences on the web. Each of the review files is parsed to read as individual sentences. Each sentence is passed as a query input to the API. We introduce the parameters, n and m, defined as:

1. Any sentence which is greater than n words is considered to be a "long sentence" in the application usage. If the sentence is a "long sentence" and the Yahoo! BOSS API returns no result, we query again using the first n words of the sentence. Here n is a configurable parameter, and in our experiments we configured $n = 10$.

2. A sentence that is commonly used on the web can return many matches, even if it was not plagiarized. Thus, we introduce another parameter, m, such that if the number of search results returned by the Yahoo! BOSS API is greater than m, then the sentence is considered common and is ignored. Our observations indicate that such frequently used sentences are likely to be short. For example: "We are tired," "No room," etc. For our usage we configured $m = 30$.

We consider a sentence to be plagiarized if the total number of results returned by the Yahoo! BOSS API is less than m. Hence each sentence is assigned a score as follows:

- *If the total number of results is greater than m: assign a score of 0*

- *If the total number of results is less than or equal to m: assign a score of 1*

We then divide the sum of the sentence scores in a review by the total number of sentences to obtain the ratio of the number of matches to total number of sentences. We use this ratio to determine whether or not a review was plagiarized.

6 Discussion and Conclusion

We have discussed several techniques for creating and labeling deceptive content, including traditional, non-gold standard, and crowdsourced approaches. We have also given an illustrative in-depth look at how one might use crowdsourcing services such as Mechanical Turk to solicit deceptive hotel reviews.

While we argue that the crowdsourcing approach to creating deceptive statements has tremendous potential, there remain a number of important limitations, some shared by the previous traditional methods laid out above. First, workers are given "permission" to lie, so these lies are sanctioned and have the same concerns as the traditional sanctioned methods, including the concern that the workers are just play-acting rather than lying. Other unique limitations include the current state of knowledge about workers. In a laboratory setting we can fairly tightly measure and control for gender, race, and even socioeconomic status, but this is not the case for the Amazon Turkers, who potentially make up a much more diverse population.

Despite these issues we believe that the approach has much to offer. First, and perhaps most importantly, the deceptions are being solicited in exactly the manner real-world deceptions are initiated. This is important in that the deception task, though sanctioned, is precisely the same task that a real-world deceiver might use, e.g., to collect fake hotel reviews for themselves. Second, this approach is extremely cost effective in terms of the time and finances required to create custom deception settings that fit a specific context. Here we looked at creating fake hotel reviews, but we can easily apply this approach to other types of reviews, including reviews of medical professionals, restaurants, and products.

Acknowledgments

This work was supported in part by National Science Foundation Grant NSCC-0904913, and the Jack Kent Cooke Foundation. We also thank the EACL reviewers for their insightful comments, suggestions and advice on various aspects of this work.

References

C.F. Bond and B.M. DePaulo. 2006. Accuracy of deception judgments. *Personality and Social Psychology Review*, 10(3):214.

B.M. DePaulo, D.A. Kashy, S.E. Kirkendol, M.M. Wyer, and J.A. Epstein. 1996. Lying in everyday life. *Journal of personality and social psychology*, 70(5):979.

P. Ekman and W. V. Friesen. 1969. *Nonverbal Leakage And Clues To Deception*, volume 32.

Forrest J. A. Feldman, R. S. and B. R. Happ. 2002. Self-presentation and verbal deception: Do self-presenters lie more? *Basic and Applied Social Psychology*, 24:163–170.

M.G. Frank and P. Ekman. 1997. The Ability To Detect Deceit Generalizes Across Different Types of High-Stake Lies. *Journal of Personality and Social Psychology*, 72:1429–1439.

J.T. Hancock, J. Thom-Santelli, and T. Ritchie. 2004. Deception and design: The impact of communication technology on lying behavior. In *Proceedings of the SIGCHI conference on Human factors in computing systems*, pages 129–134. ACM.

J.T. Hancock. 2009. Digital Deception: The Practice of Lying in the Digital Age. *Deception: Methods, Contexts and Consequences*, pages 109–120.

N. Jindal and B. Liu. 2008. Opinion spam and analysis. In *Proceedings of the international conference on Web search and web data mining*, pages 219–230. ACM.

Kim R. K. Levine, T. R. and J. P. Blair. 2010. (In)accuracy at detecting true and false confessions and denials: An initial test of a projected motive model of veracity judgments. *Human Communication Research*, 36:81–101.

F. Li, M. Huang, Y. Yang, and X. Zhu. 2011. Learning to identify review spam. In *Twenty-Second International Joint Conference on Artificial Intelligence*.

E.P. Lim, V.A. Nguyen, N. Jindal, B. Liu, and H.W. Lauw. 2010. Detecting product review spammers using rating behaviors. In *Proceedings of the 19th ACM international conference on Information and knowledge management*, pages 939–948. ACM.

R. Mihalcea and C. Strapparava. 2009. The lie detector: Explorations in the automatic recognition of deceptive language. In *Proceedings of the ACL-IJCNLP 2009 Conference Short Papers*, pages 309–312. Association for Computational Linguistics.

M.L. Newman, J.W. Pennebaker, D.S. Berry, and J.M. Richards. 2003. Lying words: Predicting deception from linguistic styles. *Personality and Social Psychology Bulletin*, 29(5):665.

M. Ott, Y. Choi, C. Cardie, and J.T. Hancock. 2011. Finding deceptive opinion spam by any stretch of the imagination. In *Proceedings of the 49th Annual Meeting of the Association for Computational Linguistics: Human Language Technologies-Volume 1*, pages 309–319. Association for Computational Linguistics.

S. Porter and J.C. Yuille. 1996. The language of deceit: An investigation of the verbal clues to deception in the interrogation context. *Law and Human Behavior*, 20:443–458.

K.B. Serota, T.R. Levine, and F.J. Boster. 2010. The prevalence of lying in america: Three studies of self-reported lies. *Human Communication Research*, 36(1):2–25.

Burggraf C. S. Stafford, L. and W.F. Sharkey. 1987. Conversational Memory The Effects of Time, Recall, Mode, and Memory Expectancies on Remembrances of Natural Conversations. *Human Communication Research*, 14:203–229.

A. Vrij. 2008. *Detecting lies and deceit: Pitfalls and opportunities*. Wiley-Interscience.

G. Wu, D. Greene, B. Smyth, and P. Cunningham. 2010a. Distortion as a validation criterion in the identification of suspicious reviews. In *Proceedings of the First Workshop on Social Media Analytics*, pages 10–13. ACM.

G. Wu, D. Greene, B. Smyth, and P. Cunningham. 2010b. Distortion as a validation criterion in the identification of suspicious reviews. Technical report, UCD-CSI-2010-04, University College Dublin.

Building a Data Collection for Deception Research

Eileen Fitzpatrick
Montclair State University
Montclair, NJ 07043
fitzpatricke@mail.montclair.edu

Joan Bachenko
Linguistech Consortium, Inc.
Oxford, NJ 07863
jbachenko@linguistech.com

Abstract

Research in high stakes deception has been held back by the sparsity of ground truth verification for data collected from real world sources. We describe a set of guidelines for acquiring and developing corpora that will enable researchers to build and test models of deceptive narrative while avoiding the problem of sanctioned lying that is typically required in a controlled experiment. Our proposals are drawn from our experience in obtaining data from court cases and other testimony, and uncovering the background information that enabled us to annotate claims made in the narratives as true or false.

1 Introduction

The ability to spot deception is an issue in many important venues: in police, security, border crossing, customs, and asylum interviews; in congressional hearings; in financial reporting; in legal depositions; in human resource evaluation; and in predatory communications, including Internet scams, identity theft, and fraud. The need for rapid, reliable deception detection in these high stakes venues calls for the development of computational applications that can distinguish true from false claims.

Our ability to test such applications is, however, hampered by a basic issue: the ground truth problem. To be able to recognize the lie, the researcher must not only identify distinctive behavior when someone is lying but must ascertain whether the statement being made is true or not.

The prevailing method for handling the ground truth problem is the controlled experiment, where truth and lies can be managed. While controlled laboratory experiments have yielded important insights into deceptive behavior, ethical and proprietary issues have put limits on the extent to which controlled experiments can model deception in the "real world". High stakes deception cannot be simulated in the laboratory without serious ethics violations. Hence the motivation to lie is weak since subjects have no personal loss or gain at stake. Motivation is further compromised when the lies are sanctioned by the experimenter who directs and condones the lying behavior (Stiff et al., 1994). With respect to the studies themselves, replication of laboratory deception research is rarely done due to differences in data sets and subjects used by different research groups. The result, as Vrij (2008) points out, is a lack of generalizability across studies.

We believe that many of the issues holding back deception research could be resolved through the construction of standardized corpora that would provide a base for expanding deception studies, comparing different approaches and testing new methods. As a first step towards standardization, we offer a set of practical guidelines for building corpora that are customized for studies of high stakes deception. The guidelines are based on our experiences in creating a corpus of real world language data that we used for testing the deception detection approach described in Bachenko et al. (2008), Fitzpatrick and Bachenko (2010). We hope that our experience will encourage other researchers to build and contribute corpora with the goal of establishing a shared resource that passes the test of ecological validity.

Section 2 of the paper describes the data collection initiative we are engaged in, section 3 describes the methods used to corroborate the claims in the data, section 4 concludes our account and covers lessons learned.

We should point out that the ethical considerations that govern our data collection are subject to the United States Code of Federal

Proceedings of the EACL 2012 Workshop on Computational Approaches to Deception Detection, pages 31–38,
Avignon, France, April 23 - 27 2012. ©2012 Association for Computational Linguistics

Regulations (CFRs) for the protection of human subjects and may differ in some respects from those in other countries.

2 Collecting High-Stakes Data

We are building a corpus of spoken and written narrative data used in real world high stakes cases in which many of the claims in the corpus have been corroborated as True or False. We have corroborated claims in almost 35,090 words of narrative. These narratives include statements to police, a legal deposition, and congressional testimony.

In assembling and managing our corpus, two issues have been paramount: the availability of data and constraints on its use. Several types of information must be publicly available, including the primary linguistic data, background information used to determine ground truth, and general information about the case or situation from which the data is taken. In addition, the data must be narrative intensive. There are also several considerations about the data that must be taken into account, including the mode (written or spoken) of the narrative, and considerations involving the needs of the users of the data.

To ensure unconstrained access, data collection must be exempt from human participant restrictions. The restrictions we must adhere to are the regulations of Title 46 of the CFRs.[1] 46 CFR 102 lists the data that is exempt from human participant restrictions. Exempt data includes "[r]esearch involving the collection or study of existing data, documents, records, pathological specimens, or diagnostic specimens, if these sources are publicly available or if the information is recorded by the investigator in such a manner that subjects cannot be identified, directly or through identifiers linked to the subjects."

46 CFR 111, section 7 covers protection of privacy: "When appropriate, there are adequate provisions to protect the privacy of subjects and to maintain the confidentiality of data."

It is conceivable that a "real world" high stakes study could involve subjects whose identifiable data would be removed from the collection, but it is highly unlikely that the subjects would consent to having their data – even if sanitized – made available on the Internet. We have therefore used only exempt data, i.e., data that is publicly available with no expectation of privacy on the part of the people involved.

2.1 Public availability of data

There is a large body of narrative data in the public domain, data that is also likely to have a rich source of ground truth evidence and general background information. Typical public sources for this data would be crime investigation websites, published police interviews, legal websites, including findlaw.com and justice.gov, quarterly earnings conference calls, and the U.S. Congressional Record. Such data includes publicly available

- Face-to-face interviews
- Depositions
- Court and other public testimony
- Phone conversations[2]
- Recorded statements to police
- Written statements to police
- Debates of political figures and candidates for public office
- Online product endorsements
- Blogs
- Webpages

High profile cases are particularly well represented on websites. In the U.S., police reports, which are a matter of public record, may also be obtained for a small fee from local police departments. Other data aggregators, like FactSet.com, provide data for higher fees.

2.2 Types of Data

2.2.1 Primary linguistic data

The narrative data is the data to be analyzed for cues to deception. Written data is, of course, available as text, but spoken data may also only be available as transcripts. Our current dataset includes recorded data only from the Enron testimony, but ideally speech data would include high quality recorded speech to enable analysis of the prosodic qualities of the speech.

To support robust analysis, it is important that the data be narrative intense. The 'yes'/'no'

[1] These regulations are enforced either by the Institutional Review Board (IRB) of the institution where the research takes place or by an independent IRB contracted by the researchers if there is no housing institution.

[2] For example, the quarterly earnings conference calls analyzed in Larcker and Zakolyukina (2010).

responses of a polygraph interview are not usable for language analysis.

Additionally, we have so far limited our collection to spontaneously produced data. Prepared, rehearsed narrative provides the opportunity to carefully craft the narrative putting the narrator in control not only of the story but of the language used to convey the story. This enables the speaker/writer to avoid the cues that we are looking for. We would be open to adding prepared data to the collection, but have not considered the guidelines for it.

2.2.2 Background data

Background information on the primary data is the basis for the ground truth annotation of the claims made in the primary data. Ground truth investigation can use various types of information, including that coming from interviews, police reports, public records posted on local and national government web sites, fact checking sites like FactCheck.org [3] and PolitiFact.com[4] that analyze political claims and provide sources for the information they use in their own judgments, and websites such as truTV.com that offer the facts of a case, the final court judgment, and interviews with the people involved in the case.

Many of these sources are available on the web – an advantage of using data where there is no expectation of privacy.[5] Some data requires filing for a police report or a court document. The sources for our current data set are given in Appendix A.

Another source of verification can be the narrative itself in situations where the narrator contradicts a prior claim. For example, one narrator, after denying a theft for most of the interview, says "All right, man, I did it," enabling us to mark his previous denials as False.

2.2.3 General information about the case/situation

Ideally, the corpus will include background information on the situation covered by the narrative. If the situation is a legal case, the background information should include the verdict of the judge or jury, the judgment of conviction given by the judge, and the sentence. If the case is on appeal, then that should be noted.

Information on the amount of control the narrator has over the story is also valuable. Is the narrative elicited or freely given? The former gives the narrator less control over the narrative, possibly increasing the odds for the appearance of cues to deception. Is the narrator offering a monologue or a written statement, both of which give the author more control of the narrative than an interview.

2.2.4 Speaker information

General information on the speaker can be valuable in gauging the performance of a deception model, including information on gender, age, and education. We found information on first language background and culture to be useful in analyzing the speech of non-native speakers of English, whose second language speech characteristics sometimes align with deception cues. Other sociolinguistic traits may also be important, although we have found that, while sociolinguistic background may determine word choice, the deceptive behavior is invariant. We have not encountered issues of competency to stand trial in the criminal cases we have included, but such evaluations should be noted if the issue arises in a legal case.

2.2.5 Spoken and written data

Two of the narratives in our current collection are written; the others are spoken. Both written statements were produced as parts of a police interview. The purpose of requesting the statement is to obtain an account in the interviewee's own words and to do this before time and questioning affect the interviewee's thinking. Hence the written statement is analogous to a lengthy interview answer, and the language used is much closer to speech than writing, as the opening of the Routier statement illustrates:

Darin and my sister Dana came home from working at the shop. The boys were playing with the neighborhood kids outside. I was finishing up dinner.

2.3 Other considerations

In providing data for general use by researchers, the collector must be aware of varying needs of researchers using the data. The general needs we

[3] FactCheck is a project of the Annenberg Public Policy Center of the University of Pennsylvania.

[4] PolitiFact is sponsored by the Tampa Bay Times.

[5] Information may be withdrawn from the web, however, if there are changes in a case, such as the filing of an appeal or simply fading interest in the case.

consider are the ground truth yield and the question of the scope of the True/False label.

2.3.1 Ground truth yield

The amount of background data that can be gathered to yield ground truth judgments can vary widely depending on the type of narrative data collected. We have worked with private criminal data where the ratio of verified propositions to words in the primary data is as high as .049 and with private job interview data where the ratio is as low as .00043. The low yield may be problematic for some types of experiment, as well as frustrating for the data collector. It is important to have some assurance that there are a reasonable number of resources that can provide ground truth data before collecting the narrative data, particularly if the narrative data is difficult to collect.

2.3.2 The Scope of the T/F label

With the exception of Fornaciari and Poesio (2011), Hirschberg et al. (2005), Bachenko et al. (2008) and Fitzpatrick and Bachenko (2010), the ML/NLP deception literature distinguishes True from False at the level of the narrative, not the proposition. In other words, most of the studies identify the liar, not the lie. For real world data, the choice to label the full narrative as True or False usually depends on the length of the narrative; a narrator giving trial testimony or a job interview will have many claims, while someone endorsing a product may have just one: this product is good.

There are high stakes narratives that are short, such as TSA airport interviews. However, the computational models of such data will be different from those of longer narratives where true and false statements are interspersed throughout. We currently have no data of this type.

3 Providing Ground Truth

In longer real-world narratives people lie selectively and the interviewer usually needs to figure out which statements, or propositions, are lies. To enable the capture of this situation in a model, we engage in a two-step process: the scope of selected verifiable propositions in the data is marked, and then the claim in each proposition is verified or refuted in the background investigation.

3.1 Marking the scope of each proposition

We currently mark the scope of verifiable propositions in the narrative that are likely to have supporting background ground truth information before we establish the ground truth. For example, statements made about a domestic disturbance that involved the police are likely to have a police report to supply background information, while "my mother walked me to school every day," while technically verifiable, will not.

A verifiable proposition, or claim, is any linguistic form that can be assigned a truth value. Propositions can be short; the transcribed answers below are all fragmented ground truth units:

{my neck%T}
{Correct%T}
{Yep%T}

Examples such as these are common in spoken dialogue. Although they do not correspond syntactically to a full proposition, they have propositional content.

Propositions can also be quite long. For example, in the 34 words of the sentence

Any LJM transaction that involved a cash disbursement that would have been within my signing authority either had to be signed by me or someone else higher in the hierarchical chain of the company.

there is only a single claim: I or someone above me had to sign LJM transactions that involved cash disbursements.

Some material is excluded from proposition tagging. Utterances that attest only to the frame of mind of the narrator, e.g. expressions such as *I think, it's my belief,* cannot be refuted or confirmed empirically. Similarly, a sentence like *Ms. Watkins said that rumor had it* contains an assertion (*rumor had it*) not made by the narrator and therefore has no value in testing a verbal deception hypothesis. For the same reason, direct quotes are excluded from verification.

3.2 Marking the Ground Truth

Once the scope of the propositions in a narrative is marked, the annotated narrative is checked against the background ground truth information, and each proposition that can be verified is marked as T or F. We represent this judgment as follows:

But as far as the relationship between {Jeff McMahon moving from the finance group into the industrial products group%T}, {there was no connection whatsoever%F} (Enron)

{At that time Philip Morris owned the Clark Gum Company%T} and {we were trying to get into the candy business%T} (Johnston)

3.2.1 The fact checker

It is critical that the person who marks the ground truth has no contact with the persons who are checking the narrative for markers of deception – to the extent that the latter task is done by hand.

We have employed a law student to fact check the claims in the one legal deposition (Johnston) we have in our current data set. We plan to employ an accounting student with a background in forensic accounting to fact check Lehmann Bros. quarterly earnings conference calls (see Larcker and Zakolyukina (2010) for similar data). For the other data, we have employed graduate assistants in linguistics who do not work on the deception markers.

3.2.2 Sources of background information

At a minimum, the background information used to mark the ground truth should include the source of the data used to establish the truth. That said, no data source is perfect. A confession may be coerced, an eyewitness may forget, a judgment may be faulty. However, at some point, we have to make a decision as to what a credible source is. We have assumed that the sources given in section 2.2.2 above, as well as claims made by the narrator that refute prior claims, all function as reliable sources of background information upon which to make decisions about the truth of a claim.

3.2.3 Verifying a claim

To verify a claim, we use both direct and circumstantial evidence. However, the latter is used only to direct us to a potentially false claim and must be supported by additional, direct facts.

Direct evidence requires no additional inferencing. In a narrative we have studied but not marked for ground truth, the police return to the apartment from which the suspect's wife has gone missing to find her body in the closet, at which point the suspect admits to suffocating his wife and describes the events leading up to the murder. His narrative prior to the confession described contrasting events that occurred in the same timeframe; this will enable us to mark these as False based on the direct evidence of the body and the confession.

Circumstantial evidence requires that a fact be inferred. For example, in his testimony before the U.S. Congress, Jeffrey Skilling claims that when he left Enron four months before the company collapsed, he thought "the company was in good shape." Circumstantial evidence of Skilling's reputation as an astute businessman and the well-known knowledge of his deep involvement with the company make this unlikely, as the interviewing congressman points out. However, we relied as well on direct testimony from other members of the Enron Board of Directors to affirm that Skilling knew the disastrous state of Enron when he left.

Verifying claims is a difficult, time consuming and sometimes tedious process. For the 35,090 words of narrative data currently in our collection, we have been able to verify 184 propositions, 110 as True and 74 as False. Appendix B gives the T/F counts for each of our narratives.

3.3 Enron: Examples of verification

Jeffrey Skilling was the Chief Operating Officer of the Enron Corporation as it was failing in 2001; he left the company in August 2001. In his testimony before the U.S. Congress the following year, which we used as our primary narrative data, Skilling made several important claims that were contradicted either by multiple parties involved in the case or by facts on record. This section illustrates how we apply the evidence to several of Skilling's claims.

1. The financial condition of Enron at the time of Skilling's departure.

MR. SKILLING: Congressman, I can just say it again – {on the date I left I absolutely, unequivocally thought the company was in good shape.F%}

Congressman Edward Markey provides circumstantial evidence that this claim is false, stating that Skilling's reputation, competence and hands-on knowledge makes this claim hard to believe. Direct evidence comes from Jeffrey McMahon, a former Enron treasurer, and Jordan Mintz, a senior attorney, who testified that they had told Skilling their concerns that limited partnerships that the company was involved in created a conflict of interest for certain Enron board members, and were damaging Enron itself.

2. The presence of Mr. Skilling at a critical meeting to discuss these limited partnerships, which enabled Enron to hide its losses.

MR. SKILLING: Well, {there's an issue as to whether I was actually at a%F} -- the particular meeting that you're talking about was in Florida, Palm Beach, Florida. . . .

But when Greenwood brandished a copy of the meeting's minutes, which confirmed Skilling's presence, the former COO hedged his answer, saying,

MR. SKILLING: "I could have been there for a portion of the meeting. Was I there for the entire meeting? I don't know."

3. The issue of whether Skilling, as Enron's Chief Operating Officer, was required to approve Enron-LJM limited partnership transactions.

Mr. SKILLING: {I was not required to approve those transactions.%F}

Minutes of the Finance Committee of Enron's Board of Directors, October 6, 2000 (referenced in the congressional testimony) show that "Misters Buy, Causey, and Skilling approve all transactions between the company and LJM funds."

4 Conclusion and lessons learned

Research in high stakes deception has been held back by the difficulty of ground truth verification. Finding suitable data "in the wild" and conducting the fact checks to obtain ground truth is costly, time-consuming and labor intensive. This is not an unknown problem in computational linguistics. Other research efforts that rely on fact checking, such as Sauri and Pustejovsky (2009), face similar ground truth challenges.

We have described our work in building a corpus customized for high stakes deception studies in hopes of encouraging other researchers to build and share similar corpora. We envision the eventual goal as a multi-language resource with standardized methods and corpora available to the community at little or no cost.

We have made several mistakes that we hope we and others can avoid in collecting high stakes data. Some errors cost us time and others aggravating work trying to correct them.

Our first lesson was to establish a strict separation between the people who annotate the data for ground truth and those who mark it for deception – if any portion of the latter is being done manually. It is important that the fact checkers are not influenced by anything in the language of the narrator that might skew them toward marking a claim one way or the other.

With respect to the narrative data, it is important in selecting new data for annotating and ground truth checking to establish that the data is of the types approved by the research institution's compliance board; in the United States, this is the Institutional Review Board of the housing institution.

It is also important to have assurance that there is a robust body of background data with which to establish ground truth. While it is impressive to be able to find 13 of the 15 verifiably false statements in 240,000 words of narrative—a situation we experienced with a private data set—it does not give us the statistical robustness we would hope for.

We also found it important to save the data sources locally. Websites disappear and the possibility of further fact checking goes with them.

Finally, it is important to provide formal training for proposition tagging and ground truth tagging to ensure consistency and quality. Tutorials, user manuals and careful supervision should be available at all times.

Acknowledgments

We are thankful to the anonymous EACL reviewers for their incisive and helpful comments. Any errors or oversights are strictly the responsibility of the authors.

References

Joan Bachenko, Eileen Fitzpatrick and Michael Schonwetter. 2008. Verification and Implementation of Language-based Deception Indicators in Civil and Criminal Narratives. *Proceedings of the 22nd International Conference on Computational Linguistics (COLING 2008).* University of Manchester, Manchester, UK.

Eileen Fitzpatrick and Joan Bachenko. 2010. Building a Forensic Corpus to Test Language-based Indicators of Deception. *Corpus Linguistics in*

North America 2008: Selections from the Seventh North American Symposium of the American Association for Corpus Linguistics. Gries, S., S. Wulff and M. Davies (eds.). *Series in Language and Computers.* Rodopi.

Tommaso Fornaciari and Massimo Poesio. 2011. Lexical vs. Surface Features in Deceptive Language Analysis, Workshop: Legal Applications of Human Language Technology. *13th International Conference on Artificial Intelligence and Law*. June 6-10. University of Pittsburgh.

Julia Hirschberg, Stefan Benus, Jason M. Brenier, Frank Enos, Sarah Friedman, Sarah Gilman, Cynthia Girand, Martin Graciarena, Andreas Kathol, Laura Michaelis, Bryan L. Pellom, Elizabeth Shriberg, Andreas Stolcke. 2005. "Distinguishing Deceptive from Non-Deceptive Speech," *INTERSPEECH 2005*, Lisbon, September.

David F. Larcker and Anastasia A. Zakolyukina. 2010. Detecting deceptive discussions in conference calls. Rock Center for Corporate Governance. Working Paper Series No. 83.

Roser Sauri and James Pustejovsky. 2009. FactBank 1.0. *Linguistic Data Consortium,* Philadelphia.

James B. Stiff, Steve Corman, Robert Krizek, and Eric Snider. 1994. Individual differences and changes in nonverbal behavior; Unmasking the changing faces of deception. *Communication Research, 21,* 555-581.

Aldert Vrij. 2008. Detecting Lies and Deceit: Pitfalls and Opportunities, 2nd. Edition. Wiley-Interscience.

Code of Federal Regulations. Retrieved Jan. 26, 2012 http://www.hhs.gov/ohrp/humansubjects/guidance/45cfr46.html#46.102

Appendix A. Sources of Background Data that has been verified[6]

Case	Source	
Johnston	Documents available from the *State of Minnesota and Blue Cross and Blue Shield of Minnesota v Philip Morris Inc et al* during the discovery process of the trial.	
Routier	Police report from first responder, Sgt. Matthew Walling. No longer available online	
Enron[7]	Kenneth L. Lay and Jeffrey K. Skilling Jury Trial – Govt. Exhibits[8] Enron Special Investigations Report (The Powers Report) Employee letters and emails	
Kennedy	Police report from Edgartown MA, and transcript of the inquest	
Peterson	Modesto Police Dept. website Gomez Peterson interview Sawyer Peterson interview Findlaw.com International call code database	Mobile number lookup Mapquest U.S. Time Zones Livermore Chevron Station

Appendix B. Distribution of T and F Propositions in Collection

Case	Words	Trues	Falses
Johnston	12,762	34	48
Routier	1,026	8	2
Enron	7,476	23	21
Kennedy	245	8	2
Peterson	13,581	37	1
TOTAL	35,090	110	74

[6] We included data from two cases of theft in the original set, which was collected prior to the creation of an IRB at our university. Incomplete documentation requires us to exclude these cases. Another case, which we called 'Guilty Nurse,' was not sufficiently sourced to be included.

[7] http://news.findlaw.com/legalnews/lit/enron/#documents

[8] http://www.justice.gov/enron/

Appendix C. Attributes of the Data Set

S=spoken; W=written

Case	Case Type	Mode	Narrator
Johnston	Civil; sale of tobacco to teens	S	Male 60+; retired tobacco CEO
Routier	Criminal; murder	W	Female 26; homemaker
Enron (Skilling)	Criminal; fraud	S	Male 53; former Enron COO
Kennedy	Criminal; leaving the scene of an accident	W	Male 37; former US Senator, deceased
Peterson	Criminal; murder	S	Male 30; agriculture chemical salesman

On the Use of Homogenous Sets of Subjects in Deceptive Language Analysis

Tommaso Fornaciari
Center for Mind/Brain Sciences
University of Trento
tommaso.fornaciari@unitn.it

Massimo Poesio
Language and Computation Group
University of Essex
Center for Mind/Brain Sciences
University of Trento
massimo.poesio@unitn.it

Abstract

Recent studies on deceptive language suggest that machine learning algorithms can be employed with good results for classification of texts as truthful or untruthful. However, the models presented so far do not attempt to take advantage of the differences between subjects. In this paper, models have been trained in order to classify statements issued in Court as false or not-false, not only taking into consideration the whole corpus, but also by identifying more homogenous subsets of producers of deceptive language. The results suggest that the models are effective in recognizing false statements, and their performance can be improved if subsets of homogeneous data are provided.

1 Introduction

Detecting deceptive communication is a challenging task, but one that could have a number of useful applications. A wide variety of approaches to the discovery of deceptive statements have been attempted, ranging from using physiological sensors such as lie detectors to using neuroscience methods (Davatzikos et al., 2005; Ganis et al., 2003). More recently, a number of techniques have been developed for recognizing deception on the basis of the communicative behavior of subjects. Given the difficulty of the task, many such methods rely on both verbal and non-verbal behavior, to increase accuracy. So for instance De Paulo et al. (2003) considered more than 150 cues, verbal and non-verbal, directly observed through experimental subjects. But finding clues indicating deception through manual inspection is not easy. De Paulo et al. asserted that "behaviors that are indicative of deception can be indicative of other states and processes as well".

The same point is made in more recent literature: thus Frank et al. (2008) write "We find that there is no clue or clue pattern that is specific to deception, although there are clues specific to emotion and cognition", and they wish for "real-world databases, identifying base rates for malfeasant behavior in security settings, optimizing training, and identifying preexisting excellence within security organizations". Jensen et al. (2010) exploited cues coming from audio, video and textual data.

One solution is to let statistical and machine learning methods discover the clues. Work such as Fornaciari and Poesio (2011a,b); Newman et al. (2003); Strapparava and Mihalcea (2009) suggests that these techniques can perform reasonably well at the task of discovering deception even just from linguistic data, provided that corpora containing examples of deceptive and truthful texts are available. The availability of such corpora is not a trivial problem, and indeed, the creation of a realistic such corpus is one of the problems in which we invested substantial effort in our own previous work, as discussed in Section 3.

In the work discussed in this paper, we tackle an issue which to our knowledge has not been addressed before, due to the limitations of the datasets previously available: this is whether the individual difference between experimental subjects affect deception detection. In previous work, lexical (Fornaciari and Poesio, 2011a) and surface (Fornaciari and Poesio, 2011b) features were employed to classify deceptive statements issued in Italian Courts. In this study, we report the results

Proceedings of the EACL 2012 Workshop on Computational Approaches to Deception Detection, pages 39–47,
Avignon, France, April 23 - 27 2012. ©2012 Association for Computational Linguistics

of experiments in which our methods were trained either over the whole corpus or over smaller subsets consisting of the utterances produced by more homogenous subsets of subjects. These subsets were identified either automatically, by clustering subjects according to their language profile, or by using meta-information about the subjects included in the corpus, such as their gender.

The structure of the paper is as follows. In Section 2 some background knowledge is introduced. In Section 3 the data set is described. In Section 4 we discuss our machine learning and experimental methods. Finally, the results are presented in Section 5 and discussed in Section 6.

2 Background

2.1 Deceptive language analysis

From a methodological point of view, to investigate deceptive language gives rise to some tricky issues: first of all, the strategy chosen to collect data. The literature can be divided in two main families of studies:

- Field studies;
- Laboratory studies.

The first ones are usually interesting in forensic applications but in such studies verifying the sincerity of the statements is often complicated (Vrij, 2005). Laboratory studies, instead, are characterized by the artificiality of participants' psychological conditions: therefore their findings may not be generalized to deception encountered in real life.

Due to practical difficulties in collection and annotation of suitable data, in literature finding papers in which real life linguistic data are employed, where truthfulness is surely known, is less common and Zhou et al. (2008) complain about the lack of "data set for evaluating deception detection models". Just recently some studies tried to fill this gap, concerning both the English (Bachenko et al., 2008; Fitzpatrick and Bachenko, 2009) and Italian language (Fornaciari and Poesio, 2011a,b). Just the studies on Italian language come from data which have constituted the first nucleus of the corpus analysed here.

2.2 Stylometry

Our own work and that of other authors that recently employed machine learning techniques to detect deception in text employs techniques very similar to that of stylometry. Stylometry is a discipline which studies texts on the basis of their stylistic features, usually in order to attribute them to an author - giving rise to the branch of author attribution - or to get information about the author himself - this is the field of author profiling.

Stylometric analyses, which relies mainly on machine learning algorithms, turned out to be effective in several forensic tasks: not only the classical field of author profiling (Coulthard, 2004; Koppel et al., 2006; Peersman et al., 2011; Solan and Tiersma, 2004) and author attribution (Luyckx and Daelemans, 2008; Mosteller and Wallace, 1964), but also emotion detection (Vaassen and Daelemans, 2011) and plagiarism analysis (Stein et al., 2007). Therefore, from a methodological point of view, Deceptive Language Analysis is a particular application of stylometry, exactly like other branches of Forensic Linguistics.

3 Data set

3.1 False testimonies in Court

In order to study deceptive language, we created the DECOUR - DEception in COURt - corpus, better described in Fornaciari and Poesio (2012). DECOUR is a corpus constituted by the transcripts of 35 hearings held in four Italian Courts: Bologna, Bolzano, Prato and Trento. These transcripts report verbatim the statements issued by a total of 31 different subjects - four of which have been heard twice. All the hearings come from criminal proceedings for **calumny** and **false testimony** (artt. 368 and 372 of the Italian Criminal Code).

In particular, the hearings of DECOUR come mainly from two situations:

- the defendant for any criminal proceeding tries to use calumny against someone;
- a witness in any criminal proceeding lies for some reason.

In both cases, a new criminal proceeding arises, in which the subjects can issue new statements or not, and having as a body of evidence the transcript of the hearing held in the previous proceeding.

The crucial point is that DECOUR only includes text from individuals who in the end have been found guilty. Hence the proceeding ends with a judgment of the Court which summarize the facts, pointing out precisely the lies told by the speaker in order to establish his punishment. Thanks to the transcripts of the hearing and to the final judgment of the Court, it is possible to annotate the statements of the speakers on the basis of their truthfulness or untruthfulness, as follows.

3.2 Annotation and agreement

The hearings are dialogs, in which the judge, the public prosecutor and the lawyer pose questions to the witness/defendant who in turn has to give them answers. These answers are the object of investigation of this study. Each answer is considered a **turn**, delimited by the end of the previous and the beginning of the following intervention of another individual. Each turn is constituted by one or more **utterances**, delimited by punctuation marks: period, triple-dots, question and exclamation marks. Utterances are the analysis unit of DECOUR and have been annotated as **false**, **true** or **uncertain**. In order to verify the agreement in the judgments about truthfulness or untruthfulness of the utterances, three annotators separately annotated about 600 utterances. The agreement study concerning the three classes of utterances, described in detail in (Fornaciari and Poesio, 2012), showed that the agreement value was k=.57. Instead, if the problem is reduced to a binary task - that is, if true and uncertain utterances are collapsed into a single category of **not-false** utterances, opposed to the category of false ones - the agreement value is k=.64.

3.3 Corpus statistics

The whole corpus has been tokenized and sensitive data have been made anonymous, according to the previous agreement with the Courts. Then DECOUR has been lemmatized and POS-tagged using a version of TreeTagger[1] (Schmid, 1994) trained for Italian.

DECOUR is made up of 3015 utterances, which come from 2094 turns. 945 utterances have been annotated as false, 1202 as true and 868 as uncertain. The size of DECOUR is 41819 tokens, including punctuation blocks.

[1] `http://www.ims.uni-stuttgart.de/projekte/corplex/TreeTagger/DecisionTreeTagger.html`

4 Methods

In this Section we first summarize our classification methods from previous work, then discuss the three experiments we carried out.

4.1 Classification methods

Each utterance is described by a feature vector. As in our previous studies (Fornaciari and Poesio, 2011a,b) three kinds of features were used.

First of all, the feature vectors include very basic linguistic information such as the length of utterances (with and without punctuation) and the number of words longer than six letters.

The second type of information are lexical features. These features have been collected making use of LIWC - Linguistic Inquiry and Word Count, a linguistic tool realized by Pennebaker et al. (2001) and widely employed in deception detection (Newman et al., 2003; Strapparava and Mihalcea, 2009). LIWC is based on a dictionary in which each term is associated with an appropriate set of syntactical, semantical and/or psychological categories. When a text is analysed with LIWC, the tokens of the text are compared with the LIWC dictionary. Every time a word present in the dictionary is found, the count of the corresponding categories grows. The output is a profile of the text which relies on the rate of incidence of the different categories in the text itself. LIWC also includes different dictionaries for several languages, amongst which Italian (Agosti and Rellini, 2007). Therefore it has been possible to apply LIWC to Italian deceptive texts, and the approximate 80 linguistic dimensions which constitute the Italian LIWC dictionary have been included as features of the vectors.

Lastly, frequencies of lemmas and part-of-speech n-grams were used. Five kinds of n-grams of lemmas and part-of-speech were taken into consideration: from unigrams to pentagrams. These frequency lists come from the part of DECOUR employed as training set. More precisely, they come from the utterances held as true or false of the training set, while the uncertain utterances have not been considered. In order to emphasize the collection of features effective in classifying true and false statements, frequency lists of n-grams have been built considering true and false utterances separately. This means that, in the training set, homologous frequency lists of n-

Table 1: The most frequent n-grams collected

N-grams	Lemmas	POS	Total
Unigrams	50	15	
Bigrams	40	12	
Trigrams	30	9	
Tetragrams	20	6	
Pentagrams	10	3	
Total	150	45	195

grams - unigrams, bigrams and so on - have been collected from the subset of true utterances *and* form the subset of false ones. From these lists, the most frequent n-grams have been collected, in a decreasing amount according to the length of the n-grams. Table 1 shows in detail the number of the most frequent lemmas and part-of-speech collected for the different n-grams. Then the couples of frequency lists were merged into one.

This procedure implies that the number of surface features is not determined *a priori*. In fact the 195 features indicated in Table 1, which are collected from true and false utterances, are unified in a list where each feature has to appear only once. Therefore, theoretically in the case of perfect identity of features in true and false utterances, a final list with the same 195 features would be obtained. In the opposite case, if the n-grams from true and false utterances would be completely different, a list of 195 + 195, then 390 n-grams would result. The aim of this procedure is to get a list of n-grams which could be as much as possible representative of the features of true and false utterances. Obviously, the smaller the overlap of the features of the two subsets, the greater the difference in the appearance of true and false utterances, and greater the hope to reach a good performance in the classification task.

We used the Support Vector Machine implementation in R (Dimitriadou et al., 2011). As specified above, the classes of the utterances are false vs. not-false, where the category of not-false utterances results from the union of the true and uncertain ones.

4.2 Corpus division

With the aim of training models able to classify the utterances of DECOUR as false or not-false, the corpus has been divided as follows:

Training set The 20 hearings coming from the Courts of Bologna and Bolzano have been employed as training set. In terms of analysis units, this means 2279 utterances, that is 75.59% of DECOUR. The features of the vectors come from this set of data.

Test set The 9 hearings of the Court of Trento have been employed as test set, in order to evaluate the effectiveness of the trained models. This test set was made up by 426 utterances, which are 14.13% of DECOUR.

Development set The 6 hearings of the Court of Prato have been employed as development set during the phase of choice and calibration of vector features, therefore this set of utterances is not directly involved in the results of the following experiments. The develpment set was constituted by 310 utterances, that is 10.28% of DECOUR.

In the various experimental conditions, some subsets of DECOUR have been taken into consideration. Hence, different hearings have been removed from the test and/or training set in order to carry out different experiments. Since the test sets vary in the different experiments, in relation to each of them different chance levels have been determined, in order to evaluate the effectiveness of the models' performance.

4.3 Experiments

Three experiments were carried out. In the first experiment, the entire corpus was used to train and test our algorithms. In the second and third experiment, sub-corpora were identified.

4.3.1 Experiment 1: whole test set

In the first experiment, the classification task has been carried out simply employing the training set and the test set as described above, in order to have a control as reference point in relation to the following experiments.

4.3.2 Experiment 2: no outliers

In the second experiment, a more homogeneous subset of DECOUR was obtained by automatically identifying and removing outliers. This was done in an unsupervised way by building vector descriptions of the hearings and clustering them. The features of these vectors were the same n-grams described above, collected from the whole

Figure 1: Multi-Dimensional Scaling of DECOURĖach entity corresponds to a hearing; the letters represent the sex of the speakers.

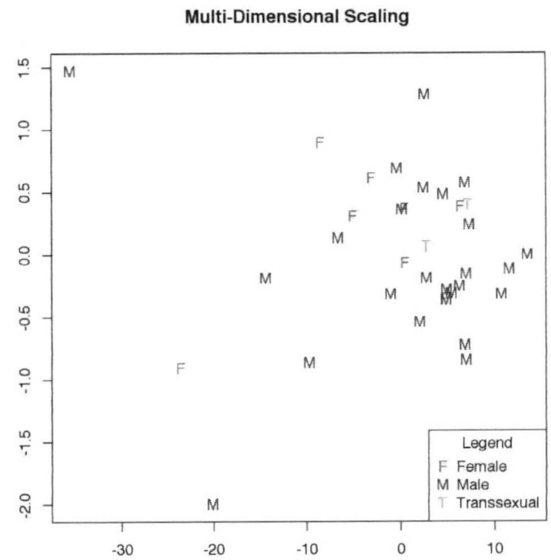

corpus (not from the only test set); their values were the mean values of the frequencies of the utterances belonging to the hearing.

This data set has been transformed into a matrix of between-hearing distances and a Multi-Dimensional Scaling - MDS function has been applied to this matrix (Baayen, 2008). Figure 1 shows the plot of MDS function. Each entity corresponds to a hearing, and is represented by a letter indicating the sex of the speaker. Getting a glimpse at Figure 1, it is possible to notice that, in general, almost all the hearings are quite close - that is, similar - to each other. Only three hearings seem to be clearly more peripheral than all the others, particularly the three most to the left in Figure 1. These hearings have been considered as outliers and shut out from the experiment. They are two hearings from Trento and one from Prato. In practice, it means that the training set, coming from the hearings of Bologna and Bolzano, remained the same as the previous experiment, while two hearings have been removed from the test set, which was constituted only by the hearings of Trento.

4.3.3 Experiment 3: only male speakers

Different from the previous one, the third experiment does not rely on a subset of data automatically identified. Instead, the subset comes from personal information concerning the subjects involved in the hearings. In fact, their sex, place of birth and age at the moment of the hearing are known. In this paper, places of birth and age have not been taken into consideration, since grouping them together in reliable categories raises issues that do not have a straightforward solution, and the size of the subsets of corpus which would be obtained must be taken into account.

Therefore this experiment has been carried out taking into consideration only the sex of the subjects, and in particular it concerned only the hearings involving men. This meant reducing the training set consistently, where seven hearings of women were present and thence removed. Instead from the test set just three hearings have been taken off, one involving a woman and two involving a transsexual.

4.4 Baselines

The chance levels for the various test sets have been calculated through Monte Carlo simulations, each one specific to every experiment. In each simulation, 100000 times a number of random predictions has been produced, in the same amount and with the same rate of false utterances of the test set employed in the single experiment. Then this random output was compared to the real sequence of false and not-false utterances of the test set, in order to count the amount of correct predictions. The rate of correct answers reached by less than 0.01% of the random predictions has been accepted as chance threshold for every experiment.

As a baseline, a simple majority baseline was computed: to classify each utterance as belonging to the most numerous class in the test set (not-false).

5 Results

The test set of the first experiemnt, carried out on the whole test set, was made up of 426 utterances, of which 190 were false, that is 44.60%. While the majority baseline is 55.40% of accuracy, a Monte Carlo simulation applied to the test set showed that the chance level was 59.60% of correct predictions. The results are shown in Table 2. The overall accuracy - almost 66% - is clearly above the chance level, being more than six points greater than the baseline.

Table 2: Whole training and test set

	Correctly classified entities	Incorrectly classified entities	Precision	Recall	F-measure
False utterances	59	131	80.82%	31.05%	44.86%
True utterances	222	14	62.89%	94.07%	75.38%
Total	281	145			
Total percent	65.96%	34.04%			
Monte Carlo simulation	59.60%				
Majority baseline	55.40%				

Table 3: Test set without outliers

	Correctly classified entities	Incorrectly classified entities	Precision	Recall	F-measure
False utterances	51	90	80.95%	36.17%	50.00%
True utterances	180	12	66.67%	93.75%	77.92%
Total	231	102			
Total percent	69.37%	30.63%			
Monte Carlo simulation	61.26%				
Majority baseline	57.66%				

Table 4: Training and test set with only male speakers

	Correctly classified entities	Incorrectly classified entities	Precision	Recall	F-measure
False utterances	32	85	74.42%	27.35%	40.00%
True utterances	179	11	67.80%	94.21%	78.85%
Total	211	96			
Total percent	68.73%	31.27%			
Monte Carlo simulation	63.19%				
Majority baseline	61.89%				

In the second experiment, the test set without outliers was made up of 333 utterances; 141 were false, which means 42.34% of the test set. The majority baseline was then at 57.66%, while the chance threshold determined with a Monte Carlo simulation had an accuracy rate of 61.26%. Table 3 shows the results of the analyses. Taking the outliers out of the test set allows tthe best performance of the three experiments to be reached. In fact the accuracy is more than 69%, which is more than eight points above the highest chance level of 61.26%.

In the third experimental condition, where only male speakers were considered, the training set was made up of 13 hearings and the test set of 6 hearings. The utterances in the test set were 307, of which 117 were false, meaning 38.11% of the test set. In this last case, the majority baseline is at 61.89% of accuracy, while according to a Monte Carlo simulation the chance level was 63.19%. The overall accuracy reached in this experiment, shown in Table 4, was more than 68%: higher than the first experiment, but in this case the lower amount of false utterances in the test set led to higher chance thresholds. Therefore the difference between performance and the chance level of 63.19% is now the smallest of all the experiments: just five points and half.

From the point of view of detection of false utterances, although with internal differences, all the experiments are placed in the same reference frame. In particular, the weak point in performance is always the recall of false utterances, which remains more or less at 30%. Instead the good news comes from the precision in recognizing them, which is close to 80%. Regarding true utterances, the recall is always good, being never lower than 93%, while the precision is close to 65%.

6 Discussion

The goal of this paper was to verify if restricting the analysis to more homogeneous subsets could improve the accuracy of our models. The results are mixed. On the one end, taking the outliers out of the corpus results in a remarkable improvement of accuracy in the classification task, in relation to the performance of the models tested on the whole test set. On the other end, in other cases - most clearly, considering only speakers of the male gender - we find no difference; our hypothesis is that any potential advantage derived from the increased homogeneity is offset by the reduction in training material (seven hearings are removed in this case). So the conclusion may be that increasing homogeneity is effective provided that the remaining set is still sufficiently large.

Regarding the models' capacity to detect false rather than true utterances, the difference between the respective recalls is noteworthy. In fact, while the recall of not-false utterances is very high, that of false ones is poor. In other words, the results indicate that an amount of false utterances is effectively so similar to the not-false ones, that the models are not able to detect them. One challenge for future studies is surely to find a way to detect some aspect currently neglected of deceptive language, which could be employed to widen the size of false utterances which can be recognized.

On the other hand, in the two more reliable experiments the precision in detecting false utterances was about 80%. This could suggest that an amount of false utterances exists, whose features are in some way peculiar and different from not-false ones. The data seem to show that this subset could be more or less one third of all the false utterances.

However, this study was not aimed to estimate the possible performance of the models in an hypothetic practical application. The experimental conditions taken into consideration, in fact, are considerably different from those that would be present in a real life analysis.

The main reason of this difference is that in a real case to classify every utterance of a hearing would not be requested. A lot of statements are irrelevant or perfectly known as true. Furthermore it would not make sense to classify all the utterances which have not propositional value, such as questions or meta-communicative acts. In the perspective of deception detection in a real life scenario, to classify this last kind of utterances is useless. Only a subset of the propositional statements should be classified. In a previous study, carried out on a selection of utterances with propositional value of a part of DeCour, machine learning models reached an accuracy of 75% in classification task (Fornaciari and Poesio, 2011b). In that study, precision and recall of false utterances are also quite similar to those of this study, the first being about 90% and the second about 50%.

From a theoretical point of view, the present study suggests that it is possible to be relatively confident in the effectiveness of the models in the analysis of any kind of utterance. This means that deceptive language is at least in part different from the truthful one and stylometric analyses can detect it. If this is true, the rate of precision with which false statements are correctly classified should clearly exceed the chance level.

Also in this case, Monte Carlo simulation is taken as reference point. Out of the 100000 random trials carried out to determine the baseline for the first experiment, less than 0.01% had a precision greater than 57.90% in classifying false utterances, in front of a precision of the models at 80.82%. Regarding the second experiment, the threshold for precision related to false utterances was 58.15% against a precision of the models at 80.95%. In the third experiment, the baseline for precision was 55.55% and the performance of models was 74.42%. In every experiment the gap is about twenty points per cent. The same cannot be said about the recall of false utterances: the baselines of Monte Carlo simulations in the three experiments were about 51-54%, while the best models' performance (of the second experiment) did not exceed 36%.

The precision reached in recognizing false statements shows that the models were reliable in detection of deceptive language. On the other hand a remarkable amount of false utterances was not identified. The challenge for the future is to understand to which extent it will be possible to improve the recall in detecting false utterances, not losing and hopefully improving the relative precision. At that point, although in specific contexts, a computational linguistics' approach could be really employed to detect deception in real life scenarios.

7 Acknowledgements

To create DeCour has been very complex, and it would not have been possible without the kind collaboration of a lot of people. Many thanks to Dr. Francesco Scutellari, President of the Court of Bologna, to Dr. Heinrich Zanon, President of the Court of Bolzano, to Dr. Francesco Antonio Genovese, President of the Court of Prato and to Dr. Sabino Giarrusso, President of the Court of Trento.

References

Agosti, A. and Rellini, A. (2007). The Italian LIWC Dictionary. Technical report, LIWC.net, Austin, TX.

Baayen, R. (2008). *Analyzing linguistic data: a practical introduction to statistics using R*. Cambridge University Press.

Bachenko, J., Fitzpatrick, E., and Schonwetter, M. (2008). Verification and implementation of language-based deception indicators in civil and criminal narratives. In *Proceedings of the 22nd International Conference on Computational Linguistics - Volume 1*, COLING '08, pages 41–48, Stroudsburg, PA, USA. Association for Computational Linguistics.

Coulthard, M. (2004). Author identification, idiolect, and linguistic uniqueness. *Applied Linguistics*, 25(4):431–447.

Davatzikos, C., Ruparel, K., Fan, Y., Shen, D., Acharyya, M., Loughead, J., Gur, R., and Langleben, D. (2005). Classifying spatial patterns of brain activity with machine learning methods: Application to lie detection. *NeuroImage*, 28(3):663 – 668.

De Paulo, B. M., Lindsay, J. J., Malone, B. E., Muhlenbruck, L., Charlton, K., and Cooper, H. (2003). Cues to deception. *Psychological Bulletin*, 129(1):74–118.

Dimitriadou, E., Hornik, K., Leisch, F., Meyer, D., and Weingessel, A. (2011). r-cran-e1071. `http://mloss.org/software/view/94/`.

Fitzpatrick, E. and Bachenko, J. (2009). Building a forensic corpus to test language-based indicators of deception. *Language and Computers*, 71(1):183–196.

Fornaciari, T. and Poesio, M. (2011a). Lexical vs. surface features in deceptive language analysis. In *Proceedings of the ICAIL 2011 Workshop Applying Human Language Technology to the Law*, AHLTL 2011, pages 2–8, Pittsburgh, USA.

Fornaciari, T. and Poesio, M. (2011b). Sincere and deceptive statements in italian criminal proceedings. In *Proceedings of the International Association of Forensic Linguists Tenth Biennial Conference*, IAFL 2011, Cardiff, Wales, UK.

Fornaciari, T. and Poesio, M. (2012). Decour: a corpus of deceptive statements in italian courts. In *Proceedings of the eighth International Conference on Language Resources and Evaluation*, LREC 2012. In press.

Frank, M. G., Menasco, M. A., and O'Sullivan, M. (2008). Human behavior and deception detection. In Voeller, J. G., editor, *Wiley Handbook of Science and Technology for Homeland Security*. John Wiley & Sons, Inc.

Ganis, G., Kosslyn, S., Stose, S., Thompson, W., and Yurgelun-Todd, D. (2003). Neural correlates of different types of deception: An fmri investigation. *Cerebral Cortex*, 13(8):830–836.

Jensen, M. L., Meservy, T. O., Burgoon, J. K., and Nunamaker, J. F. (2010). Automatic, Multimodal Evaluation of Human Interaction. *Group Decision and Negotiation*, 19(4):367–389.

Koppel, M., Schler, J., Argamon, S., and Pennebaker, J. (2006). Effects of age and gender on blogging. In *AAAI 2006 Spring Symposium on Computational Approaches to Analysing Weblogs*.

Luyckx, K. and Daelemans, W. (2008). Authorship attribution and verification with many authors and limited data. In *Proceedings of the 22nd International Conference on Computational Linguistics - Volume 1*, COLING '08, pages 513–520, Stroudsburg, PA, USA. Association for Computational Linguistics.

Mosteller, F. and Wallace, D. (1964). *Inference and Disputed Authorship: The Federalist.* Addison-Wesley.

Newman, M. L., Pennebaker, J. W., Berry, D. S., and Richards, J. M. (2003). Lying Words: Predicting Deception From Linguistic Styles. *Personality and Social Psychology Bulletin*, 29(5):665–675.

Peersman, C., Daelemans, W., and Van Vaerenbergh, L. (2011). Age and gender prediction on netlog data. *Presented at the 21st Meeting of Computational Linguistics in the Netherlands (CLIN21), Ghent, Belgium.*

Pennebaker, J. W., Francis, M. E., and Booth, R. J. (2001). *Linguistic Inquiry and Word Count (LIWC): LIWC2001.* Lawrence Erlbaum Associates, Mahwah.

Schmid, H. (1994). Probabilistic part-of-speech tagging using decision trees. In *Proceedings of International Conference on New Methods in Language Processing.*

Solan, L. M. and Tiersma, P. M. (2004). Author identification in american courts. *Applied Linguistics*, 25(4):448–465.

Stein, B., Koppel, M., and Stamatatos, E. (2007). Plagiarism analysis, authorship identification, and near-duplicate detection pan'07. *SIGIR Forum*, 41:68–71.

Strapparava, C. and Mihalcea, R. (2009). The Lie Detector: Explorations in the Automatic Recognition of Deceptive Language. In *Proceeding ACLShort '09 - Proceedings of the ACL-IJCNLP 2009 Conference Short Papers.*

Vaassen, F. and Daelemans, W. (2011). Automatic emotion classification for interpersonal communication. In *2nd Workshop on Computational Approaches to Subjectivity and Sentiment Analysis (WASSA 2.011).*

Vrij, A. (2005). Criteria-based content analysis - A Qualitative Review of the First 37 Studies. *Psychology, Public Policy, and Law*, 11(1):3–41.

Zhou, L., Shi, Y., and Zhang, D. (2008). A Statistical Language Modeling Approach to Online Deception Detection. *IEEE Transactions on Knowledge and Data Engineering*, 20(8):1077–1081.

Current and Future Needs for Deception Detection in Government Screening Environments

Daniel Baxter
U.S. Department of Defense

Abstract

The focus of this talk is on the applications and techniques currently used in government screening venues and on anticipated future applications. I will begin with a discussion of how and why the polygraph is used in a screening interview and touch on some of the newer techniques in deception detection using body movements, vocal and verbal behavior that are now being tested. We'll then look at some of the needs for deception detection and applications on our wish list. The talk will include cases where the current technology has been good and where it has not.

Proceedings of the EACL 2012 Workshop on Computational Approaches to Deception Detection, page 48,
Avignon, France, April 23 - 27 2012.

The Voice and Eye Gaze Behavior of an Imposter: Automated Interviewing and Detection for Rapid Screening at the Border

Aaron C. Elkins
University of Arizona
aelkins@cmi.arizona.edu

Douglas C. Derrick
University of Nebraska at Omaha
dcderrick@mail.unomaha.edu

Monica Gariup
Frontex, Research and Development Unit
monica.gariup@frontex.europa.eu

Abstract

Contextual differences present significant challenges when developing computational methods for detecting deception. We conducted a field experiment with border guards from the European Union in order to demonstrate that deception detection can be done robustly using context specific computational models. In the study, some of the participants were given a "fraudulent" document with incorrect data and asked to pass through a checkpoint. An automated system used an embodied conversational agent (ECA) to conduct interviews. Based on the participants' vocalic and ocular behavior our specific model classified 100% of the imposters while limiting false positive errors. The overall accuracy was 94.47%.

1 Introduction

Unlike Pinocchio, liars do not exhibit universal behavior or physiological signals in all situations. Deception is often inappropriately reduced to either simply telling the truth or lying. However, there are many strategies for lying (e.g., omission, imposters, equivocation, hedging); situations where lying occurs (e.g., rapid screening, imposter, interrogation, conversation); varying consequences and power dynamics (e.g., parents, friends, boss, border guard, law enforcement); and interviewing styles (e.g., behavioral analysis interviewer, informal chat, guilty knowledge test, short answer format). All of these factors contribute to the type of behaviors and physiological responses that are exhibited and are theoretically expected. These contextual differences present significant challenges when trying to develop computational methods for detecting deception. In order to develop systems that can be used for reliable deception detection, we must constrain the complex problem of deception and manage the factors described above.

We conducted a field experiment with border guards from the European Union in order to demonstrate that by controlling some of the above factors and by developing context specific computational models, deception detection can be achieved robustly. In the experiment, some of the participants were given a "fraudulent" document with incorrect data and asked to pass through a checkpoint. An automated system used an embodied conversational agent (ECA) to conduct interviews. The system was equipped with vocal and ocular sensors, as well as an electronic passport reader. Based on the participants' vocal and eye gaze behavior a computational classification model was developed to identify imposters while limiting the number of false positives.

2 Embodied Conversational Agent

To account for the complex interplay between liars and the deceived, Buller and Burgoon (1996) introduced Interpersonal Deception Theory (IDT). This theory expanded and conceptualized deception as a strategic interaction between a sender and receiver. Liars must simultaneously manage information, their behavior, and appearance during the interaction. Moreover, liars will use different strategies depending on their skill, relationship with the interaction partner, preparation, motivation, and time.

Proceedings of the EACL 2012 Workshop on Computational Approaches to Deception Detection, pages 49–54,
Avignon, France, April 23 - 27 2012.

Lying is undeniably a social act. One major challenge to computational deception detection is accounting for the variability introduced by human interviewers. Every interviewer has their own style (e.g., aggressive, friendly), inconsistently asks questions, and gets tired. The behavior and approach of the interviewer strongly influences the behavior and reactions of the interviewee. For example, if the interviewer is angry, the interviewee will be affected by this and artificially display reciprocal anger or even distress. Perhaps after a lunch break the interviewer is fresh and in better spirits and returns to a more friendly interaction. Any deception detection system that relies on consistent behavioral cues will have to account for the diverse range of human interviewer variability.

To address this challenge, we developed an ECA-based deception detection system that asks the same questions, in the same order, and in the same way each time. Additionally, this system can speak the native language of every interviewee.

Figure 1. ECA Interviewer

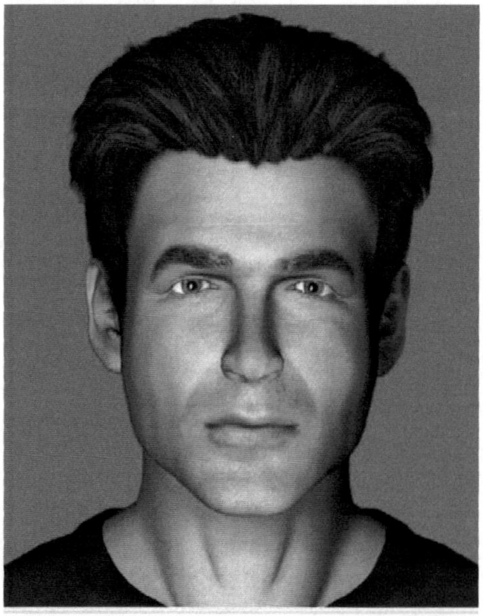

3 Sensors

The ECA depicted above (Figure 1) conducts the structured border-screening interview and integrated into this system were three sensors for detecting imposters: microphone (vocalic measures), near infrared camera (ocular behavior), and an electronic passport reader (document input).

3.1 Vocalic Measures

A unidirectional microphone was integrated into the system to capture spoken responses to the ECA's questions. Vocal features were extracted from each of these responses near real-time (i.e., seconds). Previous research has found that an increase in the fundamental frequency or pitch is related to stress or arousal (Bachorowski & Owren, 1995; Elkins & Stone, 2011; Streeter, Krauss, Geller, Olson, & Apple, 1977). Pitch is a function of the speed of vibration of the vocal folds during speech production (Titze & Martin, 1998). Females have smaller vocal folds than men, requiring their vocal chords to vibrate faster and leading to their higher pitch. When we are aroused our muscles tense and tighten. When the vocal muscles become tenser, they vibrate at a higher frequency, leading to a higher pitch. Similarly, previous research has found that when aroused or excited, our pitch also exhibits more variation and higher intensities (Juslin & Laukka, 2003).

Deceptive speech is also predicted to be more cognitively taxing, leading to non-strategic or leakage cues (Buller & Burgoon, 1996; Rockwell, Buller, & Judee K. Burgoon, 1997; Zuckerman, DePaulo, & Rosenthal, 1981). These cues, specific to cognitive effort, can be measured vocally. Cognitively taxed speakers take longer to respond (response latency) and incorporate more disfluencies (e.g., "um" "uh", speech errors). Moreover, the harmonics-to-noise ratio serves as an indicator of voice quality (Boersma, 1993). Originally intended to measure speech pathology (Yumoto, Gould, & Baer, 1982), liars have been found to speak with a lower harmonic-to-noise ratio than truth-tellers (Nunamaker, Derrick, Elkins, Burgoon, & Patton, 2011). The quality of the voice is affected by increased cognitive effort and heightened stress/emotion.

3.2 Ocular Behavior

This system was designed to be used in a rapid screening environment and to assess eye behavior during an interview typical at a port of entry. All participants were shown an image of his or her issued visa during the interview and asked if the information was correct. All of the information was correct on the visa for all participants except the imposters where the date of birth was inaccurate. This test design is based on orienting theory and predicts that measurable physiology accompanies an orienting reflex to familiar stimulus. Pavlov originally studied the orienting reflex during his classical conditioning experiments. This reflex orients attention to novel and familiar stimuli and is considered adaptive to the environment. In order to capture the eye behavior responses, we used the EyeTech Digital Systems VT2 infrared eye tracker (see figure 2) mounted directly below a computer monitor.

Figure 2. EyeTech Eye Tracker

The VT2 has two infrared light sources and an integrated infrared camera. It connects via USB to a Windows computer and captures the eye gaze location (x, y coordinates) at each instance at a rate of approximately 33-34 frames per second. During the interaction with the interviewing system, participants' eye behavior was monitored while they spoke to the ECA (e.g., for eye contact) and when they observed the image of their visa. Based on prior research (Derrick, Jenkins, & Nunamaker, 2011), we anticipated that the imposter would orient on areas of the image that contained false information about their identity. A sample of the document used by all participants is shown in Figure 3.

3.3 Electronic Passport Reader

To provide the system with additional information about each participant, a 3M AT-9000 e-passport reader was integrated into the system. Each participant placed their visa document on the scanner prior to the interview. The information from the document was read into the system using the Machine Readable Zone (MRZ) and an image of the visa was captured for use during interview.

Figure 3. Visa Issued to Participants

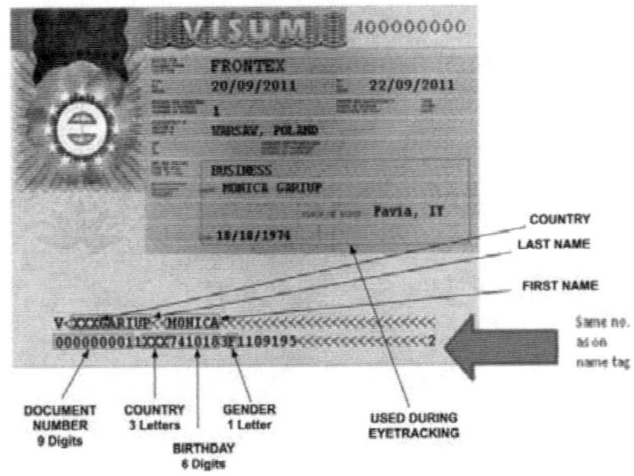

4 Final System

The final system used during the field experiment is depicted below in Figure 4. The ECA conducted the screening interview in the language of each participant's choice (English, French, German, Polish, or Spanish). The eye gaze and vocal behavior were recorded and processed during the interaction in near real-time. Immediately to the right of the monitor is a passport reader used to scan the entire participant's visas to read the information and image.

Figure 4. ECA System Screening Participants

5 Method

5.1 Participants

37 border guards from the following European Union (EU) member states participated: Austria, Belgium, Denmark, Estonia, Finland, Germany, Hungary, Italy, Latvia, Lithuania, Malta, the Netherlands, Norway, Poland, Romania, Slovakia, Spain, Sweden and the United Kingdom. In addition, two representatives from the U.S. Customs and Border Protection and the Canadian Border Services Agency also

participated. The simulation was part of a workshop on decision support for screening and risk assessment at passport control. Of the 37, four (two men from the Netherlands and Romania and two women from Sweden and Denmark respectively) were selected to be imposters with incorrect dates of birth on their visa. The selection was based on the results of an earlier survey that asked participants about their confidence in his or her ability to lie and remain undetected. Participants with the highest confidence scores were selected.

5.2 Procedure

All participants were given the visa document at their registration to use as their travel document during the simulated border check. The document consisted of personal data: name, surname, date of birth, place of birth, and nationality. For the sake of the simulation, all documents were assumed to be genuine (not counterfeited/falsified). The imposters were given basic instructions on the scenario and their role. They had acquired genuine documents of a person with a name identical to theirs who also looked like them (based on the photo of their own passport).

The goal of the imposter was to pass the border check undetected, meet with their fellow accomplices (the other imposters), and place a bomb at a reception. The imposters were explicitly instructed the day before the simulation to check his or her visa document and note that the date and location of their birth was false (not coincident with their real one).

The imposters were asked to lie and answer affirmatively when the ECA asked him or her whether the document belonged to them and if the data were correct. In order to reinforce the imposters in their role, on the day before the simulation, they were invited to meet in secret in the reception room and discuss how they would set up a bomb scare.

The other participants were simply told to behave normally. All other participants, and experimental staff were blind to the identity of the imposters.

Upon arrival to the in participants scanned their document in the e-passport reader and selected the language for the ECA to use for the interview (English, Polish, Spanish, French, or German). The ECA then asked the following questions:

1. What is your full name?
2. Where were you born?
3. Do have anything to declare?
4. What is the purpose of your visit?
5. Please carefully examine the following document
   a. Scanned document shown (15 seconds)
6. Are the data on this document correct?
   a. Scanned document shown (15 seconds)
7. Is this your document?

During each of the responses, the sensors monitored the vocal and ocular behavior of the participants and descriptive measures were calculated and presented to an experimenter and other participating border guard.

6 Results

6.1 Vocal Behavior

To assess the relationship between the voice and the participant's interview responses a multilevel model was specified with vocal quality as the response variable (N=189) regressed on condition (Guilty/Innocent) and question number (time). To reflect the repeated measure experimental design of multiple questions, both time and the Intercept of vocal quality were modeled to vary within Subject (N=38) as random effects. To calibrate each speaker each measurement of voice quality was subtracted by their starting value to reflect the deviance from a neutral starting point (Question One).

Table 1 below lists the fixed effects from this analysis. The imposters had a significantly larger drop in voice quality during the interview than innocent participants, $b=-2.18$, $p<.01$. Innocent participants and imposters both dropped their voice quality over time, likely because of the stress of the interview in contrast to the benign starting question.

Table 1. Vocal Behavior Fixed Effects (N=189, 38 Subjects)

Fixed Effects	β
Intercept	-0.136
Imposter	-2.180**
Time (Question)	-0.134*

*p<.05; **p<.01; Fit by Maximum Likelihood Estimation.

The imposters spoke with much lower vocal quality when answering questions related to their identity (questions 5, 6, and 7 above). Figure 5 below illustrates the difference in vocal quality between innocent and guilty participants.

Figure 5. Lower Vocal Quality of Imposters

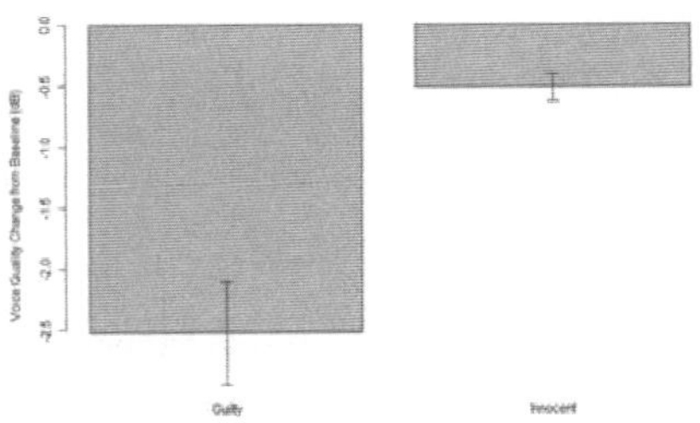

6.2 Eye Behavior

Eye contact with the ECA was not predictive of deception. However, a Between Subjects ANOVA revealed that when participants were asked to examine the image of their visa, imposters spent much more time fixating on the incorrect date of birth information, $F(1,36)=5.18$, $p=.028$, $\eta^2=.14$. Imposters spent 2.12 times more time fixating on the incorrect date of birth fields on their visa (Imposter M=29.73, SD=35.63; Innocent M=13.99, SD=8.45).

Figure 6. Eye Fixation Time on DOB Field

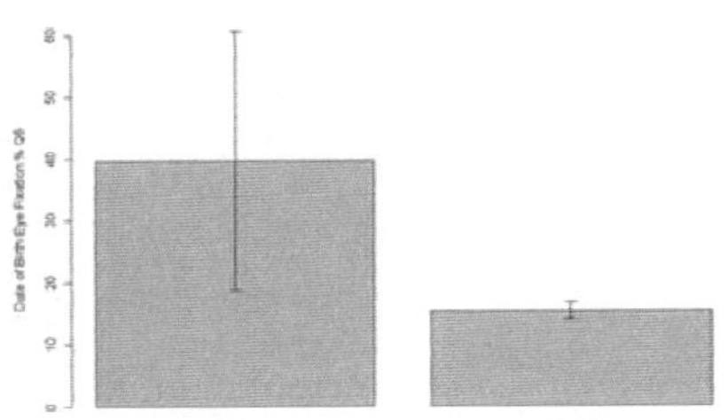

7 Summary of Predictors

To summarize the predictive potential of each of the collected vocal and eye gaze behavior measurements, each were submitted to Between Subjects ANOVA. Table 2 details the results for each measurement as a predictor of an imposter when answering question six.

Table 2. Vocal and Eye Gaze Behavior ANOVA Summary

Predictor	df	F	p
Vocal Pitch Mean	36	0.05	.83
Vocal Pitch SD	36	0.30	.58
Vocal Quality Mean	36	8.78	<.01**
Vocal Quality SD	36	0.29	.59
Vocal Intensity Mean	36	1.65	.21
Vocal Intensity SD	36	0.82	.37
DOB Eye Fixation	36	5.18	.03*
Pupil Dilation	36	0.04	.83

*p<.05; **p<.01; DOB is Date of Birth field on visa document; All vocal measurements were speaker calibrated

8 Classifying Imposters

Vocal quality and date of birth fixation were submitted to a recursive partitioning classification algorithm (Clark & Pregibon, 1992; R Development Core Team, 2011). This type of classification algorithm has the advantage of being very easy to interpret and resulted in the decision rule detailed in Figure 7 below.

Figure 7. Imposter Classification Model

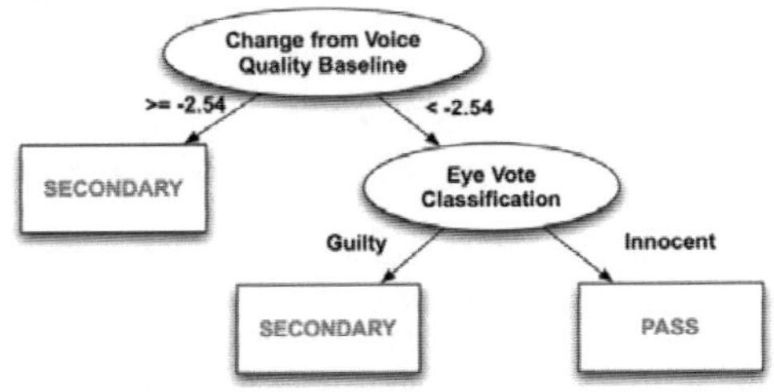

This final model had 94.47% accuracy, correctly identified all imposters, and misclassified two other participants of being imposters. When the classification model did not include the eye gaze behavior, the Voice Quality cut-off was much less conservative and resulted in many more false positives. However, after including the Eye Fixation variable, the system was calibrated to not over-rely on the voice.

This classification model illustrated the importance of additional sensors for improving overall accuracy of prediction, not just focusing entirely on true positives, or identifying imposters. Falsely accusing too many people would make the system infeasible in a high throughput, operational scenario. Given the diverse nature of the participants it should be noted that that gender, language, and potential cultural differences did not affect the results, but no support or conclusions can be drawn given the relatively small size of the various populations.

9 Conclusion

We conducted a field experiment with border guards from the European Union in order to demonstrate that by controlling some of the above factors and by developing context specific computational models, deception detection can be done robustly. We demonstrated that using both vocalic and ocular measurements we could correctly classify 100% of imposters in a limited scenario while limiting false positives. Future experimentation needs to be conducted to understand how the system compares to human judgment and if synergies exist between human and automated screening.

References

Bachorowski, J. A., & Owren, M. J. 1995. Vocal expression of emotion: Acoustic properties of speech are associated with emotional intensity and context. *Psychological Science*, 219–224.

Boersma, P. 1993. Accurate short-term analysis of the fundamental frequency and the harmonics-to-noise ratio of a sampled sound. *Proceedings of the Institute of Phonetic Sciences* (Vol. 17, pp. 97-110).

Buller, D. B., & Burgoon, J. K. 1996. Interpersonal deception theory. *Communication Theory*, *6*, 203-242.

Clark, L. A., & Pregibon, D. 1992. Tree-based models. *Statistical models in S*, 377–419.

Derrick, D. C., Jenkins, J., & Nunamaker, J. F. (2011). Design Principles for Special Purpose, Embodied, Conversational Intelligence with Environmental Sensors (SPECIES) Agents. *AIS Transactions on Human-Computer Interaction*, *3*(2), 62-81.

Elkins, A. C., & Stone, J. 2011. The Effect of Cognitive Dissonance on Argument Language and Vocalics. *Forty-Fourth Annual Hawaii International Conference on System Sciences*. Koloa, Kauai, Hawaii.

Juslin, P. N., & Laukka, P. 2003. Communication of emotions in vocal expression and music performance: Different channels, same code? *Psychological Bulletin*, *129*(5), 770-814.

Nunamaker, J. F., Derrick, D. C., Elkins, A. C., Burgoon, J. K., & Patton, M. W. 2011. Embodied Conversational Agent-Based Kiosk for Automated Interviewing. *Journal of Management Information Systems*, *28*(1), 17–48. doi:10.2753/MIS0742-1222280102

R Development Core Team. 2011. *R: A Language and Environment for Statistical Computing*. Vienna, Austria. Retrieved from http://www.R-project.org/

Rockwell, P., Buller, D. B., & Judee K. Burgoon. 1997. Measurement of deceptive voices: Comparing acoustic and perceptual data. *Applied Psycholinguistics*, *18*(04), 471-484.

Streeter, L. A., Krauss, R. M., Geller, V., Olson, C., & Apple, W. 1977. Pitch changes during attempted deception. *Journal of Personality and Social Psychology*, *35*(5), 345–350.

Titze, I. R., & Martin, D. W. 1998. Principles of voice production. *Acoustical Society of America Journal*, *104*, 1148.

Yumoto, E., Gould, W. J., & Baer, T. 1982. Harmonics-to-noise ratio as an index of the degree of hoarseness. *Journal of the Acoustical Society of America*, *71*(6), 1544-1550.

Zuckerman, M., DePaulo, B. M., & Rosenthal, R. 1981. Verbal and nonverbal communication of deception. *Advances in experimental social psychology*, *14*(1), 59.

Let's lie together: Co-presence effects on children's deceptive skills

Marc Swerts
Tilburg University
School of Humanities
Tilburg center for Communication and Cognition (TiCC)
Tilburg, The Netherlands
m.g.j.swerts@uvt.nl

Abstract

A person's expressive behavior is different in situations where he or she is alone, or where an additional person is present. This study looks at the extent to which such physical co-presence effects have an impact on a child's ability to deceive. Using an experimental digitized puppet show, truthful and deceptive utterances were elicited from children who were interacting with two story characters. The children were sitting alone, or as a couple together with another child. A first perception study in which minimal pairs of truthful and deceptive utterances were shown (vision-only) to adult observers revealed that the correct detection of deceptive utterances is dependent on whether the stimuli were produced by a child alone or together with another child (both being visible). A second perception study presented participants with videos from children of the couples condition that were edited so that only one child was visible. The study revealed that the deceptive utterances could more often be detected correctly in the more talkative children than in the more passive ones.

1 Introduction

Deceiving others is not always easy. Past research has shown that various factors can have a detrimental effect on a person's deceptive skills, as it may matter whom one tries to deceive, what kind of lie is being produced, and under what circumstances a lie is elicited (DePaulo, Lindsay, Malone, Muhlenbruck, Charlton, & Cooper 2003). The current study wants to explore whether the behavior of a deceiver is influenced by co-presence effects: i.e., is there an essential difference between a deceiver who is solely responsible for the lie he or she is producing, and someone who shares the responsibility for the deceit with another person who is physically present. We investigate such questions in data produced by children around the age of 5, and focus in particular on possible nonverbal cues to deception. As such, the current investigation fits with other studies on deceptive skills of children, given that these skills may reveal important aspects of a child's cognitive development. Indeed, telling a lie is often claimed to be mentally more demanding than telling the truth, and also presumes that one is able to understand and manipulate another person's perspective on a given state of affair. Given this, the study of lies has been thought to be potentially useful as a means to learn more about how growing children develop their metacognitive skills (e.g. Talwar, Lee, Bala, & Lindsay, 2004; Talwar, Murphy, & Lee, 2007).

Previous researchers have often explored someone's deceptive skills by running perception experiments in which independent observers have to judge in recordings of speakers whether a person is telling the truth or not. The current study explores whether the detection of a lie is different when an observer has to judge the recording of a person who is alone, or of a person who produces a lie together with another person. From the literature, it is not immediately clear whether co-presence effects are likely to maximize or diminish the perceived difference between truth and deceit. On the one hand, one could hypothesize that the presence of another person may make it easier for an observer to detect whether someone is telling the truth or not. Such an expectation could be based on studies that suggest that

Proceedings of the EACL 2012 Workshop on Computational Approaches to Deception Detection, pages 55–62,
Avignon, France, April 23 - 27 2012.

people contaminate each other's expressive behaviour, such that their facial and other nonverbal cues become more pronounced and more clearly interpretable for observers as cues to deception. In a study with game-playing children (Shahid, Krahmer, & Swerts 2008), to give an example, it was found that observers tend to find it easier to determine whether a child had won or lost a card guessing game, when it was playing together with another child, compared to a situation in which it was playing the game alone. That result is reminiscent of work on gesturing, where it is often reported that speakers become more expressive when they are directly being observed by someone else. Bavelas, Gerwing, Sutton, and Prevost (2008), for instance, found that speakers gesture more and with a larger amplitude if they are engaged in a face-to-face interaction, compared to a telephone conversation or in a setting where they talk to an answering machine. Similar findings were reported by Mol, Krahmer, Maes, and Swerts (2009).

On the other hand, findings that indicate that people become more expressive in the presence of other people may not generalize to all situational contexts, and may sometimes even be opposite to what was described above. For instance, Lee and Wagner (2002) analysed video recordings of women who were speaking about a positive or a negative experience either in the presence of an experimenter or alone. They found that women were more expressive about positive emotions when another person was present, whereas the negative emotions were less clearly expressed when someone else was present. These results show that social context can have different kinds of effects on a person's nonverbal behavior depending on a speaker's specific state of mind. This begs the question as to what happens when people are trying to deceive another person, and whether possible nonverbal correlates of their deceptive behavior become more pronounced or rather more diminished in contexts where they are alone, or physically co-present with other people. Moreover, from a perceptual perspective, it is not clear whether an observer would profit from the fact that he or she has to judge the truthfulness of only one person or of more than one person simultaneously. It could be that the exposure to multiple persons would make it easier for an observer because of having access to more resources to decide about truth or lie. But it could also be the case that the mere fact that an observer would have to judge multiple people at the same time would make the task of detecting deception more challenging than in the case where only one person is speaking, because it might be that subtle correlates of deception would escape the observer's attention.

Given the overall aim to investigate the effect of physical co-presence on a child's deceptive behavior, this study also explores whether the child's specific role in a situational context is of importance for the correct detection of deception. It has of course already been known for a few decades that a person's personality may matter, for instance in that extraverts tend to show more correlates of deception than introvert people (e.g. Bradley & Janisse 1981). Also, previous work suggests that more dominant people exhibit different kinds of nonverbal behaviour than followers (Tiedens & Fragale 2003). In line with this observation, we will look at children who are passive or active in a setting, and see whether that difference has repercussions for lie detection. On the one hand, active children in being more involved in the interaction may increase the likelihood of showing nonverbal cues to deception. On the other hand, it may that the more passive children may reveal such cues more clearly, as a result of their belief that the observer's focus of attention is directed towards the more active child, so that they leak more cues to deception.

The current research consists of two perception experiments. Experiment 1 investigates whether correlates of a child's deceptive behaviour are different for situations in which the child is either alone or co-present with another child. Experiment 2 looks at differences between participants within an interaction, in particular comparing children who are very active and talkative versus those who take less initiative. We only focus on visual cues (from which auditory features are removed), given that earlier work (Ecoff, Ekman, Mage & Frank 2000) has shown that observers can more accurately detect deception when they only have to focus on one modality (compared to tests with multimodal stimuli).

2 Interactive elicitation procedure

To obtain truthful and deceptive utterances from children, a new elicitation procedure was used, based on a computerized version of an animated puppet show. In the set-up, child participants are seated in front of a computer screen on which they see a story that unfolds. While the story is actually controlled by the experimenter (whom the child cannot see), the child is given the impression that some crucial actions of 2 main characters depend on the input of the child participant. During the interaction, the video and speech of the child are being recorded with a camera that is positioned on the top of the computer screen to which the child is looking. In this way, the recordings capture the faces and upper part of the chest (frontal view) of the child participants.

Figure 1: *A few visual materials of scenes used in the interactive puppet show*

The show starts with a longer part in which a narrating voice introduces 2 main characters, a prince (the good guy) and a dragon (the bad guy), to the participating child, in a typical fairy-tale plot. The narrator explains to the child that a bad dragon has been terrorizing a far-away country. Luckily, Prince Peter has come up with a plan to capture the dragon, for which he needs the help from the child. The narrator explains that the person who catches the dragon, receives a reward (a bag of gold) from the king. In order to increase the child's level of engagement, an actual bag of gold (actually, chocolate coins wrapped in goldish-looking paper) is clearly shown on a table in the visual field of the participant. Then the interactive part starts in which child utterances are elicited from exchanges with the 2 main characters of the story, the prince and the dragon. The interactive part contains 2 central scenes designed to elicit minimal pairs of truthful and deceptive utterances from children to be used in a perception test later on. As will become clear below, deceptive utterances are elicited from a child's interaction with the dragon, and the truthful ones from interactions with the prince.

First, the prince appears, and asks the child for its name, mainly to ensure that the latter becomes aware that it can interact with the story character. After this, the prince tells the child that he wants to capture the dragon, and needs the child's help. He tells the child that he will hide behind a tree (shown on the left of the screen), and that, if the dragon appears, the child needs to tell the dragon that the prince has entered the castle (shown on the right of the screen). Then he hides behind the tree, after which the dragon appears on stage and asks the child where the prince is. The child typically replies with a deceptive phrase like "in the castle" (first deceptive response), after which the dragon expresses some disbelief about this response, and repeats the earlier question, so that the child needs to repeat the earlier response (second deceptive response). Then, the dragon leaves, enters the castle, after which the prince appears again. He tells the child he believes he has heard the dragon, and asks where the dragon is, to which a child typically responds with a truthful "in the castle" (first truthful response). The prince says he cannot believe that response, so asks the child to repeat its truthful utterance (second truthful response). Given that both the deceptive and truthful scene contain a repeat, we obtain 4 versions from every participating child of the utterance "in the castle" (or equivalent phrases like "in the tower", or "in the church"): first and second attempts of truthful and deceptive utterances. Figure 1 depicts some representative scenes from the story.

We obtained minimal pairs (truthful and deceptive variants of the utterance "in the castle") from 38 children (18 boys; 20 girls), who had volunteered for the experiment with written consent from their parents and/or primary caretakers. The average age of these children was 5 years and 7 months (minimum: 4 years and 10 months; maximum: 6 and 4 months) in addition, we collected recordings for 10 pairs of children who did the same task as the singles, but sitting next to each other and both facing the screen. Their average age was 5 years and 5 months (minimum: 4 years and 3 months; maximum: 6 and 9 months). Note that the task given to the pairs of children was the same as the one given to the children sitting alone. It was interesting to note that there was essentially no interaction between two participants in the pairs condition, and that they basically only responded to questions and instructions from the story characters. We did observe, however, that within these pairs, there tended to be a division of labor, in that one of the children would typically take the initiative and talk to the story characters, while the other would be more passive.

3 Experiment 1: singles vs. couples

The first experiment explores whether there is a difference in the extent to which lies can be detected in children who are interacting alone with some story characters, versus children who are doing a similar task together with another child.

3.1 Method

3.1.1 Stimuli

The stimuli consisted of the children's responses to either the prince (truthful) or the dragon (deceptive), where some of the children were interacting alone, and some were interacting in couples. As said above, stimuli were presented as video-only materials, so with the sound removed.

3.1.2 Participants

The data for the singles condition were collected in an earlier study, and came from 20 observers (Swerts 2011). In addition, 121 participants took part in the couples condition of the experiment, as partial fulfillment to get course credits.

3.1.3 Procedure

Observers were presented with pairs of video recordings, i.e., a truthful and a deceptive utterance of either a single child, or similar clips in which 2 children are visible who are sitting next to each other. Pairs of recordings were either comparing the children's first time they had responded to a question from the prince or the dragon, or pairs of utterances of their second responses to those characters. Note that pairs of stimuli shown to observers were always produced by the same child. Stimuli were presented in a group experiment, although each participant had to perform the test individually (paper-and-pencil test). The task given to observers was to guess by forced choice which of the 2 clips they saw contained a child's deceptive utterance. The order of presentation of the truthful and deceptive utterance within a pair, and of the pairs within the larger test was fully randomized.

3.2 Results

The observer responses were analysed with a repeated measures ANOVA with the percentage correct detection of deceptive utterances for all stimulus pairs per observer as dependent variable, and with attempt (2 levels: first attempt, second attempt) and order (2 levels: deceptive utterance shown first, deceptive utterance shown second) as within-subject factors, and presence (2 levels: alone, together) as between-subject factors. Table 1 reveals that, while the main effects of presence and attempt are not significant, there is a significant effect of presentation order on the observers' likelihood to correctly detect the deceptive utterance: deceptive utterances could more easily be detected correctly if they were shown after the truthful utterance, rather than the other way around. In addition, we found a significant 2-way interaction between attempt and presence ($_{(1,13)} = 5.793$, $< .05$, $^{2} = .0\ 0$), which can be explained by the data shown in table 2. As can be seen, for the alone condition, observers tend to find it easier to detect the deceptive utterance in pairs of second interactions with the story characters, than in the first interactions. However, for those stimuli taken from children being together, there appears to be no difference between

Table 1: Percentage correct detection of deception (mean, standard error, 95% intervals) and F-statistics for different levels of experimental factors

Factor	Level	Correct detection	F-stats
Presence	Alone	58.0 (.24, 53.1 – 62.8)	$_{(1,13)} = .991, \; = \; . .,$
	Together	60.6 (.10, 58.7 – 62.6)	$^2 = .007$
Attempt	First	57.4 (.18, 53.9 – 61.0)	$_{(1,13)} = 2.55 \;, \; = \; . .,$
	Second	61.2 (.17, 57.8 – 64.6)	$^2 = .01$
Order	Deception first	53.2 (.18, 49.6 – 56.8)	$_{(1,13)} = 2\;.1\;3, \; < .001,$
	Deception second	65.4 (.18, 61.8 – 68.9)	$^2 = .1$

Table 2: Percentage correct detection of deception (mean, standard error) for speakers in alone or couples condition as a function of order of speaker attempt

	Attempt	
Presence	First	Second
Alone	52.3 (.33)	62.7 (.32)
Together	61.6 (.14)	59.7 (.13)

first and second attempts.

3.3 Discussion

While the experiment did not reveal a main effect of co-presence on the detection of deception, that factor turned out to be important in a 2-way interaction with attempt. This significant interaction may be explained by ceiling effects that are only true for the condition in which 2 children were being observed, but appear to be absent in the alone condition. That is, in the alone condition, the probability to correctly detect a lie appears to depend on whether observers were seeing a first or second attempt of a child interacting with the story characters. As table 2 reveals, during a second attempt, a single child was more likely to show correlates of deceptive behavior compared to its first attempt. That effect may be due to the fact that during a second attempt a child is more consciously aware of the fact that it tries to deceive which may have the ironic counter-effect that more cues to deception are leaked, as it tries harder than the first time (Swerts 2011; see also Wardlow Lane et al. 2006). However, in the together condition, it appears not to matter whether the children were interacting for the first or second time; rather, the results appears to be around 60% correct detection both during first and second attempts. Compared with related studies in this area of research (e.g. DePaulo, Lindsay, Malone, Muhlenbruck, Charlton, & Cooper, 2003), this percentage is high, so that some ceiling effects may come into play: the correct detection for first attempts is already so high that it is hard to get even better results during second attempts. While experiment 1 has provided some evidence that detection of deceit is affected by co-presence effects, it remains unclear whether observers were able to extract cues to deception from both children in the together condition or whether they were especially paying attention to certain types of children. More specifically, informal observations of the video clips suggested that some children were playing a more active role in the interactions than other children.

4 Experiment 2: active vs. passive children

Experiment 2 explores to what extent differences between the child participants (talkative vs. silent ones) may influence an observer's ability to find a deceptive utterance.

4.1 Method

4.1.1 Stimuli

The stimuli showed children from the couples condition of experiment 1, except that the clips only showed 1 child (zoomed in so that the other child was not visible). As discussed above, when two children were placed next to each other to interact with the prince and the dragon in the story, there tended to be one child who was more active

Table 3: Percentage correct detection of deception (mean, standard error, 95% intervals) and F-statistics for different levels of experimental factors

Factor	Level	Correct detection	F-stats
Speaker	Passive	50.4 (.18, 46.8 – 54.0)	$_{(1, 2)} =$ 7.1 0, $< .001$,
	Active	62.0 (.15, 59.1 – 64.9)	$^2 = .339$
Order	Deception first	47.3 (.18, 43.7 – 50.9)	$_{(1, 2)} =$ 23. 9, $< .001$,
	Deception second	65.1 (.16, 61.9 – 68.3)	$^2 = .20$

than the other when addressing the story characters. For the purpose of the current experiment, we distinguished between children who were labeled "active" as those who had been speaking in both the truthful and deceptive utterance, versus the "passive" ones as those who had been silent in at least one of the two. In doing so, we obtained 13 active and 7 passive children. Also, given that we were only interested in the effect of passive vs active children and to reduce the time it took to complete the experiment, we decided to only use stimuli from the second attempts of the children to produce a truthful or deceptive utterance.

4.1.2 Participants

In total, 93 participants took part in the experiment, as partial fulfillment to get course credits. None of them had participated in any of the perception tests of experiment 1.

4.1.3 Procedure

The procedure of this experiment was exactly the same as the one used for experiment 1.

4.2 Results

The data were again analysed with a repeated measures ANOVA with the percentage correct detection of deceptive utterances for all stimulus pairs per observer as dependent variable, and with order (2 levels: deceptive utterance shown first, deceptive utterance shown second) and speaker role (2 levels: active, passive) as independent within-subject factors. As shown in table 3, both speaker type and presentation order had a significant effect on correct detection of the deceptive utterance, such that observers found it easier to detect the lies in the more active speakers, and in those pairs in which the deceptive utterance was presented as the second one in a pair (see also experiment 1). Interestingly, the interaction between order and speaker role was not significant ($_{(1, 2)} = 2.$ 32, = . ., $^2 = .02$). As table 4 reveals, the 2 effects of speaker role and order are additive.

Table 4: Percentage correct detection of deception (mean, standard error) for passive and active speakers as a function of order of deceptive utterance

	Deceptive utterance	
Speaker	shown first	shown second
Passive	39.8 (.27)	61.0 (.27)
Active	54.8 (.22)	69.2 (.18)

4.3 Discussion

Experiment 2 has shown that the likelihood of correctly detecting whether a child is deceiving or speaking the truth depends on how active it is within a specific social context. That is, when it takes the initiative of responding to the story characters and is being relatively talkative, then this level of engagement makes it easier for an observer to decide whether or not the child is producing a lie. Further research is needed to find out why exactly it is that detection of deception is easier when people have to judge more active participants. One reason could be that children who are more active are also more expressive, which increases the chances that specific cues to deception are leaked to an observer. Such an explanation would be compatible with earlier findings that the accuracy with which lies can be detected correctly varies for deceivers who have different personalities. More specifically, it has been shown that, when comparing introvert with extravert people, it is generally easier to detect the lies in the latter group (Bradley & Janisse, 1981).

In the current set-up of the experiment, the children were not explicitly given any explicit roles in the story, for instance, in that one of them would be asked to be silent, while the other would be given the instruction to take initiative with the characters of the story. Rather, their level of engagement within the interactive story occurred spontaneously in the course of the interaction, which was thought to guarantee that their interaction was relatively natural. In future work, however, it could be worthwhile to make a participants' active or passive role within the discourse more explicit to the child and also measure aspects of their personality. This would help to decide whether the detection of deception is due to the fact that some children are more active, or to the fact that some children are more extravert, or to a combination of these factors.

5 General discussion

The current study revealed that deceiving children are affected by co-presence effects. Experiment 1, in which minimal pairs of truthful and deceptive utterances were shown (vision-only) to adult observers, brought to light that the correct detection of deceptive utterances is dependent on whether the stimuli were produced by a child alone or together with another child. This result reminds one of some practices in typical investigations of a committed crime, where it is general practice to confront various suspects with each other. Usually, the goal of letting multiple suspects meet is to confront them with each other's statements from earlier police interrogations during which they were separately interviewed independently from each other. If these earlier sessions has let to inconsistencies between the statements of the different suspects, it might be interesting to see how suspects react when they are exposed to each other's claims in a face-to-face situation. Ideally, such a confrontation might help to let one of them confess, or admit that an earlier claim was false. Obviously, the story paradigm used in the production experiment to elicit truthful and deceptive utterances is different from such a police case, but it does show that presence effects may maximize the differences between truth and deceit.

This result appears to be compatible with the idea that the presence of another person increases a liar's social awareness, which in turn might have a detrimental effect on that person's deceptive skills. Such an effect could be similar to the reported effect of an increased mental load on deceptive behaviour: lying is generally assumed to be more cognitively demanding than truth telling (e.g. DePaulo, Lindsay, Malone, Muhlenbruck, Charlton, & Cooper 2003; Vrij, Fisher, Mann, & Leal 2006), given that liars have to monitor more tasks than truth telling people, such as inventing facts and controlling their behaviour while interacting with another person. Consequently, techniques that increase cognitive load, e.g. asking people to tell a story in reverse order (Vrij, Mann, Fisher, Leal, Milne, & Bull, 2008) or instructing them to maintain eye contact with an interviewer (Vrij, Mann, Leal, & Fisher 2010), tend to lead to the effect that deception becomes more easily observable. Under conditions of such increased cognitive load, deceivers supposedly have less resources to monitor their behavior, so that they leak cues that others may pick up as indicators of deception. Similarly, an increased social awareness because of the mere presence of another person could possibly lead to leaking more cues to lies.

The second perception experiment presented participants with videos from children of the couples condition that were edited so that only one child was visible. The study revealed that the deceptive utterances could more often be detected correctly in the more talkative children compared to the more passive ones. It remains to be seen whether these results are due to the fact that the higher probability of correctly detecting deception in the more active children is due to the fact that their higher level of engagement makes them more expressive and more likely to leak cues to deception, or because these more active children have a more extravert personality that has been shown to show more cues to deception than more introvert children (Bradley & Janisse, 1981).

And finally, we found an additional order effect, as deceptive utterances can more often be detected correctly when they are presented as the second in a pair, as opposed to when they are presented as the first ones. This effect, in line with previous observations by O'Sullivan et al (1988), could be related to what is known as the truth bias in the literature on deception, which refers to "an a priori belief, expectation, or presumption that reflects the oft-observed tendency to assume communicators are truthful most of the time" (e.g. Burgoon et al. 2008, p. 575). Accordingly, this could possibly lead to the effect that an initial utterance is first processed as being truthful, and revised if an utterance contains counter-evidence to this effect. Therefore, given that the truthful utterances are more in line with default expectations of an observer, it would become more easy to detect the deceptive utterance as the more marked and deviant case, if it is presented after the truthful one.

Acknowledgments

We thank the director, teachers, parents and children of the elementary school "The Palet" in Hapert and "de Oversteek" in Liempde (both in The Netherlands) for their willingness to participate in the interactive story experiment. Many thanks also to Lennard van de Laar and Emiel Krahmer for help with setting up the elicitation procedure and perception experiment, to Marlon van Dijk, Linda Dolmans and John van den Broeck for help with collecting the stimuli and the perception results, and to Marieke Hoetjes and Lisette Mol for comments on an earlier version of this document.

6 References

Bavelas, J., Gerwing, J., Sutton, C., & Prevost, D. (2008). Gesturing on the telephone: Independent effects of dialogue and visibility. *Journal of Memory and Language* 58, 495–520.

Bradley, M. T. & Janisse, M.P. (1981) Extraversion and the detection of deception *Personality and Individual Differences* 2, 99–103

Burgoon, J.K., Blair, J.P. & Strom, R.E. (2008) Cognitive Biases and Nonverbal Cue Availability in Detecting Deception. *Human Communication Research*, 34 572–599.

DePaulo, B., Lindsay, J., Malone, B., Muhlenbruck, L., Charlton, K., & Cooper, H. (2003). Cues to deception. *Psychological Bulletin*, 129, 74–118.

Ecoff, N.L., Ekman, P., Mage, J.J. & Frank, M.G. (2000) Lie Detection And Language Comprehension. *Nature*, 405, 139.

Lee, V. & Wagner, H. (2002). The Effect of Social Presence on the Facial and Verbal Expression of Emotion and the Interrelationships Among Emotion Components. *Journal of Nonverbal Behavior*, 26, 3–25.

Mol, L., Krahmer, E., Maes, A.A., & Swerts, M. (2009). The communicative import of gestures: Evidence from a comparative analysis of human-human and human-machine interactions *Gesture* 9, 97–126.

O'Sullivan, M., Ekman, P. & Friesen, W.V. (1988). The effect of comparisons on detecting deceit *Journal of Nonverbal Behavior* 12, 203–215.

Shahid, S., Krahmer, E.J., & Swerts, M. (2008). Alone or together: Exploring the effect of physical co-presence on the emotional expressions of game playing children across cultures. In: P. Markopoulus et al. (Eds.), *Fun and Games* (pp. 94-105). Springer. (Lecture Notes in Computer Science LNCS, 5294)

Swerts, M. (2011). Correlates of social awareness in the visual prosody of growing children. *Laboratory Phonology*, 2(2), 381–402.

Talwar, V., Lee, K., Bala, N. & Lindsay, R.C.L. (2004). Children's Lie-Telling to Conceal Parents' Transgressions: Legal Implications. *Law and Human Behavior*, 28 411–435.

Talwar, V., Murphy S., & Lee, K. (2007) White lie-telling in children for politeness purposes. *International Journal of Behavioral Development*, 31, 1–11.

Tiedens, L. & Fragale, A.R. (2003) Power Moves: Complementarity in Dominant and Submissive Nonverbal Behavior. *Journal of Personality and Social Psychology* (84), 558–568.

Vrij, A., Fisher, R., Mann, S., & Leal (2006) Detecting deception by manipulating cognitive load *Trends in cognitive sciences* 10, 141–142.

Vrij, A., Mann, S., Fisher, R., Leal, S., Milne, R., & Bull, R. (2008) Increasing cognitive load to facilitate lie detection: the benefit of recalling am event in reverse order. *Law and Human Behavior* 32, 253–265.

Vrij, A., Mann, S., Leal, S. & Fisher, R. (2010) 'Look into my eyes': can an instruction to maintain eye contact facilitate lie detection? *Psychology, Crime & Law*, 16 (4), 327–348

Wagner, H., & Lee, V. (1999). Facial behavior alone and in the presence of others. In: P. Philippott et al. (eds.) *The social context of nonverbal behavior*, pp. 262–286. Cambridge University Press, New York.

Wardlow Lane, Liane, Michelle Groisman & Victor S. Ferreira. (2006). Don't Talk About Pink Elephants! Speakers' Control Over Leaking Private Information During Language Production. *Psychological Science* 17 (4), 273-277.

Argument Formation in the Reasoning Process: Toward a Generic Model of Deception Detection

Deqing Li and Eugene Santos, Jr.
Thayer School of Engineering
Dartmouth College
Hanover, N.H., U.S.A
{ Deqing.Li, Eugene.Santos.Jr }@Dartmouth.edu

Abstract

Research on deception detection has been mainly focused on two kinds of approaches. In one, people consider deception types and taxonomies, and use different counter strategies to detect and reverse deception. In the other, people search for verbal and non-verbal cues in the content of deceptive communication. However, general theories that study fundamental properties of deception which can be applied in computational models are still very rare. In this work, we propose a general model of deception detection guided by a fundamental principle in the formation of communicative deception. Experimental results using our model demonstrate that deception is distinguishable from unintentional misinformation.

Introduction

Conventional research on deception detection focuses on deception taxonomies and deception cues. Unfortunately, both of them neglect the fact that deception is rooted in the formation of arguments mainly because such formation is not directly observable. However, since the formation of arguments is where the implementation of deception starts, it is necessary to study it in depth.

The act of deceiving involves two processes: the formation of deceptive arguments (the reasoning) and the communication of deception. The communication part is intuitive to understand and has been the focus of recent research efforts in deception detection. The reasoning part is a necessary component of deception because deceiving has been found to require a heavier cognitive load than telling the truth (Greene et. Al, 1985). The reasoning process involves generating and selecting arguments while the communication process involves wording and phrasing of the arguments. Deception detection in the process of communication is not ideal because firstly, it is easy to hide deceptive cues using careful wording and phrasing, and secondly, wording and phrasing of communication are mediated by the framing of the other party's response (e.g. the answer to the question "Did you go to class today?" always starts with "Yes, I" or "No, I"). On the other hand, it is hard to hide the intent of deception by distorting arguments formed in the reasoning process because it requires higher-order deception that takes the other party's intent and even the other party's belief about the speaker's intent into consideration. Higher-order deception demands much more cognitive load than first-order deception in order to retrieve the memory about the other party's intent and leverage the original reasoning process behind it. Thus, the reasoning process provides more effective and reliable observations than the communication process. Moreover, it also guides and explains some observations in the communication process such as compellingness and level of detail of a story.

We will illustrate the formation of deceptive arguments in the next section, according to which, we propose three hypotheses of the fundamental differences between deception and non-deception. In Section 3, we describe our model of detection and the data simulation process. Experiment setting and results are

Proceedings of the EACL 2012 Workshop on Computational Approaches to Deception Detection, pages 63–71,
Avignon, France, April 23 - 27 2012. ©2012 Association for Computational Linguistics

discusses in Section 4, followed by conclusions and future work in Section 5.

1 Formation of Deceptive Argument

The reasoning process can be regarded as inference based on the conditional relationship between arguments by assuming that human reasoning is akin to informal logic. Since deceivers intentionally reach the conclusion that they target at, we propose that the act of deceiving is to reason by supposing the truth of deceivers' targeted arguments, but the truth of the targeted arguments is not actually believed by the deceivers. For example, if a person is asked to lie about his attitude on abortion, he might raise arguments such as "fetuses are human", "god will punish anyone who aborts children" and "children have the right to live". He did not raise these arguments because he believed in them but because they support the false conclusion that he is against abortion. It is thus natural to imagine that the conclusion comes into deceivers' minds before the arguments. According to Levi (1996), "*The addition of the supposition to the agent's state of full belief does not require jettisoning any convictions already fully believed. The result of this modification of the state of full belief by supposition is a new potential state of full belief containing the consequences of the supposition added and the initial state of full belief*", which means that the reasoning with a supposition is a regular reasoning with the addition of a piece of knowledge that has been assumed before the reasoning starts. It also follows that the reasoning with a supposition can be exactly the same as a regular reasoning in which the supposition in the former case is a true belief. That is to say, the reasoning in deception formation can be regarded to follow the same scheme as that in truth argumentation. However, even if deceiver and truth teller share the same reasoning scheme, their beliefs and processes of reasoning are different. In particular, if an opinion-based story is required from the speaker, truth tellers propagate beliefs from evidence, while deceivers adapt beliefs to suppositions. If an event-based story is required, truth tellers retrieve relevant memory which is based on past behavior and past behavior is based on past belief, which was propagated from past evidence, while deceivers suppose a part of the event and adapt his fantasy to the supposition. This fundamental difference in the reasoning of deceiver and truth teller is unavoidable due to the intentionality of deceivers. It provides reasoning a stable ground on which schemes of deception detection can be built.

As we have discussed, the product of reasoning from truth teller and deceiver may be exactly the same. However it is hardly true in the real world because they do not share the same belief system that supports their reasoning. If in any case they do share the same belief system, they would reach the same conclusion without any deception and there would be no need to deceive. In order to mimic truth teller's story, deceiver may manipulate his conclusion and distort other arguments to support the manipulated conclusion, but the supporting arguments are biased by his honest but untruthful belief system. **Therefore, discrepancies in arguments that deceivers are reluctant to believe but truth tellers embrace can be expected.** On the other hand, deception has been defined as "*a relationship between two statements*" (Shibles, 1988), according to which, deception is a contradiction between belief and expression. A deceiver may lie about the polarity of belief as well as the strength or extent of belief as long as his belief expression deviates from his honest reasoning. The more manipulation he did to mimic the truth, the farther he deviates from himself. **Therefore, discrepancies in arguments that are manipulated by deceivers can be expected.** The above two discrepancies in deception have been popularly embraced by existing researchers (Mehrabian, 1972; Wiener & Mehrabian, 1968; Johnson & Raye, 1981, Markus, 1977). Our focus is to explain and measure them in terms of human reasoning, and argue that these two discrepancies follow our proposal that deceptive reasoning is reasoning with presupposition, due to which the discrepancies are the fundamental difference between deception and truth that produces other observable patterns.

2 Hypotheses and Justification

We have argued that the basic discrepancy in deceptive reasoning exists in inconsistency and untruthfulness. Inconsistency means that the arguments in the story contradict with what the speaker would believe. Untruthfulness means that the arguments in the story contradict with what an honest person would believe in order to reach the conclusion. On the other hand, inconsistency indicates that an honest person should behave as he always does, which requires some familiarity with the speaker, whereas untruthfulness indicates that an honest person should behave as a reasonable and convincing person, which requires some knowledge of the topic domain. Opinion change violates the former one but not the latter one as it changes the prior knowledge but still maintains truthfulness, and innovation violates the latter one but not the former one as innovation is convincing but not expectable. They do not violate both so they are not deceptions. However, these two elements are not the unique characteristics of deception because random manipulations without any purpose to deceive such as misinformation also show inconsistency and untruthfulness. Fortunately, deceivers can be distinguished by the manner they manipulate arguments. We propose the following hypotheses that can be expected in deceptive stories but not others.

Firstly, explicit manipulations in deception continuously propagate to other arguments which become implicit manipulations. The purpose, of course, is to spread the manipulation to the conclusion. The propagation spreads to surrounding arguments and the influence of manipulation decreases as the propagation spreads farther away, which random manipulations do not exhibit. If one overlooks the abnormality of the explicit manipulations, the story would seem to flow smoothly from the arguments to the conclusion because the connection between the arguments is not broken. Inconsistency is particularly important when individual difference should be considered.

Secondly, there is a correspondence between inconsistency and untruthfulness. Some inconsistencies were manipulated significantly because the deceiver wants to convince the listener of the argument and these arguments seem more reasonable to support the conclusion after manipulation. Therefore, the significant manipulations are often convincing, but there are also exceptions in which deceivers overly manipulate arguments that are usually ignored by truth tellers. We call these Type I incredibility: incredibility due to over-manipulation. The arguments that are not convincing usually can be found in the inconsistencies that were slightly manipulated or ignored by the deceiver because deceivers do not know that they are important supports to the conclusion but truth tellers never neglect these details. This is called Type II incredibility: incredibility due to ignorance. Type I and Type II incredibility are two examples of unconvincing arguments (According to DePaulo et. al (2003), liars tell less compelling tales than truth tellers), which can be quantitatively measured in the reasoning process. On the other hand, random manipulations do not show this correspondence between inconsistency and untruthfulness. Measuring untruthfulness is particularly effective in detecting deception from general population whom the detector is not familiar with.

Thirdly, deceptions are intentional, which means the deceiver assumes the conclusion before inferring the whole story. Or in other words, deceivers fit the world to their mind, which is a necessary component of intentionality according to Humberstone (1992). They are convincers who reach arguments from conclusions, while others reach conclusions from arguments. According to the satisfaction of intention (Mele, 1992), an intention is "satisfied" only if behavior in which it issues is guided by the intention-embedded plan. Thus, deceivers choose the best behavior (argument in this case) that is guided (inferred in this case) by his desire (conclusion in this case), but not any behavior that can fulfill his desire. In particular, deceivers will choose the state of the argument in the story that is most effective compared with other states of the argument in reaching the conclusion of the story (e.g. the best state of whether 'an unborn baby is a life' towards the conclusion of supporting abortion is no). In deception, the inconsistent arguments are usually effective to the conclusion, while in random manipulation the inconsistent arguments are not.

Inconsistency, untruthfulness, propagated manipulation and intentionality are the guiding concepts of our deception detection method, which is a general model independent of the domain knowledge.

3 Methodology

In this work, we will not only test the hypotheses proposed above, but also provide a computational model to identify the discrepancy in arguments that are manipulated by deceivers and the discrepancy in arguments that are not as convincing as truth tellers'.

3.1 Computational Model of Deception Detection

We propose a generic model to detect deception through the reasoning process without assuming human's reasoning scheme. As shown in Figure

1, the model is composed of two networks: Correlation Network and Consensus Network. Correlation Network connects each agent with agents who correlate with him in a specific argument. Neighbors in the Correlation Network represent acquaintances who can anticipate each other's arguments. Consensus Network connects agents with similar conclusions. Neighbors in the Consensus Network represent people who agree with each other. We have pointed out that deception is deviation from one's own subjective beliefs, but not deviation from the objective reality or from the public. Thus Correlation Network is essential in predicting an agent's belief according to neighbors who can expect each other. This idea of measuring individual inconsistency has been discussed in our former work (Santos et. Al, 2010), which also provides details on the computation. The Consensus Network provides a sampled population of truth tellers who reach the same conclusion as the deceiver. If the deceiver told the truth, he should behave in no difference with the population. The untruthfulness of the deceiver can be evaluated by comparing the deceiver with the truth tellers. Functionality of the arguments can be revealed from the history data of the deceiver. By studying the history data, we can evaluate which arguments are effective to which from the perspective of the deceiver.

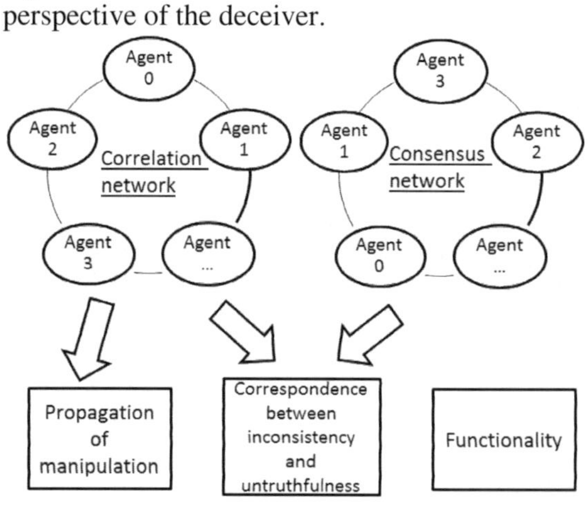

Figure 1: Architecture of the model of deception detection

3.2 Date Collection and Simulation

To test the hypotheses we proposed, we simulate the reasoning process of a deceiver according to our assumption that deceivers pre-suppose conclusions before reasoning. The deceiver we simulate is a plaintiff in a lawsuit of a rape case shown in a popular Hong Kong TV episode. The case is described as following. A female celebrity coded as *A* claims that she was raped by an Indian young man coded as *B*. *A* claims that she keeps away from *B* because both her and her mother do not like the physical odor of Indians. *A* claims that *B* once joined her birthday party without any invitation and fed *A* drugs. *B* then conveyed *A* home and raped *A*. After *A*'s boyfriend arrived, *A* called police. However, the truth is that *B* is a fan of *A* and joined *A*'s party at *A*'s invitation. *A* lied about her aversion to Indians because she used to prostitute to Indians. Besides, *B* is new to the party club, so it is unlikely for him to obtain drugs there. *A* used drugs and enticed *B* to have sex with her. This artificial scenario is a simplification of a possible legal case, which provides realistic explanations compared with simulation data that simulate deception arbitrarily without considering the intent of deceiver. We did not use real cases or lab surveys because they either do not have the ground truth of the speaker's truthfulness or lack sufficient information about the reasoning of the deceiver. Data that do have both ground truth and sufficient information such as military combat scenarios are mostly focused on behavioral deception instead of communicative deception. In addition, real cases may contain noisy data in which the communication content is mediated by factors other than reasoning. For the purpose of evaluating hypotheses about deceptive reasoning it is ideal to use clean data that only contains the semantic meaning of arguments. The evaluation of the hypotheses guides the development of our detection model, which we will apply to real data eventually.

A's belief system is represented by a Bayesian Network (BN) (Pearl, 1988). BNs have been used to simulate human reasoning processes for various purposes and have been shown to be consistent with the behavior of human (Tenenbau et. Al, 2006). A BN is a graphical structure in which a node represents a propositional argument and the conditional probability between nodes represent the conditional relationship between arguments. For example, the reasoning that *B* drives *A* home because *B* knows *A*'s address can be encoded in the conditional probability P(*B_drive_A_home*|*B_know_A_s_adr*)=0.9. In order to eliminate the variation due to wording, the semantics of the arguments instead of the phrases are encoded in the nodes. We designed a BN representing *A*'s belief system and also a BN representing the belief system of a true victim of the rape case according to the description of the scenario and some common sense. More specifically, we connect two arguments if their causal relationship is explicitly described by the deceiver or by the jury when they are analyzing the intent of the deceiver. The conditional probabilities between states of arguments are set as 0.7 to 0.99 according to the certainty of the speaker if they are explicitly described. As to the states that are not mentioned in the case, they are usually implied in or can be inferred from the scenario if their mutual exclusive states are described in the scenario, such as the probability of *A_hate_Indian* given that *B*'s relation with *A*'s mother is good and that *A* used to prostitute to Indians. Otherwise the mutual exclusive states are given the same or similar probabilities indicating that they are uncertain. To make sure that the discrepancies in deception are resulted from the manner of reasoning instead of from the inherent difference between the deceiver's belief system and the true victim's belief system, we minimize the difference between their belief systems. Specifically, we keep all their conditional probabilities the same by assuming that both are rational people with the same common sense. Only their prior probabilities of *A*'s experience as prostitute and whether *B* is new to the party or not are adjusted differently, because they are the essential truth in a true victim's perspective. That is to say, those who do not like Indians could not prostitute to them, and to obtain drugs from the party club, B has to be a regular guest. However, as a result of sharing a similar belief system with the true victim, the deceiver's story may become highly convincing. Although we expect it to be hard to detect the untruthfulness of the deceiver, the deceiver's simulation is not unrealistic because some deceivers are consistently found to be more credible than others based on the research by Bond and Depaulo (2008). It is highly likely that a randomized BN with a perturbed copy can also serve our purposes, but again, building belief systems based on the intent of deception will provide more realistic data, more convincing results and more intuitive explanations. The BN of the deceiver is depicted in Figure 2. Its conditional probability tables are shown in Appendix A.

The process of reasoning is represented by the process of inferencing, and the product of reasoning is represented by the inferred probabilities of the nodes. Computing posterior probabilities, P(A|E), is not feasible here since it does not consider the consistency over all variables. Consider the following example. Suppose 10 people join a lottery of which exactly one will win. By computing posterior probabilities, we obtain the result that no one will win because each of them wins with probability 0.1. To retain the validity of the probability of each variable as well as the consistency over all variables, we propose the following inference. We first perform a belief revision and obtain the most probable world, which is the complete inference with the highest joint probability. Then for each variable, we compute its posterior probability given that all other variables are set as evidence with the same assignment as in the most probable world. By inferring the lottery example in this way, in each of its inferred world a different person wins with equal probability. Specifically, the probability of a person winning given all others not winning is 1, and the probability of a person winning given all but one winning is 0. As we proposed earlier, the reasoning process of the deceiver presupposes her target arguments, that is, she was raped, by adding the argument as an extra piece of evidence. The inference results of *A* in both deceptive and honest cases and those of a true victim are shown in Table 1. The arguments *B_relation_with_A_s_mother=bad*, *B_drive_A_home=true*, *A_is_celebrity=true* and *A_s_boyfriend_catch_on_the_scene=true* are set as evidence as suggested by the scenario.

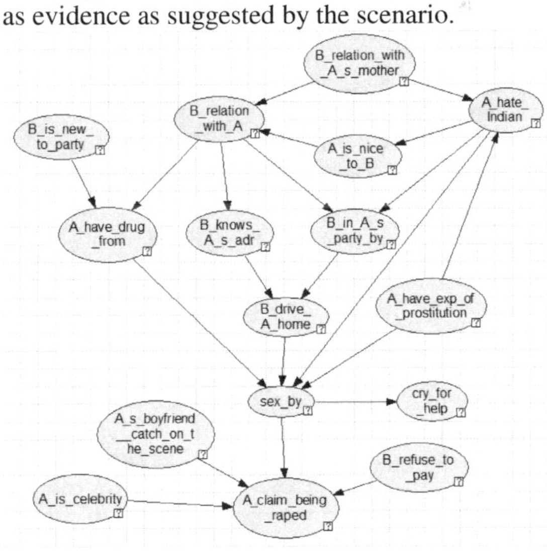

Figure 2: BN of the deceiver in the rape case

People express attitudes as binary beliefs in communication if not as beliefs with fuzzy confidence, but not as degree of belief formulated by real-valued probabilities. To map degree of belief to binary beliefs, we need to know how much confidence is sufficient for a person to believe in an attitude. Or in other words, what is the probability threshold of something being true. Research has suggested that truth threshold varies by proposition and by individual, which means it is a subjective criterion (Ferreira, 2004). Since we use simulated data, we arbitrarily choose 0.66 as the threshold since it equally spaces the interval of an argument being true, unknown and false. Then the binary beliefs in the deceptive story and honest story of the deceiver and those in the true victim's story would be the same as Table 2. To verify the inferred beliefs, we compare Table 2 with the scenario. An argument is validated if it is in the same state as described in the scenario or in the unknown state given that it is ignored in the scenario. We verified that 13 out of the 16 arguments in the deceptive story corresponds with what the deceiver claims, all of the arguments in the honest story corresponds with what is the truth. Although it is hard to verify the true victim's story because we do not have its ground truth, we observe that all the arguments are reasonable and most are contrary to the deceiver's honest story except the evidence.

Arguments	**Decept.**	**Honest**	**True**
B_relation_with_As_mother=good	0	0	0
A_have_exp_of_prostitution=T	0.66	0.88	0.11
A_hate_Indian=T	0.74	0.07	0.89
A_is_nice_to_B=T	0.18	0.88	0.18
B_relation_with_A=rape	0.98	0.16	0.96
B_in_A_s_party_by=self	0.9	0.4	0.90
B_knows_A_s_adr=T	0.95	0.95	0.95
B_drive_A_home=T	1	1	1
B_is_new_to_party=T	0.76	0.82	0.16
A_have_drug_from=B	0.76	0.07	0.92
sex_by=rape	0.93	0.08	0.98
As_boyfriend_catch_on_the_scene=T	1	1	1
A_is_celebrity=T	1	1	1
B_refuse_to_pay=T	0.8	0.85	0.50
A_claim_being_raped=T	0.6	0.7	0.60
cry_for_help=T	0.8	0.2	0.80

Table 1: Inferred results of the deceiver's deceptive story, her honest story and a true victim's story

The computation of the discrepancies assumes acquaintance of the deceiver, which requires sufficient number of history data and neighbors of the deceiver. To achieve it, we simulate 19 agents by perturbing the deceiver's BN and another 10 agents by perturbing the true victim's BN. In total, we have 29 truth telling agents and 1 deceiving agent. We simulate 100 runs of training data by inferring the network of each agent 100 times with different evidence at each run, and convert them to binary beliefs. Training data is assumed to contain no deception. This approach of inconsistency detection is borrowed from our past work (Santos et. Al, 2010).

Arguments	**Decept.**	**Honest**	**True**
B_relation_with_As_mother	bad	bad	bad
A_have_exp_of_prostitution	unknn	T	F
A_hate_Indian	T	F	T
A_is_nice_to_B	F	T	F
B_relation_with_A	rape	fan	rape
B_in_A_s_party_by	self	unknn	self
B_knows_A_s_adr	T	T	T
B_drive_A_home	T	T	T
B_is_new_to_party	T	T	F
A_have_drug_from	B	self	B
sex_by	rape	entice	rape
As_boyfriend_catch_on_the_scene	T	T	T
A_is_celebrity	T	T	T
B_refuse_to_pay	T	T	unknn
A_claim_being_raped	unknn	T	unknn
cry_for_help	T	F	T

Table 2: Binary beliefs of the deceiver's deceptive story, honest story and a true victim's story

4 Experiment and results

To test the hypotheses, we compare the result of deceptive story with the result of misinformative story. A misinformative story is simulated by adding random error to the inferred results of the arguments.

- Propagation of manipulation

To calculate inconsistency we predict binary beliefs in the deceptive story using GroupLens (Resnick et. Al, 1994) based on stories of neighboring agents in the Correlation Network. We then compare the binary beliefs in the deceptive story with predicted binary beliefs to measure deviation of each argument due to inconsistency. We measure how many standard (std.) deviations the prediction error in deceptive story deviates from the prediction error in training data, and plot them according to their locations in the BN, as shown in Figure 3. The width of the links represents the sensitivity of each variable to its neighbors.

We observe that the variables at the boundaries of the graph and not sensitive to neighbors (e.g. *B_is_new_to_party*) are ignored by the deceiver, while the variables in the center or sensitive to others (e.g. *A_hate_Indian*) are manipulated significantly. It demonstrates that manipulations propagate to closely related arguments. Unrelated arguments are probably considered as irrelevant or simply be ignored by the deceiver. On the other hand, if we compare deceptive story with honest story in Table 2, we obtain 9 arguments manipulated by the deceiver. Out of these 9 arguments, 8 are successfully identified as inconsistent by Figure 3 if we assume the suspicion threshold is 3 std. deviations.

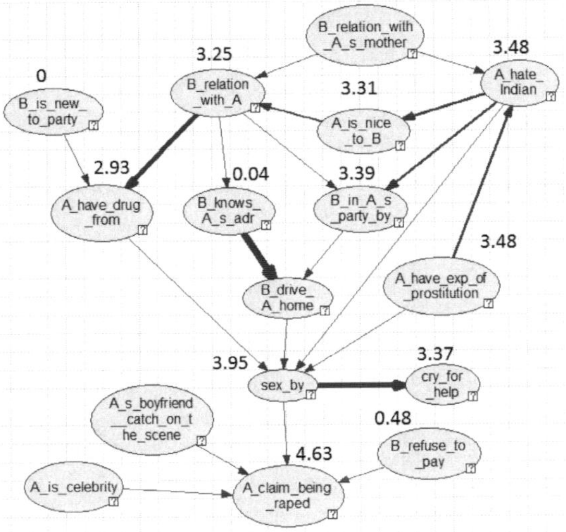

Figure 3: Inconsistency deviation of each variable

- Correspondence between inconsistency and untruthfulness

To compute untruthfulness, we calculate the deviation of the binary beliefs in the deceptive story from the population of truth teller's stories who agrees with the deceiver in the Consensus Network. We then compare the deviation due to inconsistency with respect to the deceiver herself and that due to untruthfulness with respect to truth tellers. The result is shown in Table 3.

The correlation between the deviation due to inconsistency and that due to untruthfulness is -0.5186, which means that untruthfulness has a large negative correlation with inconsistency. It credits our hypothesis that significant manipulations are often convincing and unconvincing arguments usually can be found in slightly manipulated or ignored arguments. The only exception in the result is the argument *B_knows_As_address*, which is not manipulated but convincing. It is probably because the evidence *B_drive_A_home* enforced it to remain honest. Type I incredibility does not occur in this case, but type II incredibility appears in the argument *B_is_new_to_party* and *B_refuse_to_pay*. The deceiver ignored these arguments, which results in the incredibility of the story. The correlation between inconsistency and untruthfulness in misinformative stories ranges between 0.3128 and 0.9823, which demonstrates that the negative correction cannot be found in misinformative stories. If we compare the deceptive story and the true story in Table 2, we find out that 3 arguments in the deceptive story are unconvincing. By observing the untruthfulness in Table 3, we find out that 2 of the 3 arguments are out of at least 1.44 std. deviations of the sample of true stories and all of them are out of at least 0.95 std. deviations. The small deviations indicate a high credibility of the deceiver, which is caused by the similarity between the belief systems of the deceiver and the true victim.

Belief	**Incon.**	**Untru.**
B_relation_with_As_mother=good	N/A	N/A
A_have_exp_of_prostitution=T	3.48	0.95
A_hate_Indian=T	3.48	0.28
A_is_nice_to_B=T	3.31	0.28
B_relation_with_A=rape	3.25	0
B_in_A_s_party_by=self	3.39	0.28
B_knows_A_s_adr=T	0.04	0
B_drive_A_home=T	N/A	N/A
B_is_new_to_party=T	0	1.59
A_have_drug_from=B	2.93	0
sex_by=rape	3.95	0
As_boyfriend_catch_on_the_scene =T	N/A	N/A
A_is_celebrity=T	N/A	N/A
B_refuse_to_pay=T	0.48	1.44
A_claim_being_raped=T	4.63	0.41
cry_for_help=T	3.37	0.41

Table 3: Comparison of inconsistency and untruthfulness of the deceiver

- Functionality

Functionality means that the manipulated arguments are effective in reaching the goal and at the same time satisfies the evidence. In other words, we can expect the manipulated arguments from the goal and the evidence. The calculation of functionality is as following. For each inconsistent argument, we measure its correlation with other arguments in the past using training data. We then predict each argument's binary belief based on the value of the conclusion and the evidence. If the predicted belief corresponds with the belief in the deceptive story, the variable is functional. We compare the results of deceptive story with those of misinformative story. In Table 4, all but one manipulated arguments in the deceptive story complies with the value expected by the conclusion and evidence, but none of the inconsistent arguments in misinformative stories does. Although the result shown in Table 5 comes from a random sample of misinformative story, we observed that most of the samples show the same functionality rate. Therefore, the functionality rate of deceptive story is 6/7, while the functionality rate of misinformative story is around 0/3.

Arguments	Pred.	Decept.
A_have_exp_of_prostitution=T	0.24	0.5
A_hate_Indian=T	0.85	1
A_is_nice_to_B=T	0.07	0
B_relation_with_A=rape	0.99	1
B_in_A_s_party_by=self	1	1
A_claim_being_raped=T	0.58	0.5
cry_for_help=T	0.86	1

Table 4: Functionality of the deceiver's story

Arguments	Pred.	Misinfo.
B_in_A_s_party_by=self	0.45	0
B_knows_A_s_adr=T	0.90	0.5
A_claim_being_raped=T	0.94	0.5

Table 5: Functionality of a mininformative story

5 Conclusion and future work

We proposed in this work two fundamental discrepancies in deceptive communications: discrepancies in arguments that deceivers are reluctant to believe but truth tellers embrace and discrepancies in arguments that are manipulated by deceivers. The proposal follows the following three assumptions: The act of deceiving is composed of deceptive argument formation and argument communication; Deception is formed in the reasoning process rather than the communication process; Reasoning is interaction between arguments, and deceptive reasoning is reasoning with presupposition. Then we proposed three hypotheses in order to distinguish deception from unintentional misinformation: manipulations propagate smoothly through closely related arguments, inconsistency and untruthfulness are negatively correlated, and deceptive arguments are usually functional to deceiver's goal and evidence. To evaluate and to measure these hypotheses from communication content, we designed a generic model of deception detection. In the model, agents are correlated with others to expect each other's consistency in beliefs and consenting agents are compared with each other to evaluate the truthfulness of beliefs. Our experimental results credit the hypotheses. The main contribution of this work is not to follow or reject the path that linguistic cues have laid out, but to suggest a new direction in which deeper information about the intent of deceivers is carefully mined and analyzed based on their cognitive process.

In the future, we will further develop the model by designing and implementing detection methods based on the hypotheses. Currently we use simulated data based on an artificial story, which is closer to a real legal case that provides concrete information about the reasoning of deceivers with minimum noise. In the future, we will apply the model to survey data that is commonly used in the area. Various natural language processing techniques can be utilized in the retrieval of the reasoning process. Specifically, Latent dirichlet allocation (Blei et. Al, 2002) can be used to categorize the sentences into topics (or arguments), sentiment analysis (Liu. 2010) can be used to extract the polarity of each argument, and various BN constructors such as PC algorithm (Spirtes et. Al, 1993) can be used to construct the belief systems. On the other hand, linguistic cues have been observed in past research (DePaulo et. al, 2003), but has not been defined or explained quantitatively. The study of the pattern of deceptive reasoning can ultimately provide guidance and explanations to existing observations in deception cueing.

Acknowledgments

This work was supported in part by grants from AFOSR, ONR, and DHS.

References

David M. Blei, Andrew Y. Ng, and Michael I. Jordan. 2003. Latent Dirichlet allocation. Journal of Machine Learning Research, Lafferty, John. Ed., 3 (4–5): 993–1022.

Bella M. DePaulo, James J. Lindsay, Brian E. Malone, Laura Muhlenbruck, Kelly Charlton, and

Harris Cooper. 2003. Cues to deception. Psychological Bulletin, 129(1): 74-118.

Ulisses Ferreira. 2004. On the Foundations of Computing Science. Lecture Notes in Computer Science, 3002:46-65.

John O. Greene, H. Dan O'hair, Micheal J. Cody, and Catherine Yen. 1985. Planning and Control of Behavior during Deception. Human Communication Research, 11:335-64.

I. L. Humberstone. 1992. Direction of Fit. Mind, 101(401): 59-84.

Marcia K. Johnson and Carol L. Raye. 1981. Reality Monitoring. Psychological Bulletin, 88:67–85.

Isaac Levi. 1996. For the Sake of the Argument. Cambridge University Press. New York, NY, USA.

Bing Liu. 2010. Sentiment Analysis and Subjectivity. Handbook of Natural Language Processing Issue, 1st ed., Taylor and Francis Group, Eds. CRC Press, 1-38.

Hazel Markus. 1977. Self-schemata and Processing Information about the Self. Journal of Personality and Social Psychology, 35:63–78.

Albert Mehrabian. 1972. Nonverbal Communication. Aldine Atherton, Chicago, USA.

Alfred R. Mele. 1992. Springs of Action: Understanding Intentional Behavior. Oxford University Press. New York, NY, USA.

Judea Pearl. 1988. Probabilistic Reasoning in Intelligent Systems. Morgan Kaufmann Publishers, San Francisco, CA, USA.

Paul Resnick, Neophytos Iacovou, Mitesh Suchak, Peter Bergstrom, and John Riedl. 1994. GroupLens: An Open Architecture for Collaborative Filtering of Netnews. Proc. of the Conference on Computer Supported Cooperative Work, 175-186. ACM Press, Chapel Hill, NC, USA.

Eugene Santos, Jr. and Deqing Li. 2010. Deception Detection in Multi-Agent Systems. IEEE Transactions on Systems, Man, and Cybernetics: Part A, 40(2):224-235.

Warren Shibles. 1988. A Revision of the Definition of Lying as an Untruth Told with Intent to Deceive. Argumentation, 2:99-115.

Peter Spirtes, Clark N. Glymour, and Richard Scheines, 1993. Causation, Prediction, and Search. Springer-Verlag, New York, NY, USA.

Morton Wiener and Albert Mehrabian. 1968. Language within Language: Immediacy, a Channel in Verbal Communication. Meredith Corporation, New York, NY, USA.

Pastiche detection based on stopword rankings. Exposing impersonators of a Romanian writer

Liviu P. Dinu
Faculty of Mathematics
and Computer Science
University of Bucharest
ldinu@fmi.unibuc.ro

Vlad Niculae
Faculty of Mathematics
and Computer Science
University of Bucharest
vlad@vene.ro

Octavia-Maria Şulea
Faculty of Foreign Languages
and Literatures
Faculty of Mathematics
and Computer Science
University of Bucharest
mary.octavia@gmail.com

Abstract

We applied hierarchical clustering using Rank distance, previously used in computational stylometry, on literary texts written by Mateiu Caragiale and a number of different authors who attempted to impersonate Caragiale after his death, or simply to mimic his style. Their pastiches were consistently clustered opposite to the original work, thereby confirming the performance of the method and proposing an extension of the method from simple authorship attribution to the more complicated problem of pastiche detection.

The novelty of our work is the use of frequency rankings of stopwords as features, showing that this idea yields good results for pastiche detection.

1 Introduction

The postulated existence of the human stylome has been thoroughly studied with encouraging results. The term *stylome*, which is currently not in any English dictionaries, was recently defined as a linguistic fingerprint which can be measured, is largely unconscious, and is constant (van Halteren et al., 2005).

Closely related to the problem of authorship attribution lies the pastiche detection problem, where the fundamental question is: Can the human stylome be faked in order to trick authorship attribution methods? There are situations where certain authors or journalists have tried to pass their own work as written by someone else. A similar application is in forensics, where an impersonator is writing letters or messages and signing with someone else's name, especially online.

It is important to note that sometimes pastiches are not intended to deceive, but simply as an exercise in mimicking another's style. Even in this case, the best confirmation that the author of the pastiche can get is if he manages to fool an authorship attribution algorithm, even if the ground truth is known and there is no real question about it.

Marcus (1989) identifies the following four situation in which text authorship is disputed:

- A text attributed to one author seems non-homogeneous, lacking unity, which raises the suspicion that there may be more than one author. If the text was originally attributed to one author, one must establish which fragments, if any, do not belong to him, and who are their real authors.
- A text is anonymous. If the author of a text is unknown, then based on the location, time frame and cultural context, we can conjecture who the author may be and test this hypothesis.
- If based on certain circumstances, arising from literature history, the paternity is disputed between two possibilities, A and B, we have to decide if A is preferred to B, or the other way around.
- Based on literary history information, a text seems to be the result of the collaboration of two authors, an ulterior analysis should establish, for each of the two authors, their corresponding text fragments.

We situate ourselves in a case similar to the third, but instead of having to choose between two authors, we are asking whether a group of texts were indeed written by the claimed author or by someone else. Ideally, we would take samples authored by every possible impersonator and run a

Proceedings of the EACL 2012 Workshop on Computational Approaches to Deception Detection, pages 72–77,
Avignon, France, April 23 - 27 2012.

multi-class classifier in order to estimate the probability that the disputed work is written by them or by the asserted author. Such a method can give results if we know who the impersonator can be, but most of the time that information is not available, or the number of possible impersonators is intractabally large.

In the case of only one impersonator, the problem can simply be stated as authorship attribution with a positive or a negative answer. However, when there are a number of people separately writing pastiches of one victim's style, the extra information can prove beneficial in an unsupervised learning sense. In this paper we analyze the structure induced by the Rank Distance metric using frequencies of stopwords as features, previously applied for authorship attribution, on such a sample space. The assumption is that trying to fake someone else's stylome will induce some consistent bias so that new impersonators can be caught using features from other pastiche authors.

2 The successors of Mateiu Caragiale

Mateiu Caragiale, one of the most important Romanian novelists, died in 1936, at the age of 51, leaving behind an unfinished novel, *Sub pecetea tainei*. Some decades later, in the 70's, a rumor agitated the Romanian literary world: it seemed that the ending of the novel had been found. A few human experts agreed that the manuscript is in concordance with Mateiu's style, and in the next months almost everybody talked about the huge finding. However, it was suspicious that the writer who claimed the discovery, Radu Albala, was considered by the critics to be one of the closest stylistic followers of Mateiu Caragiale. When the discussions regarding the mysterious finding reached a critical mass, Albala publically put a stop to them, by admitting that he himself had written the ending as a challenge - he wanted to see how well he could deceive the public into thinking the text in question was written by Mateiu himself.

Other authors attempted to write different endings to the novel, but without claiming Caragiale's paternity, like Albala did. Around the same time, Eugen Bălan also set to continue the unfinished novel, as a stylistic exercise. He addressed a separate storyline than Albala's. Later, Alexandru George also attempted to finish the novel, claiming that his ending is the best. Unfortunately there is only one copy of George's work, and we couldn't obtain it for this study.

In 2008, Ion Iovan published the so-called *Last Notes of Mateiu Caragiale*, composed of sections written from Iovan's voice, and another section in the style of a personal diary describing the life of Mateiu Caragiale, suggesting that this is really Caragiale's diary. This was further strengthened by the fact that a lot of phrases from the diary were copied word for word from Mateiu Caragiale's novels, therefore pushing the style towards Caragiale's. However, this was completely a work of fiction, the diary having been admittedly imagined and written by Iovan.

Another noteworthy case is the author Ştefan Agopian. He never attempted to continue Mateiu Caragiale's novel, but critics consider him one of his closest stylistic successors. Even though not really a pastiche, we considered worth investigating how such a successor relates to the impersonators.

3 Simple visual comparisons

The pioneering methods of Mendenhall (Mendenhall, 1901) on the subject of authorship attribution, even though obsolete by today's standards, can be used to quickly examine at a glance the differences between the authors, from certain points of view. The Mendenhall plot, showing frequency versus word length, does not give an objective criterion to attribute authorship, but as an easy to calculate statistic, it can motivate further research on a specific attribution problem.

A further critique to Mendenhall's method is that different distributions of word length are not necessary caused by individual stylome but rather by the genre or the theme of the work. This can further lead to noisy distributions in case of versatile authors, whereas the stylome is supposed to be stable.

Even so, the fact that Mateiu Caragiale's Mendenhall distribution has its modes consistently in a different position than the others, suggests that the styles are different, but it appears that Caragiale's successors have somewhat similar distributions. This can be seen in figure 3. In order to evaluate the questions *How different, how similar?*, and to make a more objective judgement on authorship attribution, we resort to pairwise distance-based methods.

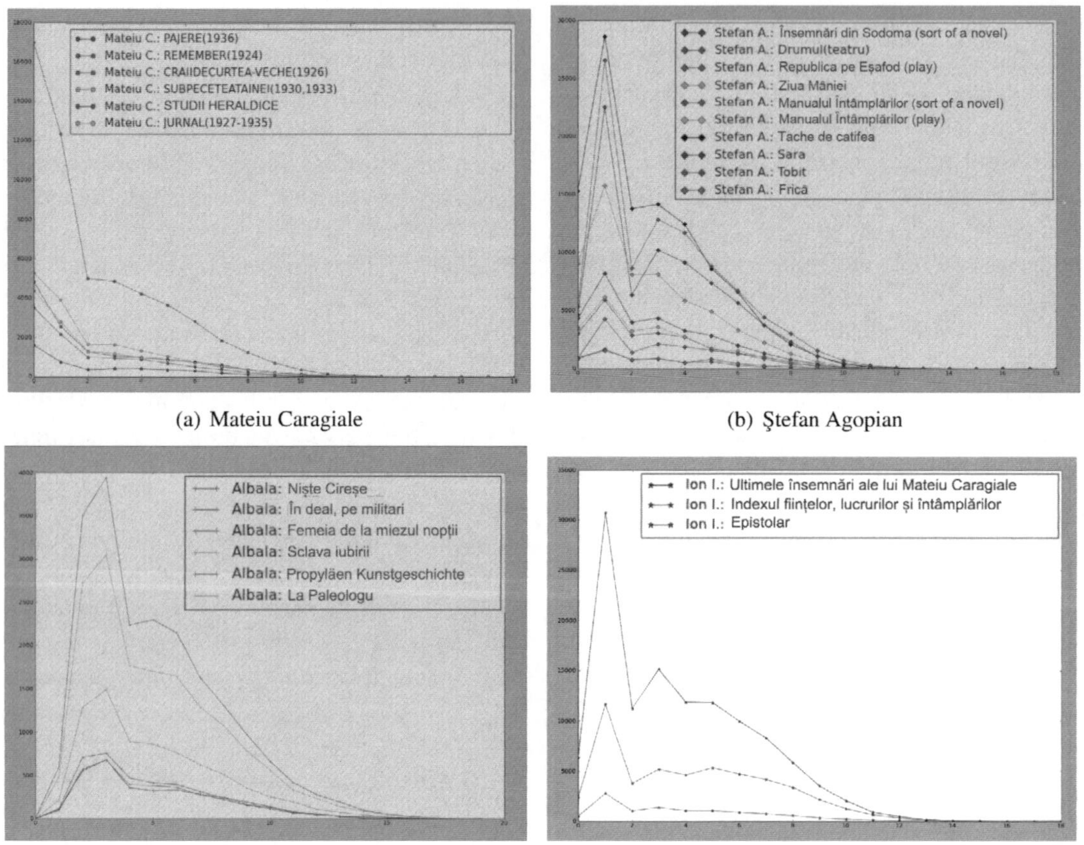

(a) Mateiu Caragiale (b) Ştefan Agopian

(c) Radu Albala (d) Ion Iovan

Figure 1: Mendenhall plots: frequency distribution of word lengths, showing similarities between the other authors, but differences between them and Mateiu Caragiale.

şi în să se cu o la nu a ce mai din pe un că ca mă fi care era lui fără ne pentru el ar dar îl tot am mi însă într cum când toate al aa după până decât ci nici numai dacă cu avea fost le sau spre unde unei atunci mea prin ai atât au chiar cine iar noi sunt acum ale are asta cel fie fiind peste această a cele face fiecare nimeni încă între aceasta aceea acest acesta acestei avut ceea cât da făcut noastră poate acestui alte celor cineva către lor unui altă aţi dintre doar foarte unor vă aceste astfel avem aveţi cei ci deci este suntem va vom vor de

Table 1: The 120 stopwords extracted as the most frequent words in the corpus.

In order to speak of distances, we need to represent the samples (the novels) as points in a metric space. Using the idea that stopword frequencies are a significant component of the stylome, and one that is difficult to fake (Chung and Pennebaker, 2007), we first represented each work as a vector of stopword frequencies, where the stopwords are chosen to be the most frequent words from all the concatenated documents. The stopwords can be seen in table 1. Another useful visualisation method is the Principal Components Analysis, which gives us a projection from a high-dimensional space into a low-dimensional one, in this case in 2D. Using this stopword frequency representation, the first principal components plane looks like figure 3.

4 Distances and clustering

In (Popescu and Dinu, 2008), the use of rankings instead of frequencies is proposed as a smoothing method and it is shown to give good results for computational stylometry. A ranking is simply an ordering of items; in this case, the representation of each document is the ranking of the stopwords in that particular document. The fact that a specific function word has the rank 2 (is the second most frequent word) in one text and has the rank 4 (is the fourth most frequent word) in another text can be more directly relevant than the fact that the respective word appears 349 times in the first text and only 299 times in the second.

Rank distance (Dinu, 2003) is an ordinal metric able to compare different rankings of a set of objects. In the general case, Rank distance works for

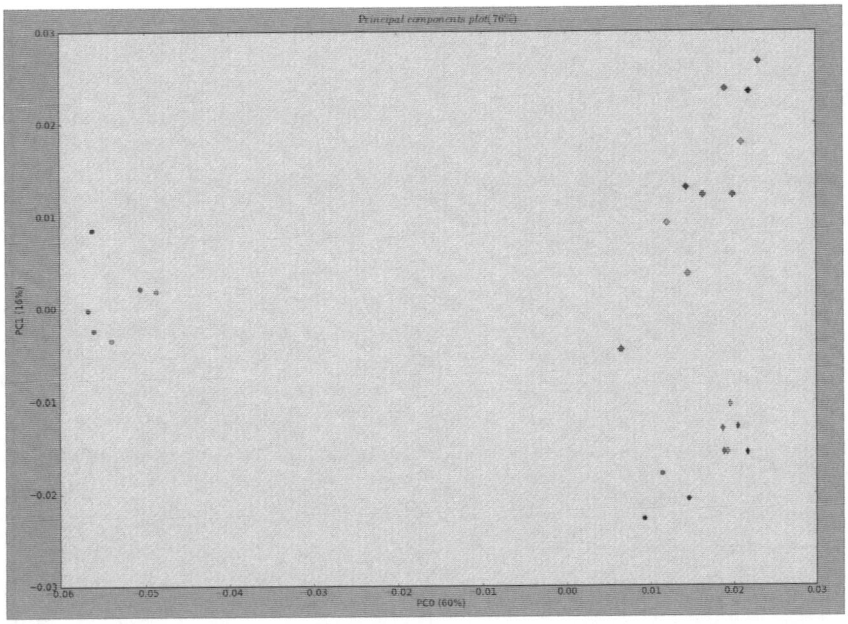

Figure 2: Principal components plot. Works are colour coded like in figure 3. The cluster on the left consists only of novels by Mateiu Caragiale. Individual authors seem to form subclusters in the right cluster.

rankings where the support set is different (for example, if a stopword would completely be missing from a text). When this is not the case, we have the following useful property:

A ranking of a set of n objects is a mapping $\sigma : \{1, 2, ..., n\} \rightarrow \{1, 2, ..., n\}$ where $\sigma(i)$ will represent the place (rank) of the object indexed as i such that if $\sigma(q) < \sigma(p)$ word q is more frequent than word p. The Rank distance in this case is simply the distance induced by L_1 norm on the space of vector representations of permutations:

$$D(\sigma_1, \sigma_2) = \sum_{i=1}^{n} |\sigma_1(i) - \sigma_2(i)| \qquad (1)$$

This is a distance between what is called full rankings. However, in real situations, the problem of *tying* arises, when two or more objects claim the same rank (are ranked equally). For example, two or more function words can have the same frequency in a text and any ordering of them would be arbitrary.

The Rank distance allocates to tied objects a number which is the average of the ranks the tied objects share. For instance, if two objects claim the rank 2, then they will share the ranks 2 and 3 and both will receive the rank number $(2+3)/2 = 2.5$. In general, if k objects will claim the same rank and the first x ranks are already used by other objects, then they will share the ranks $x + 1, x + 2, \ldots, x + k$ and all of them will receive as rank the number: $\frac{(x+1)+(x+2)+...+(x+k)}{k} = x + \frac{k+1}{2}$. In this case, a ranking will be no longer a permutation ($\sigma(i)$ can be a non integer value), but the formula (1) will remain a distance (Dinu, 2003).

Even though computationally the formula (1) allows us to use the L_1 distance we will continue using the phrase Rank distance to refer to it, in order to emphasize that we are measuring distances between rankings of stopwords, not L_1 distances between frequency values or anything like that.

Hierarchical clustering (Duda et al., 2001) is a bottom-up clustering method that starts with the most specific cluster arrangement (one cluster for each sample) and keeps joining the *nearest* clusters, eventually stopping when reaching either a stopping condition or the most general cluster arrangement possible (one cluster containing all the samples). When joining two clusters, there are many possible ways to specify the distance between them. We used *complete linkage*: the distance between the most dissimilar points from the two clusters. The resulting clustering path, visualised a dendrogram, is shown in figure 4.

The use of clustering techniques in authorship attribution problems has been shown useful by Labbé and Labbé (2006); Luyckx et al. (2006). Hierarchical clustering with Euclidean distances

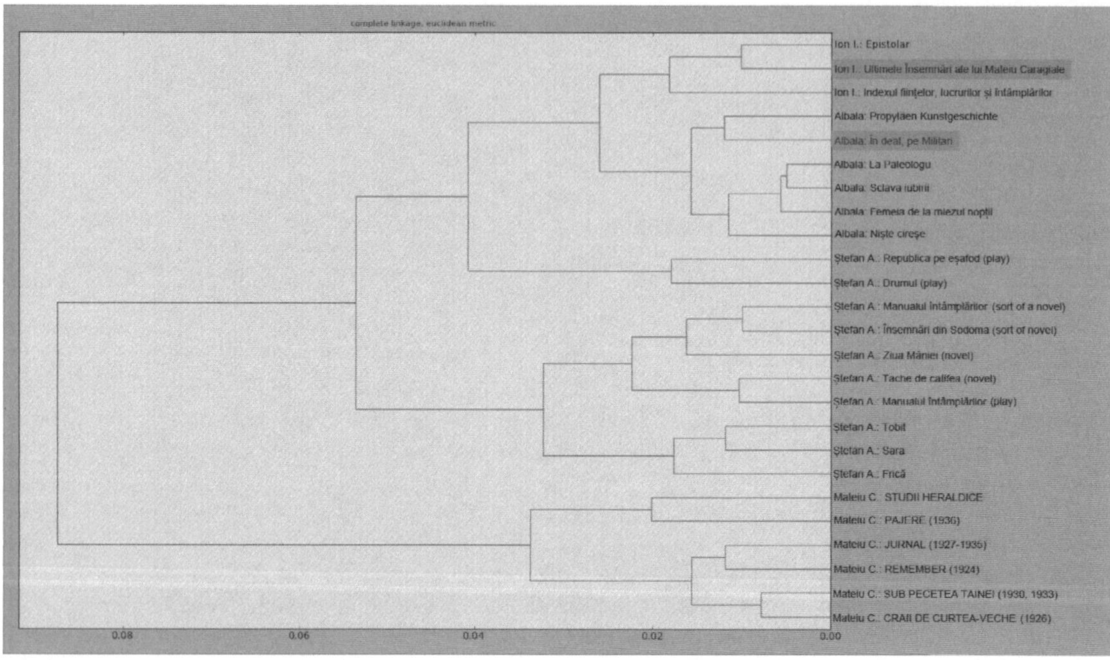

Figure 3: Dendrogram showing the results of hierarchical clustering using the L_2 (euclidean) distance.

has been used for pastiche detection in (Somers and Tweedie, 2003). The novelty of our work is the use of rankings as features, and using the L_1 distance (equivalent to the Rank distance for this particular case). (Somers and Tweedie, 2003) shows how the Euclidean distance clusters mostly works by the same author at the finest level, with a few exceptions. On the data from our problem, we observed a similar problem. The Euclidean distance behaves in a less than ideal fasion, joining some of Agopian's works with the cluster formed by the other authors (see figure 3), whereas the Rank distance always finds works by the same author the most similar at the leaves level (with the obvious exception of Eugen Bălan's text, because it is his only available text).

Reading the dendrogram in the reverse order (top to bottom), we see that for $k = 2$ clusters, one corresponds to Mateiu Caragiale and the other to all of his successors. In a little finer-grained spot, there is a clear cluster of Ştefan Agopian's work, the (single) text by Eugen Bălan, and a joint cluster with Radu Albala and Ion Iovan, which also quickly breaks down into the separate authors. The fact that there is no k for which all authors are clearly separated in clusters can be attributed to the large stylistic variance exhibited by Ştefan Agopian and Mateiu Caragiale, whose clusters break down more quickly.

These results confirm our intuition that rankings of stopwords are more relevant than frequencies, when an appropriate metric is used. Rank distance is well-suited to this task. This leads us to believe that if we go back and apply our methods to the texts studies in (Somers and Tweedie, 2003), an improvement will be seen, and we intend to further look into this.

5 Conclusions

We reiterate that all of the authors used in the study are considered stylistically similar to Mateiu Caragiale by the critics. Some of their works, highlighted on the graph, were either attributed to Caragiale (by Albala and Iovan), or intended as pastiche works continuing Caragiale's unfinished novel.

A key result is that with this models, all of these successors prove to be closer to each other than to Mateiu Caragiale. Therefore, when faced with a new problem, we don't have to seed the system with many works from the possible authors (note that we used a single text by Bălan): it suffices to use as seeds texts by one or more authors who are stylistically and culturally close to the claimed author (in this case, Mateiu Caragiale). Clustering with an appropriate distance such as Rank dis-

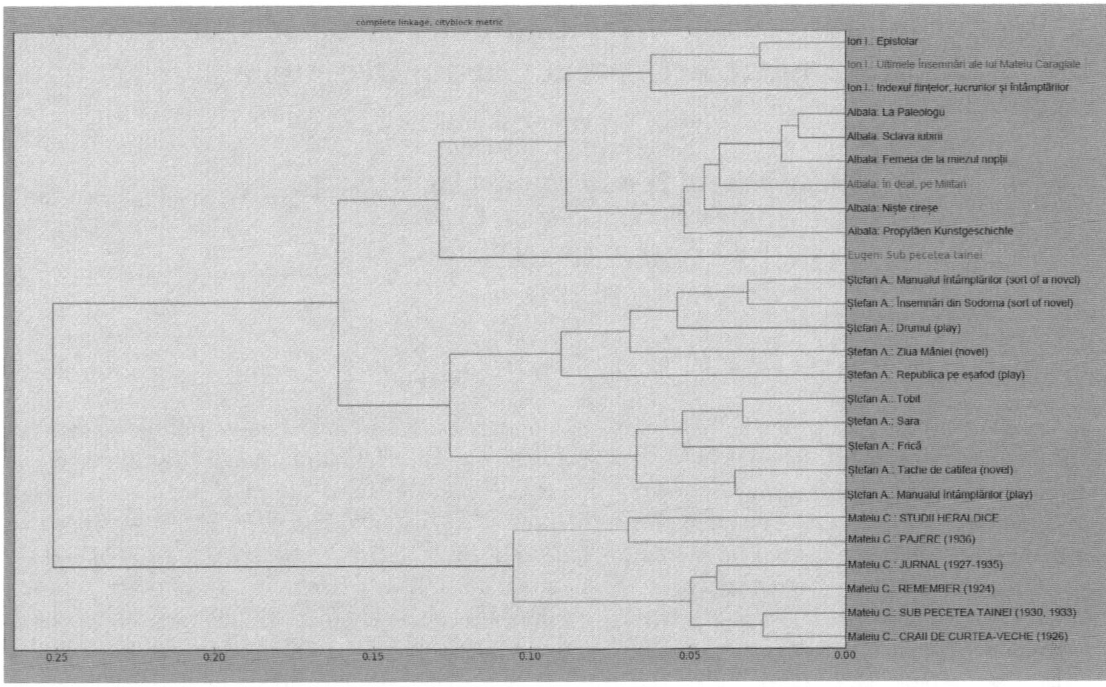

Figure 4: Dendrogram showing the results of hierarchical clustering using L_1 distance on stopword rankings (equivalent to Rank distance).

tance will unmask the pastiche.

References

Cindy Chung and James Pennebaker. The psychological functions of function words. *Social communication: Frontiers of social psychology*, pages 343–359, 2007.

Liviu Petrisor Dinu. On the classification and aggregation of hierarchies with different constitutive elements. *Fundamenta Informaticae*, 55 (1):39–50, 2003.

R. O. Duda, P. E. Hart, and D. G. Stork. *Pattern Classification (2nd ed.)*. Wiley-Interscience Publication, 2001.

Cyril Labbé and Dominique Labbé. A tool for literary studies: Intertextual distance and tree classification. *Literary and Linguistic Computing*, 21(3):311–326, 2006.

Kim Luyckx, Walter Daelemans, and Edward Vanhoutte. Stylogenetics: Clustering-based stylistic analysis of literary corpora. In *Proceedings of LREC-2006, the fifth International Language Resources and Evaluation Conference*, pages 30–35, 2006.

Solomon Marcus. *Inventie si descoperire*. Ed. Cartea Romaneasca, Bucuresti, 1989.

T C Mendenhall. A mechanical solution of a literary problem. *Popular Science Monthly*, 60(2): 97–105, 1901.

Marius Popescu and Liviu Petrisor Dinu. Rank distance as a stylistic similarity. In *COLING (Posters)'08*, pages 91–94, 2008.

Harold Somers and Fiona Tweedie. Authorship attribution and pastiche. *Computers and the Humanities*, 37:407–429, 2003. ISSN 0010-4817. 10.1023/A:1025786724466.

Hans van Halteren, R. Harald Baayen, Fiona J. Tweedie, Marco Haverkort, and Anneke Neijt. New machine learning methods demonstrate the existence of a human stylome. *Journal of Quantitative Linguistics*, pages 65–77, 2005.

Making the Subjective Objective? Computer-Assisted Quantification of Qualitative Content Cues to Deception

Siegfried L. Sporer
Department of Psychology and Sports Science
University of Giessen, Germany
Siegfried.L.Sporer@psychol.uni-giessen.de

Abstract

Research syntheses suggest that verbal content cues are more diagnostic than other cues in discriminating between truth and deception. In many studies on content cues, raters are trained to rate the presence of specific content cues, an inherently subjective process. This necessitates to demonstrate inter-coder reliability first. Depending on the statistical coefficient used, establishing adequate inter-rater reliabilities for these subjective judgments often creates a problem. To address some of these problems, a new method for coding these content cues with a computer program developed for qualitative research, MaxQDA (www.maxqda.de), is proprosed. The application of the program is demonstrated using the Aberdeen Report Judgment Scales (ARJS; Sporer, 2004) with a set of 72 deceptive and true accounts of a driving examination. Data on different types of inter-coder reliabilities are presented and implications for future research with computer-assisted qualitative coding procedures as well as training of coders are outlined.

Credits

This research has been supported by a grant from the German Science Foundation (Deutsche Forschungsgemeinschaft (DFG): Sp262/3-2) to the present author. The author would like to thank Edda Niederstadt and Nina F. Petermann for the coding of the data, and to Jaume Masip, Valerie Hauch, and Sarah Treiber for comments on an earlier version of this manuscript.

Introduction

Human judges are often only slightly better than chance at discriminating between truths and lies (Bond, & DePaulo, 2006). Likewise, a recent meta-analysis of training programs designed to teach lie detection has shown only small to medium effect sizes in improving judges' detection accuracy (e.g., Hauch, Sporer, Michael, & Meissner, 2010). This meta-analysis has also shown that training effects are larger when the content of messages are considered than when only relying on nonverbal or paraverbal cues. In a series of studies, Reinhard, Sporer, Scharmach, and Marksteiner (2011) further demonstrated that paying attention to verbal content cues improved lie detection accuracy compared to participants who relied on heuristic nonverbal cues. Therefore, particular attention should be paid to find valid content cues to detect deception (DePaulo, Lindsay, Malone, Muhlenbruck, Charlton, & Cooper, 2003; Sporer, 2004; Vrij, 2008).

Most of the research to date has relied on Criteria-based Content Analysis (CBCA; Steller & Koehnken, 1989; for a review, see Vrij, 2005) or reality monitoring approaches (e.g., Sporer, 1997; for reviews, see Masip, Sporer, Garrido, & Herrero, 2005; Sporer, 2004).

Usually, a small set of raters is trained more or less extensively with these content criteria to apply them to transcripts of oral accounts. Due to the subjective nature of these codings, establishing inter-coder reliability of any such coding system is a necessary prerequisite for its validity (Anson, Golding, & Gully, 1993).

1.1 The Problem of Inter-Coder Reliability

Whenever content cues are to be coded from transcripts, raters usually assign a binary code (0/1) regarding the presence of a certain criterion to the *whole* account. Alternatively, coders rate the extent of the presence of a criterion on some scale (0/1/2; 0-4; 1-7), which is usually treated as

Proceedings of the EACL 2012 Workshop on Computational Approaches to Deception Detection, pages 78–85,
Avignon, France, April 23 - 27 2012. ©2012 Association for Computational Linguistics

a Likert type scale and analyzed statistically as if it were an interval-scale measurement.

Using frequency counts of criteria. Other researchers have raters count the frequencies of occurrences of a given criterion and use this as a dependent variable, similarly treating it as an interval-scale measurement. In other words, not the overall presence vs. absence in an account is coded, but specific instances of occurrencies of a given criterion throughout a text corpus are noted which are subsequently added up.

One problem with this method is that the resulting distributions may be skewed which will obfuscate the use of Pearson's *r* as a measure of inter-rater agreement. Therefore, in case of skewness, Spearman *rho* may be a preferred method for ordinal-scale data. Another potential problem with the frequency count method is that the frequency of occurrence of a given criterion depends on the length of a given account (i.e., the number of words it contains). To the extent to which true accounts are likely to be longer than deceptive accounts (e.g., Colwell, Hiscock-Anisman, Memon, Taylor, & Prewett, 2007; but see the meta-analyses by DePaulo et al., 2003; Sporer & Schwandt, 2006), using frequency counts may yield erroneous conclusions. For example, if longer accounts contain more details, which are considered as an indicator of truthfulness, merely counting the number of details may be an artefact of story length.

To our knowledge, in most studies the length of the accounts (i.e., the number of words) has not been considered in the resulting statistical analyses although standardizing frequencies per minute (or per 100 words) appears to be a common procedure when investigating nonverbal and paraverbal cues; see DePaulo et al., 2003; Sporer & Schwandt, 2006, 2007; for a noteworthy exception see Granhag, Stroemwall, & Olsson, 2001).

Binary coding of criteria. Some authors dichotomize the obtained frequency distributions via a median-split, resulting in a binary judgment regarding the presence/absence of a given criterion for the whole account (e.g., Vrij, Akehurst, Soukara, & Bull, 2004). For binary judgments, percentage agreement is usually reported as a measure of inter-coder reliability, yielding usually quite high levels of agreement, which in turn are interpreted as being highly satisfactory (see Vrij, 2005, 2008). However, it has long been known that percentage agreement is a problematic measure of inter-rater reliability because it does not correct for chance agreement (Cohen, 1960, 1973; Rosenthal, 1995; Shrout & Fleiss, 1974; Wirtz & Caspar, 2002). Here, Cohen's (1960) *kappa* would be preferable. In addition, *phi* should be reported to make results more comparable with other studies' reporting of reliabilty coefficients like Pearson *r* for continuous ratings.

Reliability of coding of specific occurrencies. A problem inherent to frequency counts is the fact that even though two raters may have agreed upon the presence of some criterion (e.g., "Unusual detail") in a given account, this agreement may or may not refer to the same factual aspect of a statement. Thus, different segments of a transcript may be assigned a specific code by different raters. This begs the question regarding the segment length and the semantic boundaries of a given cue in this text corpus.

A given cue may occur at a specific location in a given text corpus, which has to be marked by a coder. Hence, it is possible that raters may not agree on the specific text passage where a criterion occurs although they may both conclude that a given criterion is present in an account.

To my knowledge, this issue has never even been addressed in the literature on deception of detection (except for a German legal dissertation that illustrated this problem with a case of perjury in the Appendix; Bender, 1987). Thus, in practically all empirical studies to date, inter-rater reliability for any given content cue is only established for each account as a whole--not for specific text passages.

This is where computer programs developed for qualitative research can be useful. For example, the program MAXQDA (see below) allows different coders to mark specific text passages in a text corpus (either words, phrases, sentences or longer passages) and assign a given code, which is shown at the margin. Different codes for different criteria, as well as codes from different raters, can be entered in different colors which allows comparisons between raters. This way, reliability can be established not only across accounts but for any single account.

Adding up occurrences of a given criterion. When raters code the presence of certain criteria rater in a given account, and researchers subsequently add up the frequencies for this account, another problem arises. For example, rater A may observe the occurrence of a given criterion in sentence 1, 3, 5, 7, and 9, while rater B observes this criterion in sentences 2, 4, 6, 8, and 10 in the same account. For each rater, 5 occurences will be noted. This may lead to an illusion of perfect agreement, as both raters report an agreement of 5 occurrences for this account, even though they did not actually agree in a single instance. Again, computerized coding as demonstrated here could help to detect such problems. Here, we only report overall agreement as in previous studies across accounts, not separately for each account as suggested in this example, which would be very tedious for a large number of accounts.

1.2 Goal of the Present Study

These issues will be addressed in the present study. Using the computer program MaxQDA (www.maxqda.de) which was developed for qualitative research in the social sciences, accounts of true and fabricated experiences were coded by two independent raters with respect to specific occurrences of the Aberdeen Report Judgment Scales criteria (ARJS; Sporer, 2004) at specific text passages. In the following, the adaptation of MaxQDA applied to these content criteria is demonstrated and results for different reliability coefficients are presented.

Method

1.3 Design

In a 2 x 2 x 2 factorial design, truth status (experienced vs. deceptive) and format of questions (W-questions vs. Content-criteria questions) were manipulated as between-, and report form (free report vs. subsequent interview) as within-participants factor. Questions varied only during the interview.

1.4 Participants and Procedure

Young adults (N = 72; 36 male, 36 female) between 17 and 45 years of age (*Mdn* = 18 years; mostly high school students) were asked to provide a convincing story of their driving test for obtaining their driver's license, which they either had recently passed (true condition), or which was immediately ahead of them (deceptive condition). Participants first provided a free report and subsequently were randomly assigned to one of two question types in the following interview. During the interview, participants answered either a series of W-questions (Who? What? Where? etc.; cf., Camparo, Wagner, & Saywitz, 2001) or questions that specifically asked for information typically used to evaluate the presence of content criteria of credibility.
Importantly, the interviewer was blind with respect to truth status. To enhance participants' motivation they were promised 5 Euros (in addition to the participation fee of 8 Euros) if their account was judged to be truthful by the experimenter at the end of the interview.

1.5 Stimulus Material and Coding

All interviews were both video- and audiotaped, and transcripts were typed from audiotapes according to specified transcription rules. The transcripts were coded by two independent raters who were blind with respect to the truth status of the accounts.

1.6 Computer-based Coding

In the following, we explain the different menus of the program and explain step by step the coding procedure.

1. Accounts are entered into MaxQDA as Microsoft Word *.rtf files (in a newer version of the program, *.doc files can also be used).
2. A list of codes is entered into MaxQDA using short labels which later can be used as variable labels in Excel spreadsheets or in SPSS analyses. Figure 1 lists codes to be assigned to text passages. New codes can be added via a context menu.
3. Codes are assigned to specific text passages by highlighting a passage in the text browser and then assigning a specific code (see Figure 2). More than one code can be assigned to a specific code, and the codes assigned are visible in the margin of the text window.

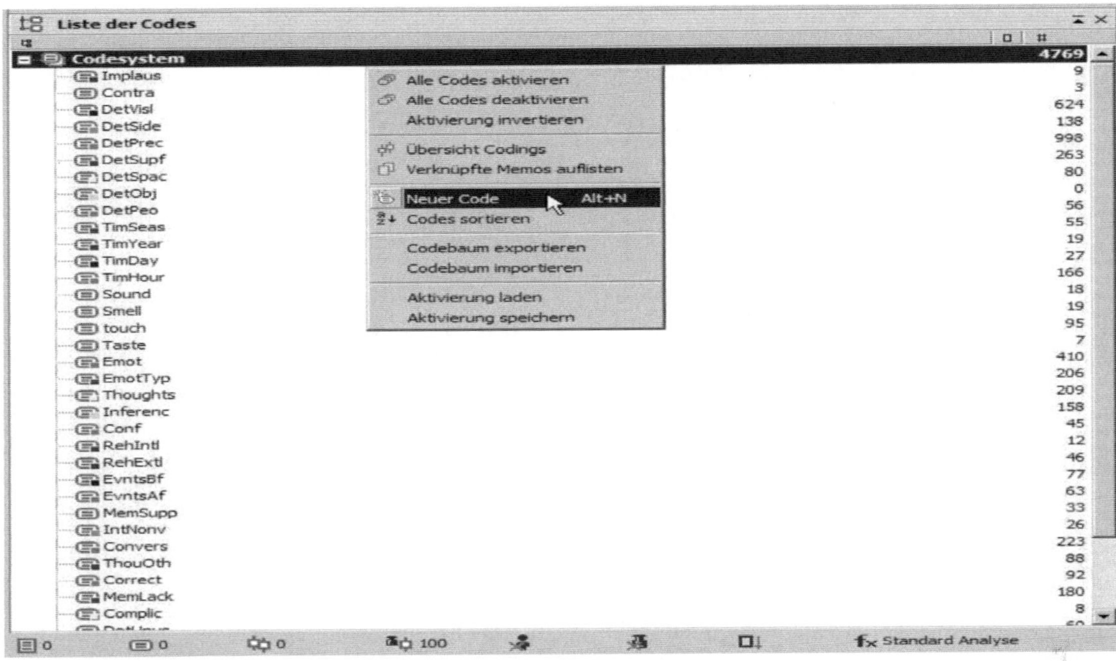

Figure 1. Menu of list of codes to be assigned to text passages. New codes can be added via a context menu.

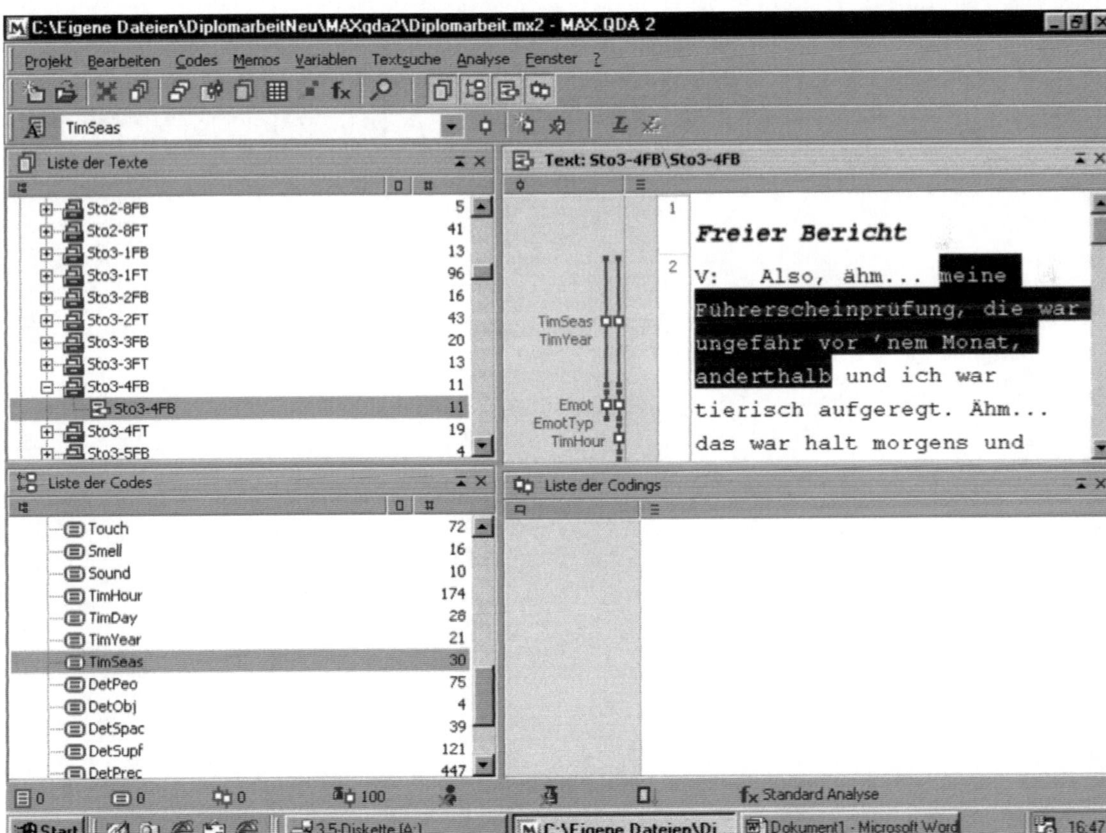

Figure 2. Assigning a specific code to a selected text passage.

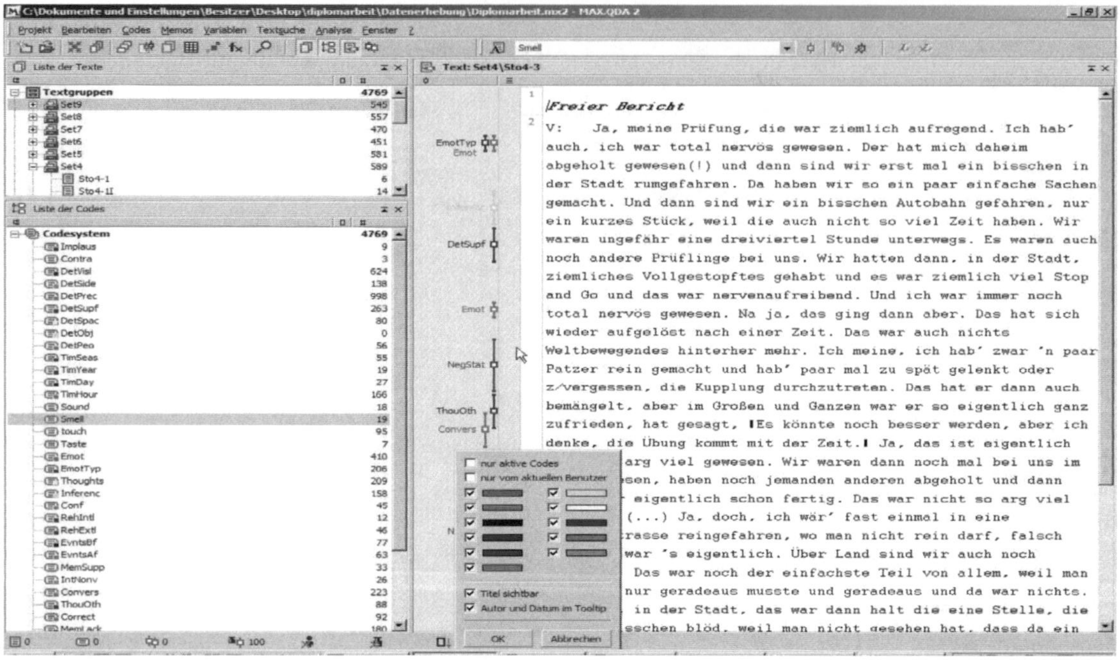

Figure 3. Codes and frequencies of codes assigned to a given text. Codes can be viewed separately per rater as indicated by the context menu.

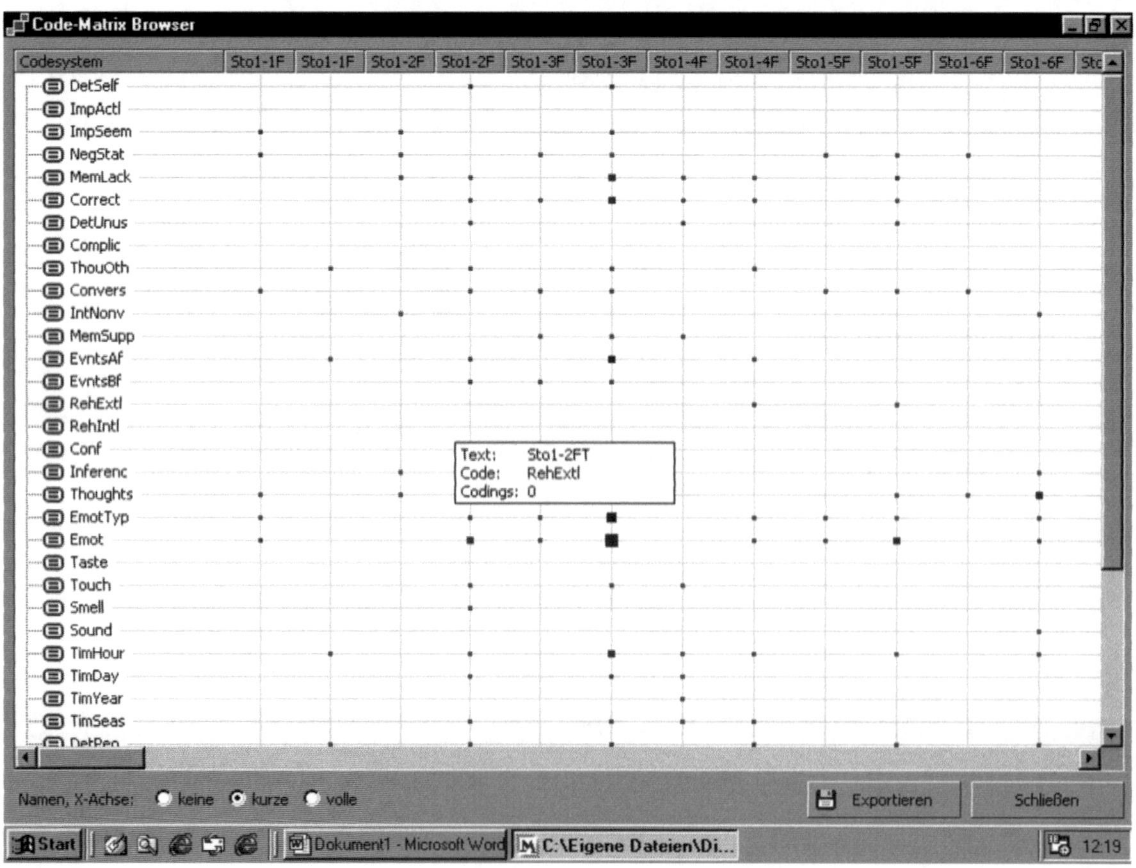

Figure 4. Relative frequencies of codes in different accounts (stories). Size of symbols represents relative frequencies.

4. The frequencies of codes assigned can be listed for all raters together, or separately for different raters. This feature is particularly useful for comparing ratings of specific passages (see Figure 3).
5. An overview of the relative frequencies of all variables coded in different accounts can also be obtained in the Matrix Browser (see Figure 4). The size of symbols corresponds to the relative frequencies in each account (story).
6. Data can be exported as Excel files, which in turn can be imported into statistical programs directly or as ASCII files.

All codes assigned by the two raters for each account were exported into SPSS and different types of reliability coefficients were computed. Table 1 displays means (and *SDs*) of all accounts as well as the inter-coder reliabilities (percentage agreement, Cohen's *kappa* for binary coding after a Median split, Spearman *rho*, Pearson's *r*, and two types of intra-class correlation coefficients [ICC]; see McGraw & Wong, 1996; Orwin & Vevea, 2009; Shrout & Fleiss, 1974; Wirtz & Caspar, 2002).

Results and Discussion

All codes assigned by the two raters for each account were exported into SPSS and different types of reliability coefficients were computed. Table 1 displays means (and *SDs*) of all accounts as well as the inter-coder reliabilities (percentage agreement, Cohen's *kappa* for binary coding after a Median split, Spearman *rho*, Pearson's *r*, and two types of intra-class correlation coefficients [ICC]; see McGraw & Wong, 1996; Orwin & Vevea, 2009; Shrout & Fleiss, 1974; Wirtz & Caspar, 2002).

Most noteworthy, for "Implausible Details and Contradictions", which showed a very low baserate, percentage agreement was very high, whereas all other coefficients suggest that reliability for this scale is very poor. How can we explain this discrepancy?

Here, 2 raters coded all 72 accounts regarding the presence of "Implausible Details and Contradictions", which resulted in a 2 x 2 Table (see Table 1). Both raters agreed on 66 nonoccurrences. Furthermore, rater A found some implausible details in 3 accounts, and rater B found Implausible Details in 3 other accounts, totalling in 6 disagreements. In other words, they really did not agree at all on the occurrence of these types of details. Nonetheless, this resulted in a percentage agreement of 91.7%--which most authors would consider quite impressive.

Table 1

Raw Freqencies of Ratings of Implausible Details

	Rater B		
Rater A	Not Present	Present	Sum
Not Present	66	3	69
Present	3	0	3
Sum	69	3	72

In contrast, using Cohen's *kappa*, which corrects for chance agreement, resulted in *kappa* = -.04, that is, no agreement at all. Other coefficients similarly showed very low inter-coder reliabilities for this variable. This discrepancy makes it clear that asymmetric marginal distributions as shown in Table 1, that is, scales with either floor or ceiling effects, are likely to render divergent results for different types of reliability coefficients. Thus, none of the coefficients should be interpreted in isolation. We recommend always to calculate other supplementary coefficients in addition to percentage agreement for comparison.

Table 2 displays the different types of reliabilities for this and the remaining variables. In line 2, the coefficients for the interview condition (W-questions) are inserted for comparison which appear somewhat higher. This is likely to have resulted from the higher baserate.

Some of the differences between the Spearman *rho* and Pearson *r* coefficients may be a function of the skewness of the underlying frequency distributions of the two raters. We recommend always to examine the scatter plots before

Table 2

Base Rates of Raw Frequencies and Reliability Coefficients of ARJS Criteria Corrected for the Number of Words

ARJS Scales	*M*	*SD*	*PA*	*kappa*	*rho*	*r*	*ICC-s*	*ICC-av*
Implausible Elements and Contradictions (a)	**0.05**	**0.17**	**91.7**	**-.04**	**-.04**	**-.04**	**.00**	**.00**
Implausible Elements and Contradictions (b)	**0.09**	**0.23**	**91.7**	**.36**	**.40**	**.76**	**.76**	**.86**
Clarity and vividness	0.74	1.18	75.0	.49	.68	.68	.59	.74
Details	3.29	2.65	65.3	.31	.57	.45	.30	.46
Spatial Details	0.39	0.65	100.0	1.00	.63	.67	.65	.79
Time Details	1.26	1.53	97.2	.94	.95	.93	.92	.96
Sensory Impressions	0.26	0.48	94.4	.85	.86	.83	.83	.91
Emotions and Feelings	3.01	2.43	87.5	.75	.87	.82	.79	.88
Thoughts	1.08	1.58	72.2	.45	.52	.68	.67	.80
Memory Processes and Rehearsal	0.42	0.63	72.2	.37	.44	.47	.34	.50
Nonverbal and Verbal Interactions	1.64	1.77	79.2	.58	.73	.66	.60	.75
Complications/Unusual details	0.38	0.54	72.2	.31	.35	.41	.40	.57
Errors and Lack of Social Desirability	1.58	1.58	70.8	.42	.58	.63	.63	.77
Personal Significance	0.54	0.73	66.7	.30	.35	.35	.29	.45
Mean (a)			**80.3**		**.65**	**.64**	**.59**	**.73**
Mean (b)			**80.3**		**.67**	**.68**	**.64**	**.77**
Mean (without Implausible Elements)			**79.8**		**.68**	**.67**	**.63**	**.77**

Note. (a) Free report; (b) After "W"-questions.
ICC-s = single measure ICC
ICC-av = average measure ICC

employing Pearson's *r*, and, in case of outliers, to use Spearman's *rho* or Kendall's *tau* instead. The intra-class coefficient *ICC* has the additional advantage that it also takes systematic differences between raters into account (i.e., when one rater gives generally higher ratings than another). *ICC*s can also be calculated for more than two raters. When two (or more raters) rate all accounts, the *ICC-av* provides an estimate of inter-coder reliability for a given study which is higher than that for single raters (analogously to the Spearman-Brown formula in testing theory; Rosenthal, 1995). Different types of *ICC*s are available depending on how many coders rated either all or only portions of the accounts (see Orwin & Vevea, 2009; Shrout & Fleiss, 1974; Winer, 1971; Wirtz & Caspar, 2002).

In conclusion, this study demonstrated that it seems well worth to use a computer-assisted coding system. A particular value of this system may also lie in the possibility to train raters where a supervisor can point out agreements and discrepancies in specific accounts to further improve inter-rater agreement. Specific discrepancies can also be resolved by two or more coders by comparing the color codes in a MAXQDA file. Such a procedure with this or similar computer programs should improve inter-rater reliabilities of any type of verbal content cues to deception.

References

Anson, D. A., Golding, S. L., & Gully, K. J. (1993). Child sexual abuse allegation: Reliability of criteria-based content analysis. *Law and Human Behavior, 17,* 331-341.

Bender, H. (1987). *Merkmalskombinationen in Aussagen* [Criteria combinations in statements]. Tuebingen: J. C. B. Mohr.

Bond, C. F., & DePaulo, B. M. (2006). Accuracy of deception judgments. *Personality and Social Psychology Review, 10,* 214-234.

Camparo, L. B., Wagner, J. T., & Saywitz, K. J. (2001). Interviewing children about real and fictitious events: Revisiting the narrative elaboration procedure. *Law and Human Behavior, 25,* 63-80.

Colwell, K., Hiscock-Anisman, C. K., Memon, A., Taylor, L., & Prewett, J. (2007). Assessment Criteria Indicative of Deception (ACID): An Integrated System of Investigative Interviewing and Detecting Deception. *Journal of Investigative Psychology and Offender Profiling, 4,* 167-180.

DePaulo, B. M., Lindsay, J. J., Malone, B. E., Muhlenbruck, L., Charlton, K., & Cooper, H. (2003). Cues to deception. *Psychological Bulletin, 129,* 74-118.

Granhag, P. A., Stroemwall, L., & Olsson, C. (2001, June). *Fact or fiction? Adults' ability to assess children's veracity.* Paper presented at the 11th European Conference on Psychology and Law in Lisbon, Portugal.

Hauch, V., Sporer, S. L., Michael, S. W., & Meissner, C. A. (2010, June). *Does training improve detection of deception? A meta-analysis.* Paper presented at the 20th Conference of the European Association of Psychology and Law, Gothenburg, Sweden.

Masip, J., Bethencourt, M., Lucas, G., Sánchez-San Segundo, M., & Herrero, C. (2011). Deception detection from written accounts. Scandinavian Journal of Psychology. DOI: 10.1111/j.1467-9450.2011.00931.x

Masip, J., Sporer, S. L., Garrido, E., & Herrero, C. (2005). The detection of deception with the reality monitoring approach: A review of the empirical evidence. *Psychology, Crime, and Law, 11,* 99-122.

McGraw, K. O., & Wong, S. P. (1996). Forming inferences about some intraclass correlations coefficients. *Psychological Methods, 1,* 31-43.

Newman, M. L., Pennebaker, J. W., Berry, D. S., & Richards, J. M. (2003). Lying words: Predicting deception from linguistic styles. *Personality and Social Psychology Bulletin, 29,* 665–675.

Orwin, R. G., & Vevea, J. L. (2009). Evaluating coding decisions. In H. Cooper, L. V., Hedges, & J. C. Valentine (Eds.), *The handbook of research synthesis and meta-analysis* (2nd ed., pp. 177-203). New York, NY: Russell Sage Foundation.

Reinhard, M. A., Sporer, S. L., Scharmach, M., & Marksteiner, T. (2011, June 27). Listening, not watching: Situational familiarity and the ability to detect deception. *Journal of Personality and Social Psychology.* Advance online publication. doi: 10.1037/a0023726

Rosenthal, R. (1995). Methodology. In A. Tesser (Ed.), *Advanced social psychology* (pp. 17-49). New York: McGraw-Hill.

Sporer, S. L. (1997). The less traveled road to truth: Verbal cues in deception detection in accounts of fabricated and self-experienced events. *Applied Cognitive Psychology, 11,* 373-397.

Sporer, S. L. (2004). Reality monitoring and the detection of deception. In P.-A. Granhag & L. Stromwall (Eds.), *Deception detection in forensic contexts* (pp. 64-102). Cambridge University Press.

Sporer, S. L., & Schwandt, B. (2006). Paraverbal indicators of deception: A meta-analytic synthesis. *Applied Cognitive Psychology, 20,* 421 - 446.

Sporer, S. L., & Schwandt, B. (2007). Moderators of nonverbal indicators of deception: A meta-analytic synthesis. Psychology, Public Policy, and Law, 13, 1-34.

Vrij, A. (2005). Criteria-Based Content Analysis. A qualitative review of the first 37 studies. *Psychology, Public Policy, and Law,* 11, 3-41.

Vrij, A. (2008). *Detecting lies and deceit: Pitfalls and opportunities*. Chichester, England: Wiley.

Vrij, A., Akehurst, L., Soukara, S., & Bull, R. (2004). Let me inform you how to tell a convincing story: CBCA and Reality Monitoring scores as a function of age, coaching and deception. *Canadian Journal of Behavioral Science, 36,* 113-126.

Winer, B. J. (1971). *Statistical principles in experimental design.* New York: McGraw-Hill.

Wirtz, M., & Caspar, F. (2002). Beurteilerübereinstimmung und Beurteilerreliabilität [Inter-rater agreement and inter-rater reliability]. Göttingen: Hogrefe.

Modelling Fixated Discourse in Chats with Cyberpedophiles

Dasha Bogdanova
University of
Saint Petersburg
dasha.bogdanova
@gmail.com

Paolo Rosso
NLE Lab. - ELiRF,
Univ. Politécnica de Valencia
prosso@dsic.upv.es

Thamar Solorio
University of
Alabama at Birmingham
solorio@cis.uab.edu

Abstract

The ability to detect deceptive statements in predatory communications can help in the identification of sexual predators, a type of deception that is recently attracting the attention of the research community. Due to the intention of a pedophile of hiding his/her true identity (name, age, gender and location) its detection is a challenge. According to previous research, fixated discourse is one of the main characteristics inherent to the language of online sexual predation. In this paper we approach this problem by computing sex-related lexical chains spanning over the conversation. Our study shows a considerable variation in the length of sex-related lexical chains according to the nature of the corpus, which supports our belief that this could be a valuable feature in an automated pedophile detection system.

1 Introduction

Child sexual abuse is not a rare problem. The statistical analysis by the National Incident-Based Reporting System data (FBI, 1995) revealed that in the majority of all sexual assaults (67%) the victims were underage (Snyder, 2000). Child sexual abuse and pedophilia are related to each other and both are of great social concern. On the one hand, law enforcement is working on prosecuting and preventing child sexual abuse. On the other hand, psychologists and mental specialists are investigating the phenomenon of pedophilia. Even though pedophilia has been studied from different research perspectives, it remains to be a very important problem that requires further research.

The widespread availability of the Internet, and the anonymity enabled by it has brought about new forms of crime. According to the research conducted by Mitchell (2001), 19% of children have been sexually approached over the Internet. However, only 10% of such cases were reported to the police. Attempts to solicit children have become common in chat rooms, but manual monitoring of each conversation is impossible, due to the massive amount of data and privacy issues. Therefore, development of reliable tools for detecting pedophilia in social media is of great importance.

Another related issue is that Internet makes it very easy to provide false personal information. Therefore, many online sexual predators create false profiles where they hide their identity and age. Thus, detection of online sexual predation also involves age and gender detection in chats.

From the Natural Language Processing (NLP) perspective, there are additional challenges to this problem because of the chat data specificity. Chat conversations are very different, not only from the written text, but also from other types of Internet communication, such as blogs and forums. Since online chatting usually involves very fast typing, mistakes, misspellings, and abbreviations occur frequently in chats. Moreover, specific slang (e.g. “kewl” is used instead of “cool” and “asl” stands for “age/sex/location”) and character flooding (e.g. *greeeeeat!*) are used. Therefore, modern NLP tools often fail to provide accurate processing of chat language.

Previous research on cyberpedophiles reports that they often copy juveniles' behavior (Egan et al., 2011), in particular, they often use colloquialisms and emoticons. Other important characteristics reported previously include the unwillingness of the predator to step out of the sex-related conversation, even if the potential victim wants to change the topic. This is called fixated discourse (Egan et al., 2011). In this paper we present preliminary experiments on modelling this phenomenon. To approach the problem we apply lexical chaining techniques. The experiments show the difference in the length of sex-related lexical chains between different datasets. We believe this fact could be then utilized in detecting pedophiles.

The following section overviews related work on the topic. Section 3 briefly describes previous research on pedophiles, the language of online sexual predation and the fixated discourse phenomenon in particular. Our approach to modelling fixated discourse is presented in Section 4. We describe the data set used in the experiments in Section 5, followed by preliminary experiments presented in Section 6. We finally draw some conclusions and plans for future work in Section 7.

Proceedings of the EACL 2012 Workshop on Computational Approaches to Deception Detection, pages 86–90,
Avignon, France, April 23 - 27 2012. ©2012 Association for Computational Linguistics

2 Related Work

The problem of detecting pedophiles in social media is difficult and relatively novel. New ways of meeting new friends are offered: chatting with webcam (http://chatroulette.com/) or picking another user at random and let you have a one-on-one chat with each other (http://omegle.com/) in a completely anonymous way.

Some chat conversations with online sexual predators are available at www.perverted-justice.com. The site is run by adult volunteers who enter chat rooms as juveniles (usually 12-15 year old) and if they are sexually solicited by adults, they work with the police to prosecute this. Related to the problem of pedophile detection in social media, a study of Perverted Justice Foundation revealed that since 2007, they have been working on identifying sex offenders on Myspace and in 2008, they expanded that effort to Facebook. The results are sadly staggering in terms of sex offenders that have misused the two social media: Myspace (period 2007- 2010) and Facebook (2008-2010) deleted respectively 10,746 and 2,800 known sex offenders. Although both social media have been helpful and responsive towards removing danger users from their communities, an automatic identification of sex offenders would certainly help and make the process faster.

Only few attempts to automatic detection of online sexual predation have been done. Pendar (2007) proved that it is possible to distinguish between predator and pseudo-victim with quite high accuracy. The experiments were conducted on perverted-justice data. The authors used a kNN classifier to distinguish between lines written by predators and the lines posted by pseudo-victims. As features they used word unigrams, bigrams and trigrams.

Another attempt has been done by McGhee et al. (2011). They manually annotated the chat lines from perverted-justice.com with the following labels:

1. Exchange of personal information
2. Grooming
3. Approach
4. None of the above listed classes

In order to distinguish between these types of lines they used both a rule-based and a machine learning (kNN) classification approach. Their experiments showed that the machine learning approach provides better results and achieves up to 83% accuracy.

Another research work closely related to detection of cyberpedophilia has been carried by Peersman et al. (**?**). As it was already mentioned, pedophiles often create false profiles and pretend to be younger or of another gender. Moreover, they try to copy children's behaviour. Therefore, there is a need to detect age and gender in chat conversation. Peersman et al. (**?**) have analyzed chats from Belgium Netlog social network. Discrimination between those who are older than 16 from those who are younger based on Support Vector Machine classification yields 71.3% accuracy. The accuracy is even higher with increasing the gap between the age groups (e.g. the accuracy of classifying those who are less than 16 from those who are older than 25 is 88.2%). They have also investigated the issues of the minimum required dataset. Their experiments have shown that with 50% of the original dataset the accuracy remains almost the same and with only 10% it is still much better than random baseline performance.

3 Profiling the Pedophile

Pedophilia is a "disorder of adult personality and behaviour" which is characterized by sexual interest in prepubescent children (International statistical classification of diseases and related health problems, 1988). Even though solicitation of children is not a medical diagnosis, Abel and Harlow (2001) reported that 88% of child sexual abuse cases are committed by pedophiles. Therefore, we believe that understanding behaviour of pedophiles could help detecting and preventing online sexual predation. Even though online sexual offender is not always a pedophile, in this paper we use these terms as synonyms.

3.1 Predator's Linguistic Behavior

The language sexual offenders use was analyzed by Egan et al. (2011). The authors considered the chats published at www.perverted-justice.com. The analysis of the chats revealed several characteristics of predators' language:

- Fixated discourse. Predators impose a sex-related topic on the conversation and dismiss attempts from the pseudo-victim to switch topics.
- Implicit/explicit content. On the one hand, predators shift gradually to the sexual conversation, starting with more ordinary compliments. On the other hand, conversation then becomes overtly related to sex. They do not hide their intentions.
- Offenders often understand that what they are doing is not moral.
- They transfer responsibility to the victim.
- Predators often behave as children, copying the language: colloquialisms often appear in their messages.
- They try to minimize the risk of being prosecuted: they ask to delete chat logs and warn victims not to tell anyone about the talk, though they finally stop being cautious and insist on meeting offline.

In this paper we consider only the first characteristic: fixated discourse. The conversation below, taken from perverted-justice.com, illustrates fixated discourse: the predator almost ignores what the victim says and comes back to the sex-related conversation:

Predator: licking dont hurt
Predator: its like u lick ice cream
Pseudo-victim: do u care that im 13 in march and not yet? i lied a little bit b4
Predator: its all cool
Predator: i can lick hard

4 Our Approach

We believe that lexical chains are appropriate to model the fixated discourse of the predators chats.

4.1 Lexical Chains

A lexical chain is a sequence of semantically related terms (Morris and Hirst, 1991). It has applications in many tasks including Word Sense Disambiguation (WSD) (Galley and McKeown, 2003) and Text Summarization (Barzilay and Elhadad, 1997).

To estimate semantic similarity we used two metrics: the similarity of Leacock and Chodorow (Leacock and Chodorow, 2003), and that of Resnik (Resnik, 1995). Leacock and Chodorow's semantic similarity measure is defined as:

$$Sim_{L\&Ch}(c_1, c_2) = -\log\frac{length(c_1, c_2)}{2 * depth}$$

where *length*(c_1, c_2) is the length of the shortest path between the concepts c_1 and c_2 and *depth* is depth of the taxonomy.

The semantic similarity measure that was proposed by Resnik (Resnik, 1995) relies on the Information Content concept:

$$IC(c) = -\log P(c)$$

where *P(c)* is the probability of encountering the concept *c* in a large corpus. Thus, Resnik's similarity measure is defined as follows:

$$Sim_{Resnik}(c_1, c_2) = IC(lcs(c_1, c_2))$$

where *lcs*(c_1, c_2) is the least common subsumer of c_1 and c_2.

4.2 Modelling Fixated Discourse

To model the fixated discourse phenomenon, we estimate the length of the longest sex-related lexical chain in a text. In particular, we start the construction of a chain with an anchor word "sex" in the first WordNet meaning: "sexual activity, sexual practice, sex, sex activity (activities associated with sexual intercourse)". Then we continue the chain construction process until the end of the text. We compare the relative lengths (in percentage to the total number of words) of the constructed chains: we believe that the presence of a long sex-related lexical chain in a text indicates fixated discourse.

5 Data

Pendar (2007) has summarized the possible types of chat interactions with sexually explicit content:

1. Predator/Other
   (a) Predator/Victim (victim is underage)
   (b) Predator/Volunteer posing as a children
   (c) Predator/Law enforcement officer posing as a child
2. Adult/Adult (consensual relationship)

The most interesting from our research point of view is data of the type 1(a), but obtaining such data is not easy. However, the data of type 1(b) is freely available at the web site www.perverted-justice.com (PJ). For our study, we have extracted chat logs from the perverted-justice website. Since the victim is not real, we considered only the chat lines written by predators.

As the negative dataset, we need data of type 2. Therefore, we have downloaded cybersex chat logs available at www.oocities.org/urgrl21f/. The archive contains 34 one-on-one cybersex logs. We have separated lines of different authors, thereby obtaining 68 files.

We have also used a subset of the NPS chat corpus (Forsythand and Martell, 2007), though it is not of type 2, we believe it will make a good comparison. We have extracted chat lines only for those adult authors who had more than 30 lines written. Finally the NPS dataset consisted of 65 authors.

6 Experiments

We carried out preliminary experiments on estimating the length of lexical chains with sexually related content in PJ chats, and compare our results with the corpora described above. Our goal is to explore the feasibility of including fixated discourse as a feature in pedophile detection.

We used Java WordNet Similarity library (Hope, 2008), which is a Java implementation of Perl Wordnet:Similarity (Pedersen et al., 2008). The average length of the longest lexical chains (with respect to the total number of words in a document) found for different corpora are presented in Table 1 and Table 2. As we expected, sex-related lexical chains in the NPS corpus are much shorter regardless of the similarity metric used. The chains in the cybersex corpus are even longer than in PJ corpus. This is probably due

	Threshold			
	0.5		0.7	
	mean	**st.dev.**	**mean**	**st.dev.**
PJ	12.21	3.63	9.3	5.68
Cybersex	18.28	16.8	9.98	12.76
NPS	5.66	5.9	2.42	4.77

Table 1: Average length of the longest lexical chain (percentage in the total number of words) computed with Leacock and Chodorow semantic similarity.

	Threshold			
	0.5		0.7	
	mean	**st.dev.**	**mean**	**st.dev.**
PJ	8.24	4.51	6.68	5.06
Cybersex	12.04	15.86	9.13	11.64
NPS	0.67	0.96	0.41	0.66

Table 2: Average length of the longest lexical chain (percentage in the total number of words) computed with Resnik semantic similarity.

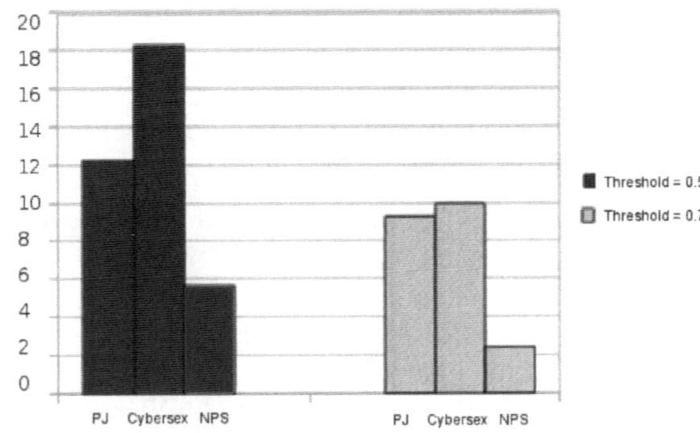

Figure 1: Average length of lexical chains calculated with Leacock and Chodorow semantic similarity

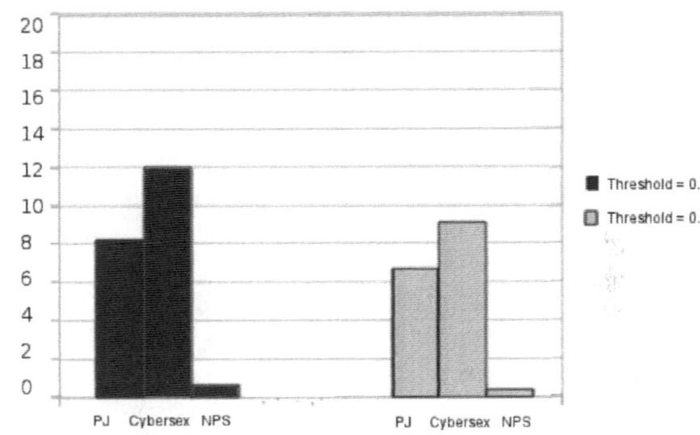

Figure 2: Average length of lexical chains calculated with Resnik semantic similarity

to the fact that whilst both corpora contain conversations about sex, cyberpedophiles are switching to this topic gradually, whereas cybersex logs are entirely sex-related.

7 Conclusions and Future Work

Detection of online sexual predation is a problem of great importance. In this small scale study we have focused on modelling fixated discourse using lexical chains as a potential feature in the automated detection of online sex predators. The preliminary experiments revealed that the lengths of sex-related lexical chains vary with the nature of the corpus, with the pedophiles logs having longer lexical chains than chat logs not related to sex, while the cybersex chat logs had the longest sex-related lexical chains of the three corpora.

As it was mentioned in Section 1, chat language is very informal and has a lot of abbreviations, slang words, mistakes etc. Hence a fair amount of words used there do not appear in WordNet and, therefore, can not be included into the lexical chains. For example, the word "ssex" is obviously related and should appear in the chain, though because of the different spelling it is not found in WordNet and, therefore, is not included into the chain. We plan to add a normalization step prior to computing lexical chains. We have used only one anchor word ("sex") to start the lexical chain. But several other words could also be good candidate for this.

Fixated discourse is not only about keeping the sexual topic throughout all the conversation, it is also about unwillingness to step out of the sexual conversation and ignoring victim's attempts to do it. Therefore, the chat lines of the pseudo-victim should be analyzed as well in order to find out if there were failed attempts to switch the topic. This may also help to distinguish predation from cybersex conversation, since in the cybersex conversation both participants want to follow the topic. However, during this preliminary experiments we have not yet considered this. Moreover, perverted-justice is run by volunteers posing as potential victims. It is then possible that the volunteers' behavior differ from the responses of real children (Egan et al., 2011). Their goal is to build a legal case against the pedophile and, therefore, they are more willing to provoke the predator than to avoid sex-related conversation.

Another way to distinguish cybersex fixed topic from the predator's unwillingness to step out of it is could be to use emotion classification based on the Leary Rose model proposed by Vaassen and Daelemans (Vaassen and Daelemans, 2011). Their approach is based on Interpersonal Circumplex suggested by Leary (Leary, 1957). This is a model of interpersonal communication that reflects whether one of the participants is dominant and whether the participants are cooperative. It was already mentioned that cyberpedophiles tend to be dominant. Therefore, we believe that the Leary Rose model can be useful in detecting online sexual predation.

Once the model of fixated discourse is improved, we plan to use it as an additional feature to detect pedophiles in social media.

Acknowledgements

The first author was partially supported by a Google Research Award and by a scholarship from the University of St. Petersburg. The second author was supported by WIQ-EI IRSES project (grant no. 269180) from the European Commission, within the FP 7 Marie Curie People, the MICINN research project TEXT-ENTERPRISE 2.0 TIN2009-13391-C04-03(Plan I+D+i), and the VLC/CAMPUS Microcluster on Multimodal Interaction in Intelligent Systems. The last author was partially supported by the UPV program PAID-02-11, award no. 1932.

References

Gene G. Abel and Nora Harlow. The Abel and Harlow child molestation prevention study. Philadelphia, Xlibris, 2001.

Regina Barzilay and Michael Elhadad. Using lexical chains for text summarization. *In Proceedings of the Intelligent Scalable Text Summarization Workshop*, 1997.

Vincent Egan, James Hoskinson, and David Shewan. Perverted justice: A content analysis of the language used by offenders detected attempting to solicit children for sex. *Antisocial Behavior: Causes, Correlations and Treatments*, 2011.

Eric N Forsythand and Craig H Martell. Lexical and discourse analysis of online chat dialog. *International Conference on Semantic Computing ICSC 2007*, pages 19–26, 2007.

Michel Galley and Kathleen McKeown. Improving word sense disambiguation in lexical chaining. *In Proceedings of IJCAI-2003*, 2003.

David Hope. Java wordnet similarity library. http://www.cogs.susx.ac.uk/users/drh21.

Claudia Leacock and Martin Chodorow. C-rater: Automated scoring of short-answer questions. *Computers and the Humanities*, 37(4):389–405, 2003.

Timothy Leary. *Interpersonal diagnosis of personality; a functional theory and methodology for personality evaluation*. Oxford, England: Ronald Press, 1957.

India McGhee, Jennifer Bayzick, April Kontostathis, Lynne Edwards, Alexandra McBride and Emma Jakubowski. Learning to identify Internet sexual predation. *International Journal on Electronic Commerce* 2011.

Kimberly J. Mitchell, David Finkelhor, and Janis Wolak. Risk factors for and impact of online sexual solicitation of youth. *Journal of the American Medical Association*, 285:3011–3014, 2001.

Jane Morris and Graeme Hirst. Lexical cohesion computed by thesaural relations as an indicator of the structure of text. *Computational Linguistics*, 17(1):21–43, 1991.

Federal Bureau of Investigation. Nibrs flatfile tape master record descriptions. 1995.

Ted Pedersen, Siddharth Patwardhan, Jason Michelizzi, and Satanjeev Banerjee. Wordnet:similarity. http://wn-similarity.sourceforge.net/.

Nick Pendar. Toward spotting the pedophile: Telling victim from predator in text chats. pages 235–241, Irvine, California, 2007.

Philip Resnik. Using information content to evaluate semantic similarity in a taxonomy. In *IJCAI*, pages 448–453, 1995.

Howard N. Snyder. Sexual assault of young children as reported to law enforcement: Victim, incident, and offender characteristics. a nibrs statistical report. *Bureau of Justice Statistics Clearinghouse*, 2000.

Frederik Vaassen and Walter Daelemans. Automatic emotion classification for interpersonal communication. In *Proceedings of the 2nd Workshop on Computational Approaches to Subjectivity and Sentiment Analysis (WASSA 2.011)*, pages 104–110. Association for Computational Linguistics, 2011.

World health organization, international statistical classification of diseases and related health problems: Icd-10 section f65.4: Paedophilia. 1988.

Detecting Stylistic Deception

Patrick Juola
Evaluating Variation in Language Laboratory
Duquesne University
Pittsburgh, PA 15282 USA
juola@mathcs.duq.edu

Abstract

Whistleblowers and activists need the ability to communicate without disclosing their identity, as of course do kidnappers and terrorists. Recent advances in the technology of stylometry (the study of authorial style) or "authorship attribution" have made it possible to identify the author with high reliability in a non-confrontational setting. In a confrontational setting, where the author is deliberately masking their identity (i.e. attempting to deceive), the results are much less promising. In this paper, we show that although the specific author may not be identifiable, the intent to deceive and to hide his identity can be. We show this by a reanalysis of the Brennan and Greenstadt (2009) deception corpus and discuss some of the implications of this surprising finding.

1 Introduction

Deception can occur in many different ways; it is possible to deceive not only about the content of a message, but about its background or origin. For example, a friendly invitation can become sexual harassment when sent from the wrong person, and very few ransom notes are signed by their authors. Recent research into stylometry has shown that it is practical to identify authors based on their writing style, but it is equally practical (at present technology) for authors to use a deliberately deceptive style, either obfuscating their own style or mimicking that of another writer, with a strong likelihood of avoiding identification.

In this paper, we investigate the possibility of identifying, not the specific author of a text, but whether or not the author of a text wrote with the (deceptive) intent to disguise their style. Our results strongly suggest that this deceptive intent can itself be identified with greater reliability than the actual author can be.

2 Background

Stylometric authorship attribution — assessing the author of a document by statistical analysis of its contents — has its origins in the 19th century (Mendenhall, 1887; de Morgan, 1851), but has experienced tremendous resurgence since the work of (Mosteller and Wallace, 1964) and the beginnings of the corpus revolution. With the exponential growth of digital-only texts and the increasing need to validate or test the legitimacy of questioned digital documents, this is obviously an area with many potential applications.

The most commonly cited stylometric study is of course that of Mosteller and Wallace (1964), who examined the frequency of appearance of approximately thirty function words within the collection of documents known as *The Federalist Papers*. Using a form of Bayesian analysis, they were able to show significant differences among the various authors in their use of these words and hence infer the probabilities that each document had been written by each author – i.e. infer authorship. Another classic in this field is the study of the *Oz* books by Binongo (2003), where he applied principal component analysis (PCA) to the frequencies of the fifty most frequent words in these books and was able to demonstrate (via the first two principle components) a clear visual separation between the books written by Baum and those written later by Thompson. Recent surveys of this field (Argamon et al., 2009; Koppel et al., 2005; Rudman, 1998; Koppel et al.,

Proceedings of the EACL 2012 Workshop on Computational Approaches to Deception Detection, pages 91–96,
Avignon, France, April 23 - 27 2012.

2009; Juola, 2006; Jockers and Witten, 2010; Stamatatos, 2009) illustrate many techniques of increasing sophistication and accuracy.

What, however, of the person who doesn't want to be identified? Chaski (2005) cites several real-world instances where authorship attribution was applied to the task of detecting miscreants, and in one case a murderer. We assume that these miscreants would have preferred to hide their identities if possible. On a more positive note, activists who fear a tyrannical government would do well to avoid being identified by the political police. Intuitively, it seems plausible that one would be able to write "in a different style," although it also seems intuitively plausible that at least part of one's writing style is fixed and immutable (van Halteren et al., 2005) — you can't pretend, for example, to a bigger vocabulary than you have, as you can't use words that you don't know. On the other hand, the long tradition of pastiche and parody suggests that at least some aspects of style can be copied.

It should be noted that this type of "deception" is different than what most research project study. Traditionally, a "deceptive" statement occurs when a speaker or writer offers an untruth; we instead suggest that another form of "deception" can occur when a speaker or writer offers a statement *that he or she does not want to be identified with.* This statement may be true (a whistleblower identifying a problem, but not wanting to risk being fired) or false (a criminal writing a false confession to incriminate someone else) — the key deception being the identity of the author.

There is little research on the success of "deceptive style" and what little there is should lend hope to activists and whistleblowers. A team of Drexel researchers (Brennan and Greenstadt, 2009; Afroz et al., 2012) developed a small corpus of deceptive writing (described in detail later), but were unable to find any methods to pierce the deception. Larger scale analyses (Juola and Vescovi, 2010; Juola and Vescovi, 2011) similarly failed. '[N]o method [out of more than 1000 tested] was able to perform "significantly" above chance at the standard 0.05 level.... We [...] observe that, yes, there is a confirmed problem here. Although these analyses performed (on average) above chance, they did not do so by robust margins, and there is enough variance in individual performance that we cannot claim even to have "significant" improvement.'

In light of these results, the Drexel team have proposed and developed a tool ["Anonymouth", (Afroz and Brennan, 2011; Perlroth, 2012)] that provides a more formal and systematic method of disguising their writing style. Based in part on the JGAAP tool (Juola et al., 2009; Juola, 2006), this system allows would-be activists to see what aspects of their linguistic fingerprints are more obvious in a document, and guides these same activists to make changes to neutralize their personal style, or even to assume a specific other's style. In some sense, Anonymouth is the "evil twin" countermeasure to JGAAP – while JGAAP detects style, Anonymouth in theory renders style indetectable.

Does it work? The tool is still too new for substantial testing, but we assume based on the earlier work that it will still be difficult to detect the original author under the deception. However, it may be possible to detect the act of deception itself. As will be seen in the following sections, standard stylometric tools themselves can do that.

3 Materials and Methods

One of the most powerful and flexible tools for text analysis and classification is the JGAAP (Java Graphical Authorship Attribution Program) software package. Available for download from `www.evllabs.com`, it is a modular Java-based freeware program that implements a simple pipelined architecture for text classification. We have applied it to the Brennan-Greenstadt (Brennan and Greenstadt, 2009) Adversarial corpus of imitative and obfuscative essays, to determine whether these "imitative and obfuscative" essays have themselves a stable style.

JGAAP itself (Juola, 2006) follows a standard model for statistical authorship attribution. Documents are pre-processed ("canonicized") to eliminate distracting or uninformative variation (for example, the length of a printed line is set by the editor, not the author, so "normalizing whitespace" removes some editorial distraction). Following this, they are broken up into individual events which are subject to some form of statistical analysis and classification.

As an example, Binongo's experiment could be captured within the JGAAP framework as follows: preprocess the *Oz* books to remove extraneous materials (including punctuation), unify case to neutralize syntax-based case distinctions (like capital letters at the beginning of a sentence), and normalize whitespace as described above. Binongo then broke the books up into individual words and selected only the top fifty most common words as his events of interest. Finally, he applied PCA to get a visual picture of how the documents separated in abstract event space.

The B/G corpus (as published) collects the writings of twelve people, with approximately ten essays (totaling about 5000 words) per person. In addition, it has twelve passages from *The Road* by the professional author Cormac McCarthy. This establishes a baseline of 126 essays of "normal" writing, writing where there is no attempt to disguise style (and hence no deception). Each subject was then asked to write two additional essays: one deliberately written "in such a way that their personal writing style will not be recognized" (a so-called "obfuscation"), and another in the style of Cormac McCarthy as expressed in *The Road* ("imitation"). This creates another twenty-four instances of "deceptive" writing where the writer is attempting to conceal their style.

Of the twelve (thirteen including McCarthy) writers in the sample, we used nine (plus McCarthy) as training data, labeling all instances of the writer using their own style as "HONEST" and all instances of obfuscation/imitation as "DECEPTIVE." The writings of three subjects (Andrew, Chris, and Sara) were used as test subjects, creating six unknown "deceptive" documents and twenty-eight unknown "honest" documents. (This is obviously an unbalanced corpus as the number of honest documents is more than five times the number of deceptive ones; this will be discussed later.)

These documents were analyzed by JGAAP using the following settings, which previous testing (Noecker and Juola, 2009) has shown to work well:

- Canonicizer : Unify Case & Punctuation Separator
- Event Driver : Character 3-grams (Character N-grams with N set to 3)
- Event Culler : <none>
- Analysis Driver : Nearest Neighbor Driver
- Distance : (Normalized) Cosine Distance

"Unify Case" converts all (alphabetic) characters to lower case, thus removing any apparent differences between sentence-initial words and their sentence-internal equivalents. "Punctuation Separator" breaks up groups of consecutive punctuation characters by inserting spaces (e.g. "(!)" would become "(!)"). The events analyzed were strings of three consecutive characters (e.g. the word "there" contains three such 3-grams ("the" "her" and "ere"). These 3-grams were not culled (unlike the Binongo experiment, where the events were culled to include only the top 50) and instead were all used in the analysis. These 3-grams were collected into a histogram for each document and inter-document distances were calculated using the normalized cosine distance (aka dot product distance). Finally, each testing document attributed to (considered to be the same deceptiveness type as) the closest training document.

4 Results

The results are summarized in table 1. Of the six deceptive documents, five (or 83%) were correctly identified, while of the twenty-eight non-deceptive documents, twenty-two (or 79%) were correctly identified. (Of course, due to the imbalance in the test set, only 44% of the documents labeled "deceptive" actually were; we consider this statistic something of an artifact.) This result is of course far above chance: baseline performance would be only two correct on deceptive documents and 19 correct on honest ones. Fisher's exact test on the 2×2 contingency matrix shows a one-tailed probability of $p < 0.00790$ (or a two-tailed probability of double that, of course), confirming the high significance of this result.

Preliminary error analysis is attached as table 2. Most notable is that none of the imitation Cormac McCarthy analyses were misclassified as "normal" writing.

5 Discussion and Future Work

Previous work [(Brennan and Greenstadt, 2009; Juola and Vescovi, 2010; Juola and Vescovi, 2011)] has shown that identifying the author of "deceptively" written materials is extremely difficult. We thus have the highly surprising result that, while identifying the specific author may be difficult, uncovering the mere fact that the author

		Actual Deception	
		Y	N
Detected Deception	Y	5	6
	N	1	22

Table 1: Results from deception-detection experiment

	FP	FN (obfusc)	FN (imit)
Andrew	3	0	0
Chris	1	1	0
Sara	2	0	0

Table 2: Number of incorrect classifications by type

is concerned about being identified is relatively easy. This of course parallels the rather commonplace situation in detective fiction where the fact that the criminal has wiped the fingerprints off the murder weapon is both easy to learn and highly significant, even if the criminal's actual identity must wait five more chapters for the big reveal. Similarly, it appears to be fairly easy to detect the attempt to wipe one's authorial "fingerprints" off of the writing.

This result is all the more surprising in light of the heterogeneity of the corpus; the writing style of ten different people, collectively, created our sample of "normal" writing. The writings of three entirely different people fit that sample relatively well. Astonishingly, the attempts of all twelve people to write "differently" fit into a recognizable and distinctive stylistic pattern; these twelve people seem to have a relatively uniform sense of "the other." This sense of "the other," in turn, persists even when these people model the writings of a professional writer *whose style itself is part of the "normal" sample!*

Put more strongly, when "Chris" (or any of the other test subjects) attempted to write in the style of Cormac McCarthy, the result was actually closer to a third party's attempt to write deceptively than it was to McCarthy's writing himself. In the specific case of "Andrew's" imitative writing, all six of the six closest samples were of deceptive writing, suggesting that "deceptive writing" is itself a recognizable style.

Further investigation is clearly required into the characteristics of the style of deception. For example, there may not be one single style; it may instead be the case that "imitation McCarthy" is a recognizable and distinct style from McCarthy's, but also from "obfuscated style." There may be one or several "obfuscated styles." It is not clear from this study what the characteristics of this style are, and in fact, the inability of JGAAP (and JGAAP's distance-based measures in particular) to produce explanations for what are evidently clear-cut categorizations is one of the major weaknesses of the JGAAP system as currently envisioned. Even simple replication of this experiment would be of value, as while we consider it unlikely that our arbitrary choice of test subjects would have created an unrepresentative result, we can't (yet) confirm that. Indeed, we hope that this finding provides encouragement for the development of larger-scale corpora than the simple twelve-subject Brennan-Greenstadt corpus.

We also hope this finding spurs research into exactly what the stylistic "other" is, and in particular, research from a psychological or psycholinguistic standpoint. For example, Chaski (2005) [see also (Chaski, 2007)] argues that the linguistic concept of "markedness" is a key aspect of author identification. Chaski in particular suggests that the use or non-use of "marked" constructions is a good feature to capture. Following her line of reasoning, if I try to write as "not-myself," does this mean I will deliberately use concepts that I consider to be "marked" and therefore unusual? (If this were true, this would have significant implications for the theory of markedness, as this concept is usually held to be a property of a language as a whole and not of individual idiolects. In particular, if I personally tend to use "marked" constructions, and consider traditionally "unmarked" construtions to be unusual, does this imply that traditional notions of "markedness' are reversed *in my idiolect*, or that my cognitive processing of this construction is atypical?) Alternatively, if authorship is defined more computationally in terms of probability spaces, can we relate "otherness" to a notion of prototypicality (Rosch and Mervis, 1975) of language?

Even without explanations, our basic results have significant implications for the stylometric arms race. We acknowledge the legitimate need for the good guys to analyze the writings of the bad guys to help find them, while also acknowledging the needs of the good guys (human rights advocates, corporate whistleblowers, etc.) to be free to expose the abuses of the bad guys without fear of retribution. We applaud the development of tools like *Anonymouth* for this reason. On the other hand, if an attempt even to disguise one's style is detectable, it may equally be suspicious — especially in the mind of one who believes that the innocent have no reason to disguise themselves. In this regard tools like *Anonymouth* may be similar to encryption programs like PGP. Encrypted email may be suspected due to its very rarity. Zimmermann (nd) has suggested that "it would be nice if everyone routinely used encryption for all their E-mail, innocent or not, so that no one drew suspicion by asserting their [right to] E-mail privacy with encryption."

This result may also have significant implications for (linguistic) forensic practices. The question of reliability is key for any evidence. Any defense lawyer will ask whether or not it's possible that someone could have imitated the style of his client when writing the incriminating document. The results of repeated analysis of the Brennan-Greenstadt corpus suggest that it is, in fact, possible to fool stylometric analysis. The results presented here, however, show that such deception is detectable — the analyst can respond "yes, it may be possible, but such imitation would leave traces that were not found in the document." By showing a lack of deceptive intent, one can enhance the *de facto* reliability of a report.

A key technical question that remains is whether tools like *Anonymouth* will produce "strongly" stylistic masking – and whether the use of such tools is as detectable as more freestyle approaches to stylistic matching, where the author is simply told "write like so-and-so." In theory *Anonymouth* could guide a writer to specific types of stylistic difference ("you use words that are too short; use longer words") – in practice (Greenstadt, personal communication) this has so far been shown to be very cumbersome. (Of course, *Anonymouth* itself is barely out of prototype stage and can probably be improved.) A worst-case scenario would be where the use of *Anonymouth* itself left the equivalent of stylistic "toolmarks," allowing people to identify that the message had been altered by this specific software package (and possibly even a specific version). This could, in turn, provide investigators with information and evidence that actually makes it easier to identify the origin of a given text (e.g., how many people have *Anonymouth* on their systems?).

6 Conclusions

The results of this study, despite being preliminary, show that attempts to disguise one's writing style can be detected with relatively high accuracy. While these results technically only apply to freestyle deception as opposed to tool-based deception, we expect that similar findings would apply to the use of anti-stylometric tools. Similarly, we have only shown one particular method is capable of performing this detection, but we expect that there are others as well and invite large-scale testing to find the most accurate way to detect deceptive writing, which may or may not be the best way to identify the author of non-deceptive writing (or the author of deceptive writing, for that matter).

From the standpoint of security technologies, this creates another level in the countermeasures/counter-countermeasures/etc. loop. If the use of a tool provides security at one level, it is likely to create a weakness at another; disguising one's writing style may at the same time make it obvious to an appropriate observer that you are trying to conceal something. With interest in stylometry and stylometric security growing, we acknowledge the need for stylistic masking, but argue here that using such tools may actually put the masked writer at risk.

Acknowledgments

This material is based in part upon work supported by the National Science Foundation under Grant Numbers OCI-0721667 and OCI-1032683. Any opinions, findings, and conclusions or recommendations expressed in this material are those of the author(s) and do not necessarily reflect the views of the National Science Foundation.

References

Sadia Afroz and Michael Brennan. 2011. Deceiving authorship detection. In *28th Annual Meeting of the Chaos Computer Club (28C3)*, Berlin.

Sadia Afroz, Michael Brennan, and Rachel Greenstadt. 2012. Detecting hoaxes, frauds, and deception in writing style online. In *Proceedings of the 33rd conference on* IEEE Symposium on Security and Privacy, *pages=To appear*. IEEE.

Shlomo Argamon, Moshe Koppel, James W. Pennebaker, and Jonathan Schler. 2009. Automatically profiling the author of an anonymous text. *CACM*, 52(2):119–123, February.

Jose Nilo G. Binongo. 2003. Who wrote the 15th book of Oz? an application of multivariate analysis to authorship attribution. *Chance*, 16(2):9–17.

Michael Brennan and Rachel Greenstadt. 2009. Practical attacks against authorship recognition techniques. In *Proceedings of the Twenty-First Conference on Innovative Applications of Artificial Intelligence (IAAI)*, Pasadena, CA.

Carole E. Chaski. 2005. Who's at the keyboard: Authorship attribution in digital evidence invesigations. *International Journal of Digital Evidence*, 4(1):n/a. Electronic-only journal: http://www.ijde.org, accessed 5.31.2007.

Carole E. Chaski. 2007. The keyboard dilemma and forensic authorship attribution. Advances in Digital Forensics III.

Augustus de Morgan. 1851. Letter to Rev. Heald 18/08/1851. In Sophia Elizabeth. De Morgan (Ed.) *Memoirs of Augustus de Morgan by his wife Sophia Elizabeth de Morgan with Selections from his Letters.*

M. L. Jockers and D.M Witten. 2010. A comparative study of machine learning methods for authorship attribution. *LLC*, 25(2):215–23.

Patrick Juola and Darren Vescovi. 2010. Empirical evaluation of authorship obfuscation using JGAAP. In *Proceedings of the Third Workshop on Artificial Intelligence and Security*, Chicago, IL USA, October.

Patrick Juola and Darren Vescovi. 2011. Authorship attribution for electronic documents. In Gilbert Petersen and Sujeet Shenoi, editors, *Advances in Digital Forensics VII*, International Federal for Information Processing, chapter 9, pages 115–129. Springer, Boston.

Patrick Juola, John Noecker, Jr., Mike Ryan, and Sandy Speer. 2009. Jgaap 4.0 — a revised authorship attribution tool. In *Proceedings of Digital Humanities 2009*, College Park, MD.

Patrick Juola. 2006. Authorship attribution. *Foundations and Trends in Information Retrieval*, 1(3).

Moshe Koppel, Johnathan Schler, and K. Zigdon. 2005. Determining an author's native language by mining a text for errors (short paper). In *Proceedings of KDD*, Chicago,IL, August.

Moshe Koppel, Jonathan Schler, and Shlomo Argamon. 2009. Computational methods in authorship attribution. *Journal of the American Society for Information Science and Technology*, 60(1):9–26.

T. C. Mendenhall. 1887. The characteristic curves of composition. *Science*, IX:237–49.

F. Mosteller and D. L. Wallace. 1964. *Inference and Disputed Authorship : The Federalist*. Addison-Wesley, Reading, MA.

John Noecker, Jr. and Patrick Juola. 2009. Cosine distance nearest-neighbor classification for authorship attribution. In *Proceedings of Digital Humanities 2009*, College Park, MD.

Nicole Perlroth. 2012. Software helps identify anonymous writers or helps them stay that way, January. New York Times article of 3 January, 2012.

Eleanor Rosch and Carolyn B. Mervis. 1975. Family resemblances: Studies in the internal structure of categories. *Cognitive Psychology*, 7(4):573–605.

J. Rudman. 1998. The state of authorship attribution studies: Some problems and solutions. *Computers and the Humanities*, 31:351–365.

Efstathios Stamatatos. 2009. A survey of modern authorship attribution methods. *Journal of the American Society for Information Science and Technology*, 60(3):538–56.

Hans van Halteren, R. Harald Baayen, Fiona Tweedie, Marco Haverkort, and Anneke Neijt. 2005. New machine learning methods demonstrate the existence of a human stylome. *Journal of Quantitative Linguistics*, 12(1):65–77.

Phil Zimmermann. n.d. Why do you need PGP? `http://www.pgpi.org/doc/whypgp/en`. Retrieved 18 January, 2012.

Identification of Truth and Deception in Text: Application of Vector Space Model to Rhetorical Structure Theory

Victoria L. Rubin and **Tatiana Vashchilko**
Language and Information Technology Research Lab (LiT.RL)
Faculty of Information and Media Studies, University of Western Ontario
London, Ontario, Canada
{vrubin,tvashchi}@uwo.ca

Abstract

The paper proposes to use Rhetorical Structure Theory (RST) analytic framework to identify systematic differences between deceptive and truthful stories in terms of their coherence and structure. A sample of 36 elicited personal stories, self-ranked as completely truthful or completely deceptive, is manually analyzed by assigning RST discourse relations among a story's constituent parts. Vector Space Model (VSM) assesses each story's position in multi-dimensional RST space with respect to its distance to truth and deceptive centers as measures of the story's level of deception and truthfulness. Ten human judges evaluate if each story is deceptive or not, and assign their confidence levels, which produce measures of the human expected deception and truthfulness levels. The paper contributes to deception detection research and RST twofold: a) demonstration of discourse structure analysis in pragmatics as a prominent way of automated deception detection and, as such, an effective complement to lexico-semantic analysis, and b) development of RST-VSM methodology to interpret RST analysis in identification of previously unseen deceptive texts.

Introduction

Automated deception detection is a challenging task (DePaulo, Charlton, Cooper, Lindsay, and Muhlenbruck, 1997), only recently proven feasible with natural language processing and machine learning techniques (Bachenko, Fitzpatrick, and Schonwetter, 2008; Fuller, Biros, and Wilson, 2009; Hancock, Curry, Goorha, and Woodworth, 2008; Rubin, 2010; Zhou, Burgoon, Nunamaker, and Twitchell, 2004). The idea is to distinguish truthful information from deceptive, where deception usually implies an intentional and knowing attempt on the part of the sender to create a false belief or false conclusion in the mind of the receiver of the information (e.g., Buller and Burgoon, 1996; Zhou, et al., 2004). In this paper we focus solely on textual information, in particular, in computer-mediated personal communications such as e-mails or online posts.

Previously suggested techniques for detecting deception in text reach modest accuracy rates at the level of lexico-semantic analysis. Certain lexical items are considered to be predictive linguistic cues, and could be derived, for examples, from the Statement Validity Analysis techniques used in law enforcement for credibility assessments (as in Porter and Yuille, 1996). Though there is no clear consensus on reliable predictors of deception, deceptive cues are identified in texts, extracted and clustered conceptually, for instance, to represent diversity, complexity, specificity, and non-immediacy of the analyzed texts (e.g., Zhou, Burgoon, Nunamaker, and Twitchell (2004)). When implemented with standard classification algorithms (such as neural nets, decision trees, and logistic regression), such methods achieve 74% accuracy (Fuller, et al., 2009). Existing psycholinguistic lexicons (e.g., LWIC by Pennebaker and Francis, 1999) have been adapted to perform binary text classifications for truthful versus deceptive opinions, with an average classifier demonstrating 70% accuracy rate (Mihalcea and Strapparava, 2009).

These modest results, though usually achieved on restricted topics, are promising since they supersede notoriously unreliable human abilities in lie-truth discrimination tasks. On average, people are not very good at spotting lies (Vrij, 2000), succeeding generally only about half of the time (Frank, Paolantinio, Feeley, and

Proceedings of the EACL 2012 Workshop on Computational Approaches to Deception Detection, pages 97–106,
Avignon, France, April 23 - 27 2012.

Servoss, 2004). For instance, a meta-analytical review of over 100 experiments with over 1,000 participants, showed a 54% mean accuracy rate at identifying deception (DePaulo, et al., 1997). Human judges achieve 50 – 63% success rates, depending on what is considered deceptive on a seven-point scale of truth-to-deception continuum (Rubin and Conroy, 2011, Rubin and Conroy, 2012), but the higher the actual self-reported deception level of the story, the more likely a story would be confidently assigned as deceptive. In other words, extreme degrees of deception are more transparent to judges.

The task for current automated deception detection techniques has been formulated as binary text categorization – is a message deceptive or truthful – and the decision applies to the whole analyzed text. Since it is an overall discourse level decision, it may be reasonable to consider discourse or pragmatic features of each message. Thus far, discourse is surprisingly rarely considered, if at all, and the majority of the effort has been restricted to lexico-semantic verbal predictors. A rare exception up to date has been a Bachenko, Fitzpatrick and Schonwetter's (2008) study that focuses on truth or falsity of individual propositions, achieving a finer-grained level of analysis[1], but the propositional inter-relations within the discourse structure are not considered. To the best of our knowledge there have been no advances in that automation deception detection task to incorporate discourse structure features and/or text coherence analysis at the pragmatic levels of story interpretation.

Study Objective

With the recent advances in the identification of verbal cues of deception in mind, and the realization that they focus on linguistic levels below discourse and pragmatic analysis, the study focuses on one main question:

- What is the impact of the relations between discourse constituent parts on the discourse composition of deceptive and truthful messages?

We hypothesize that if the relations between discourse constituent parts in deceptive messages differ from the ones in truthful messages, then systematic analysis of such relations will help to detect deception. To investigate this question, we propose to use a novel methodology for deception detection research, Rhetorical Structure Theory (RST) analysis with subsequent application of the Vector Space Model (VSM). RST analysis is promising in deception detection, since RST analysis captures coherence of a story in terms of functional relations among different meaningful text units, and describes a hierarchical structure of each story (Mann and Thompson, 1988). The result is that each story is a set of RST relations connected in a hierarchical manner with more salient text units heading this hierarchical tree. We also propose to utilize the VSM model for conversion of the derived RST relations' frequencies into meaningful clusters of diverse deception levels. To evaluate the proposed RST-VSM methodology of deception detection in texts, we compare human assessment to the RST-analysis of deception levels for the sets of deceptive and truthful stories. The main findings demonstrate that RST resembles, to some degree, human judges in deceptive and truthful stories, and RST deception detection in self-rated deceptive stories has greater consistency than in truthful ones, which signifies the prominence of using RST-VSM methodology for deception detection[2]. However, RST conclusions regarding levels of deception in the truthful stories requires further research about the diversity of RST relations for the expressions of truths and deception as well as the types of clustering algorithms most suitable for clustering unevaluated by human judges' written communication in RST space to detect deception with certain degree of precision.

The paper has three main parts. The next part discusses methodological foundations of RST-VSM approach. Then, the data and collection method describe the sample. Finally, the results section demonstrates the identified levels of deception and truthfulness as well as their distribution across truthful and deceptive stories.

RST-VSM Methodology: Combining Vector Space Model and Rhetorical Structure Theory

Vector space model (VSM) seemed to be very useful in the identification of truth and deception types of written stories especially if the meaning

[1] Using a corpus of criminal statements, police interrogations and legal testimonies, their regression and tree-based classification automatic tagger performs at average 69% recall and 85% precision rates, as compared to the performance of human taggers on the same subset (Bachenko, et al., 2008).

[2] The authors recognize that the results are preliminary and should be generalized with caution due to very small dataset and certain methodological issues that require further development.

of the stories is represented as RST relations. RST differentiates between rhetorically stand-alone parts of a text, some of which are more salient (nucleolus) than the others (satellite). In the past couple of decades, empirical observations and previous RST research confirmed that writers tend to emphasize certain parts of a text in order to express their most essential idea to reach the purpose of the written message. These parts can be systematically identified through the analysis of the rhetorical connections among more and less essential parts of a text. RST helps to describe and quantify text coherence through a set of constraints on nucleolus and satellites. The main function of these constraints is to describe in the meaningful way why and how one part of a text connects to the others within a hierarchical tree structure, which is an RST representation of a coded text. The names of the RST relations also resemble the purpose of using the connected text parts together.

For example, one of the RST relations, which appear in truthful stories and never appear in the deceptive stories in our sample, is EVIDENCE. The main purpose of using EVIDENCE to connect two parts of text is to present additional information in satellite, so that the reader's belief about the information in the nucleolus increases. However, this can happen only if the information in the satellite is credible from reader's point of view. For some reason, the RST coding of 18 deceptive stories has never used EVIDENCE, but used it rather often in 18 truthful stories. This might indicates that either 1) writers of deceptive stories did not see any purpose in supplying additional information to the readers to increase their beliefs in communicating writer's essential ideas, or 2) the credibility of presented information in satellite was not credible from the readers' points of view, which did not qualify the relationship between nucleolus and satellite for "EVIDENCE" relation, or 3) both (See an example of RST diagram in Appendix A).

Our premise is that if there are systematic differences between deceptive and truthful written stories in terms of their coherence and structure, then the RST analysis of these stories can identify two sets of RST relations and their structure. One set is specific for the deceptive stories, and the other one is specific for the truthful stories.

We propose to use a vector space model for the identification of these sets of RST relations. Mathematically speaking, written stories have to be modeled in a way suitable for the application of various computational algorithms based on linear algebra. Using a vector space model, the written stories could be represented as RST vectors in a high dimensional space (Salton and McGill 1983, Manning and Schutse 1999). According to the VSM, stories are represented as vectors, and the dimension of the vector space equals to the number of RST relations in a set of all written stories under consideration. Such representation of written stories makes the VSM very attractive in terms of its simplicity and applicability (Baeza-Yates and Ribeiro-Neto 1999).

Vector space model[3] is the basis for almost all clustering techniques when dealing with the analysis of texts. Once the texts are represented according to VSM, as vectors in an n-dimensional space, we can apply the myriad of cluster methods that have been developed in Computational Science, Data Mining, Bioinformatics. Cluster analysis methods can be divided into two big groups (Zhong and Ghosh 2004): discriminative (or similarity based) approaches (Indyk 1999, Scholkopf and Smola 2001, Vapnik 1998) and generative (or model-based) approaches (Blimes 1998, Rose 1998, Cadez et al. 2000).

The main benefit of applying vector space model to RST analysis is that the VSM allows a formal identification of coherence and structural similarities among stories of the same type (truthful or deceptive). For this purpose, RST relations are vectors in a story space. Visually we could think about the set of stories or RST relations as a cube (Figure 1), in which each dimension is an RST relation.

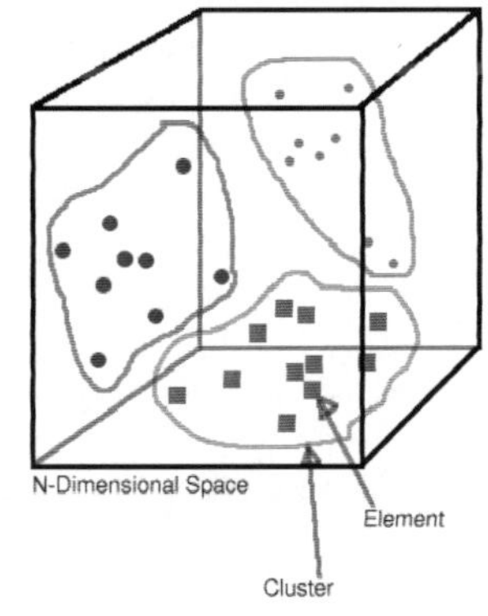

Figure 1: Cluster Representation of Story Sets or RST Relations (Cluto Graphical Frontend Project, 2002).

[3] Tombros (2002) maintains that most of the research related to the retrieval of information is based on vector space model.

The main subsets of this set of stories are two clusters, deceptive stories and truthful stories. The element of a cluster is a story, and a cluster is a set of elements that share enough similarity to be grouped together, the deceptive stories or truthful stories (Berkhin 2002). That is, there is a number of distinctive features (RST relations, their co-occurrences and positions in a hierarchical structure) that make each story unique and being a member of a particular cluster. These distinctive features of the stories are compared, and when some similarity threshold is met, they are placed in one of two groups, deceptive or truthful stories.

Similarity [4] is one of the key concepts in cluster analysis, since most of the classical techniques (k-means, unsupervised Bayes, hierarchical agglomerative clustering) and rather recent ones (CLARANS, DBSCAN, BIRCH, CLIQUE, CURE, etc.) "are based on distances between the samples in the original vector space" (Strehl et al 2000). Such algorithms form a similarity based clustering framework (Figure 1) as it is described in Strehl et al (2000) , or as Zhong and Ghosh (2004) define it as discriminative (or similarity – based) clustering approaches.

That is why, this paper modifies Strehl et al's (2004) similarity based clustering framework (Figure 2) to develop a unique RST-VSM methodology for deception detection in text. The RST-VSM methodology includes three main steps:

1) The set of written stories, *X*, is transformed into the vector space description, X, using some rule, *Y*, that in our case corresponds to an RST analysis and identification of RST relations as well as their hierarchy in each story.

2) This vector space description X is transformed into a similarity space description, S, using some rule, Ψ , which in our case is the Euclidian distance of every story from a deception and truth centers correspondingly based on normalized frequency of RST relations in a written story[5].

3) The similarity space description, S, is mapped into clusters based on the rule Φ , which we define as the relative closeness of a story to a deception or a truth center: if a story is closer to the truth center, then a story is placed in a truth cluster, whereas if a story is closer to a deception center, then a story is placed in a deception cluster.

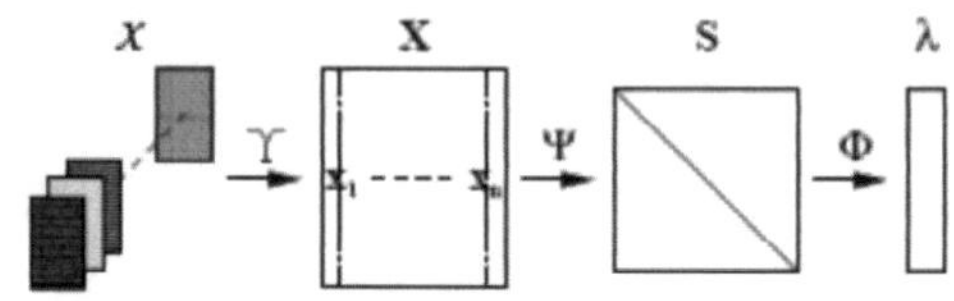

Figure 2: Similarity Based Clustering Framework (Strehl et al, 2004)

Data Collection and Sample

The dataset contains 36 rich unique personal stories, elicited using Amazon's online survey service, Mechanical Turk (www.mturk.com). Respondents in one group were asked to write a rich unique story, which is completely true or with some degree of deception. Respondents in another group were asked to evaluate the stories written by the respondents in the first group (For further details on the data collection process and the discussion of associated challenges, see Rubin and Conroy 2012).

Two groups of 18 stories each compile the data sample. The first group consists of 18 stories that were self-ranked by their authors as completely deceptive on a seven-point Likhert scale from complete truth to complete deception (deceptive self-reported group). The second group includes stories, which their authors rated as completely truthful stories (truthful self-reported group). The second group was matched in numbers for direct comparisons to the first group by selecting random 18 stories from a larger group of 39 completely truthful stories (Rubin and Conroy, 2011, Rubin and Conroy, 2012). Each story in both groups, truthful self-reported and deceptive self-reported, has 10 unique human judgments associated with it. Each judgment is binary ("judged truthful" or "judged deceptive"), and has an associated confidence level assigned by the judge (either "totally uncertain", "somewhat uncertain", "I'm guessing", "somewhat certain", or "totally certain"). Each writer and judge was encouraged to provide explanations for defining a story as truthful or deceptive, and assigning a particular confidence level. In total, 396 participants contributed to the study, 36 of them were story authors, and 360 – were judges performing lie-truth discrimination task by confidence level.

[4] "Interobject similarity is a measure of correspondence or resemblance between objects to be clustered" (Hair et al. 1995, p. 429).

[5] Since RST stories as vectors differ in length, the normalization assures their comparability. The coordinates of every story (the frequency of an RST relation in a story) are divided on the vector's length.

We combine the 10 judges' evaluations of a story into one measure, the expected level of a story's deception or truthfulness. Since judges' confidence levels reflect the likelihood of a story being truthful or deceptive, the probability of a story being completely true or deceptive equals one and corresponds to a "totally certain" confidence level that the story is true or deceptive[6]. Two dummy variables are created for each story. One dummy, a deception dummy, equals 1, if a judge rated the story is "judged deceptive", and 0 otherwise. The second dummy, the truthfulness dummy, equals 1 if a judge rated the story as "judged truthful", and 0 otherwise. Then the expected level of deception of a story equals the product of the probability (confidence level) of deception and the deception dummy across 10 judges. Similarly, the expected level of truthfulness is equals the product of the probability of truthfulness (confidence level) and the truthfulness dummy across 10 judges. The distribution of expected levels of deception and the expected levels of truthfulness of the deceptive and truthful subsets of the sample are in Appendix B1-B2.

Thirty six stories, evenly divided between truthful and deceptive self-report groups, were manually analyzed using the classical set of Mann and Thompson's (1988) RST relations, extensively tested empirically (Taboada and Mann, 2006). As a first stage of RST-VSM methodology development, the manual RST coding was required to deepen the understanding of the rhetorical relations and structures specific for deceptive and truthful stories. Moreover, manual analysis aided by Mick O'Donnell's RSTTool (http://www.wagsoft.com/RSTTool/) might ensure higher reliability of the analysis and avoid compilation of errors, as the RST output further served as the VSM input. Taboada (2004) reports on the existence of Daniel Marcu's RST Annotation Tool: www.isi.edu/licensed-sw/RSTTool/ and Hatem Ghorbel's RhetAnnotate (lithwww.epfl.ch/~ghorbel/rhetannotate/) and provides a good overview of other recent RST resources and applications. The acquired knowledge during manual coding of deceptive stories along with recent advances in automated RST analysis will help later on to evaluate RST-VSM methodology and design a completely automated deception detection tool relying on the automated procedures to recognize rhetorical relations, which utilize the full rhetorical parsing (Marcu 1997, 2002).

[6] In the same way, the other levels of confidence have the following probability correspondences: "totally uncertain" has probability 0.2 of a story being deceptive or truthful, "somewhat uncertain" – 0.4, "I'm guessing" – 0.6, and "somewhat certain" – 0.8.

Results

The preliminary clustering of 36 stories in RST space using various clustering algorithms shows that RST dimensions can systematically differentiate between truthful and deceptive stories as well as diverse levels of deception (Figure 3).

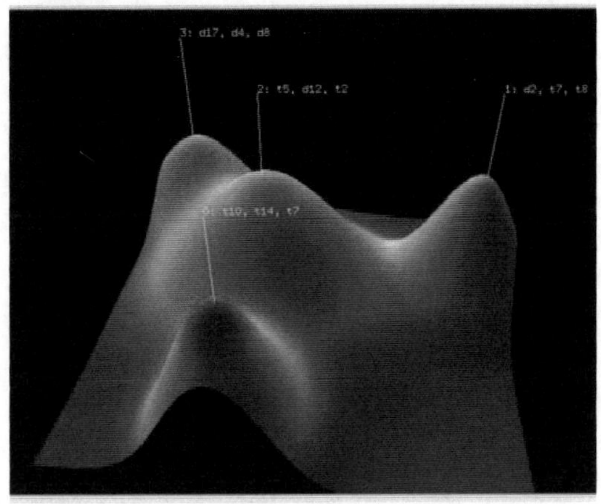

Figure 3. Four Clusters in RST Space by Level of Deception.

The visualization uses GLUTO software (http://glaros.dtc.umn.edu/gkhome/cluto/gcluto/overview), which finds the clustering solution as a result of the optimization of a "particular function that reflects the underlying definition of the "goodness" of the cluster" (Rasmussen and Karypis 2004, p.3). Among the four clusters in RST space, two clusters are composed of completely deceptive stories (far back left peak in green) or entirely truthful stories (front peak in red), the other two clusters have a mixture with the prevalence of either truthful or deceptive stories. This preliminary investigation of using RST space for deception detection indicates that the RST analysis seems to offer a systematical way of distinguishing between truth and deceptive features of texts.

This paper develops an RST-VSM methodology by using RST analysis of each story in N-dimensional RST space with subsequent application of vector space model to identify the level of a story's deception. A normalized frequency of an RST relation in a story is a distinct coordinate in the RST space. The authors' ratings are used to calculate the centers for the truth and deception clusters based on corresponding authors' self-rated deception and truthful sets of stories in the sample. The normalized Euclidian distances between a story and each of the centers are defined as the degree of deception of that story depending on its closeness to the deception center. The closer a story is to the deception center, the higher is its level of deception. The closer a story is to the truthful center, the higher is its level of truthfulness[7].

RST seems to differentiate between truthful and deceptive stories. The difference in means test demonstrates that the truthful stories have a statistically significantly lower average number of text units per statement than the deceptive stories (t= -1.3104), though these differences are not large, only at 10% significance level. The normalized frequencies of the RST relations appearing in the truthful and deceptive stories differ for about one third of all RST relations based on the difference in means test (Appendix C).

The comparison of the distribution of RST relations across deceptive and truth centers demonstrates that on average, the frequencies and the usage of such RST relations as conjunction, elaboration, evaluation, list, means, non-volitional cause, non-volitional result, sequence, and solutionhood in deceptive stories exceeds those in the truthful ones (Figure 4). On the other hand, the average usage and frequencies of such RST relations as volitional result, volitional cause, purpose, interpretation, concession, circumstance and antithesis in truthful stories exceeds those in the deceptive ones. Some of the RST relations are only specific for one type of the story: enablement, restatement and evidence appear only in truthful stories, whereas summary, preparation, unconditional and disjunction appear only in deceptive stories.

The histograms of distributions of deception (truthfulness) levels assigned by judges and derived from RST-VSM analysis demonstrate some similarities between the two for truth and for deceptive stories (Appendices D-E). More rigorous statistical testing reveals that only truthfulness levels in deceptive stories assigned by judges do not have statistically significant difference from the RST-VSM ones[8]. For other groups, the judges' assessments and RST ones do differ significantly.

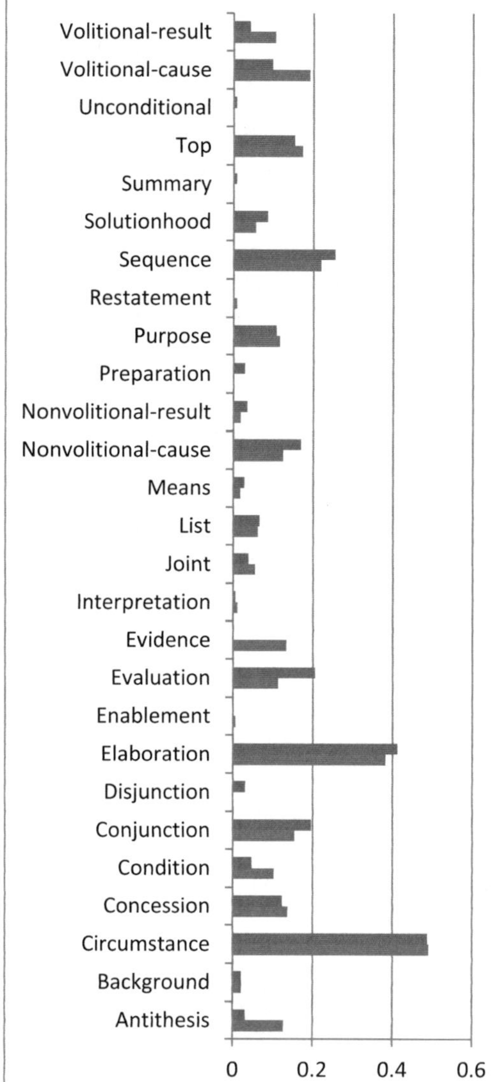

Figure 4: Comparison of the RST Relations' Composing the Deceptive Cluster Center (top red bar) and the Truthful Cluster Center (bottom blue bar).

The difference is especially apparent in the distributions of deception and truthfulness in truthful stories. Among them, RST-VSM methodology counted 44.44% of stories having 50% deception level, whereas judges counted 61.11 percent of the same stories having low deception level of no more than 20%. The level of truthfulness was also much higher in judges' assessment than based on RST-VSM calculations.

[7] All calculations are performed in STATA.

[8] We use the Wilcoxon signed rank sum test, which is the non-parametric version of a paired samples t-test (STATA command signrank (STATA 2012)).

The distribution of the levels of deception and truthfulness across all deceptive stories (Appendices D1-D4) and across all truthful stories (Appendices E1-E4) shows variations in patterns of deception levels based on RST-VSM. In deception stories, the RST-VSM levels of deception are consistently higher than the RST-VSM levels of truthfulness. Assuming that the authors of the stories did make them up, the RST-VSM methodology seems to offer a systematic way of detecting a high level of deception with rather good precision.

The RST-VSM deception levels are not as high as human judges' ones, with human judges assigning much higher levels of deception to deceptive stories than to truthful stories. Assuming that the stories are indeed made up, the human judges have greater precision than the RST-VSM methodology. Nevertheless, RST-VSM analysis assigns higher deception levels to stories, which also receive higher human judges' deception levels. This pattern is consistent across all deceptive stories.

Discussion

The analysis of truthful stories shows some systematic and some slightly contradictory findings. On one hand, the levels of truthfulness assigned by judges are predominantly higher than the levels of deception. Again, assuming that the stories in the truthful set are completely true because the authors ranked them so, the human judges have greater likelihood of rating these stories as truthful than as deceptive. This can be an indicator of a good precision of deception detection by human judges.

On the other hand, the RST-VSM analysis also demonstrates that large subsample (but not as large as indicated by human judges) of truthful stories is closer to the truth center than to the deceptive one. However, it seems that RST-VSM methodology overestimates the levels of deception in the truthful stories compared to human judges

Overall, however, the RST-VSM analysis demonstrates a positive support for the proposed hypothesis. The apparent and consistent closeness of deceptive stories to RST deception center (compared to the closeness of the deceptive stories to the truthful center) and truthful stories to RST truthful center can indicate that the relations between discourse constituent parts differ between truthful and deceptive messages. Thus, since the truthful and deceptive relations exhibit systematic differences in RST space, the proposed RST-VSM methodology seemed to be a prominent tool in deception detection. The results, however, have to be interpreted with caution, since the sample was very small, and only one expert conducted RST coding.

The discussion, however, might be extended to the case, where the assumption of self-ranked levels of deception and truthfulness do not hold. In this case we still suspect that even deceptive story might contain elements of truth (though much less), and the truth story will have some elements of deception. RST-VSM analysis demonstrated greater levels of deception in truth and deceptive stories compared to the human judges. This might indicate that RST-VSM potentially offers an alternative to human judges way of detecting deception when it is least expected in text (as in the example of supposedly truthful stories) or detecting it in a more accurate way (if some level of deception is assumed as in the completely deceptive stories). The advantage of RST-VSM methodology is in its rigorous and systematic approach of coding discourse relations and their subsequent analysis in RST space using vector space models. As a result, the relations between units exhibiting different degrees of salience in text because of writers' purposes with their subsequent readers' perceptions become indicators of diversity in deception levels.

Conclusions

To conclude, relations between discourse parts along with its structure seem to have different patterns in truthful and deception stories. If so, RST-VSM methodology can be a prominent way of detecting deception and complementing the existing lexical ones.

Our contribution to deception detection research and RST twofold: a) we demonstrate that discourse structure analysis and pragmatics as a promising way of automated deception detection and, as such, an effective complement to lexico-semantic analysis, and b) we develop the unique RST-VSM methodology of interpreting RST analysis in identification of previously unseen deceptive texts.

Acknowledgments

This research is funded by the New Research and Scholarly Initiative Award (10-303) from the Academic Development Fund at Western.

References

Bachenko, J., Fitzpatrick, E., and Schonwetter, M. 2008. Verification and implementation of language-based deception indicators in civil and criminal narratives. In *Proceedings of the 22nd International Conf. on Computational Linguistics.*

Baeza-Yates, R. and B. Ribeiro-Neto. 1999. *Modern Information Retrieval.* New York:Addison-Wesley

Buller, D. B., and Burgoon, J. K. 1996. Interpersonal Deception Theory. *Communication Theory, 6*(3), 203-242.

Berkhin, P. 2002. Survey of Clustering Data Mining Techniques. DOI: 10.1.1.18.3739.

Blimes, J. A. 1998. *A Gentle Tutorial of the EM Algorithm and Its Application to Parameter Estimation for Gaussian Mixture and Hidden Markov Models*: Univ. of California, Berkeley.

Cadez, I. V, Gaffney, S. and P. Smyth. 2000. A General Probabilistic Framework for Clustering Individuals and Objects. In *Proceedings of the 6th ACM SIGKDD International Conference on Knowledge Discovery and Data Mining.*

DePaulo, B. M., Charlton, K., Cooper, H., Lindsay, J. J., and Muhlenbruck, L. 1997. The Accuracy-Confidence Correlation in the Detection of Deception. *Personality and Social Psychology Review, 1*(4), 346-357.

Frank, M. G., Paolantinio, N., Feeley, T., and Servoss, T. 2004. Individual and Small Group Accuracy in Judging Truthful and Deceptive Communication. *Group Decision and Negotiation, 13*, 45-59.

Fuller, C. M., Biros, D. P., and Wilson, R. L. 2009. Decision support for determining veracity via linguistic-based cues. *Decision Support Systems 46*(3), 695-703.

gCLUTO: Graphical Clustering Toolkit 1.2. Dept. of Computer Science, University of Minnesota.

Hair, J.F., Anderson, R.E., Tathman, R.L. and W.C. Black. 1995. *Multivariate Data Analysis with Readings*. Upper Saddle River, NJ: Princeton Hall.

Hancock, J. T., Curry, L. E., Goorha, S., and Woodworth, M. 2008. On lying and being lied to: A linguistic analysis of deception in computer-mediated communication. *Discourse Processes, 45*(1), 1-23.

Indyk, P. 1999. A Sublinear- time Approximation Scheme for Clustering in Metric Spaces. In *Proceedings of the 40th Annual Symposium on Foundations of Computer Science.*

Karypis, G. 2003. Cluto: A Clustering Toolkit. Minneapolis: Univ. of Minnesota, Comp. Sci. Dept.

Mann, W. C., and Thompson, S. A. 1988. Rhetorical Structure Theory: Toward a Functional Theory of Text Organization. *Text, 8*(3), 243-281.

Manning, C.D. and H. Schutze. 1999. *Foundations of Statistical Natural Language Processing*. Cambridge, MA: MIT Press.

Mihalcea, R., and Strapparava, C. 2009. The Lie Detector: Explorations in the Automatic Recognition of Deceptive Language. In *Proceedings of the ACL*, Aug. 2-7, Singapore.

Pennebaker, J., and Francis, M. 1999. *Linguistic inquiry and word count: LIWC.* Erlbaum Publisher

Porter, S., and Yuille, J. C. 1996. The language of deceit: An investigation of the verbal clues to deception in the interrogation context. *Law and Human Behavior, 20*(4), 443-458.

Rasmussen, M. and G. Karypis. 2004. gCLUTO: An Interactive Clustering, Vizualization and Analysis System. *UMN-CS TR-04-021.*

Rose, K. 1998. Deterministic Annealing for Clustering, Compression, Classification, Regression, and Related Optimization Problems. In *Proceedings of the IEEE 86(11).*

Rubin, V.L. 2010. On Deception and Deception Detection: Content Analysis of Computer-Mediated Stated Beliefs. In *Proceedings of the American Soc. for Information Science and Tech. Annual Meeting,* Oct. 22-27, Pittsburgh.

Rubin, V.L., and Conroy, N. 2011. Challenges in Automated Deception Detection in Computer-Mediated Communication. In *Proceedings of the American Soc. for Information Science and Tech. Annual Meeting,* Oct. 9-12, New Orleans.

Rubin V.L., Conroy, N. 2012. Discerning Truth from Deception: Human Judgments and Automation Efforts. *First Monday 17*(3), http://firstmonday.org

Salton, G. and M.J. McGill. 1983. *Introduction to Modern Information Retrieval.* New York: McGraw-Hill.

Scholkopf, B. and A. Smola. 2001. *Learning With Kernels*. Cambridge, MA: MIT Press.

Strehl, A., Ghosh, J. and R. Mooney. 2000. In *AAAI Workshop of Artificial Intelligence for Web Search,* July 30, 58-64.

Taboada, M. 2004. *Building Coherence and Cohesion: Task-Oriented Dialogue in English and Spanish*. Amsterdam, Netherlands: Benjamins.

Taboada, M. and W.C. Mann. (2006). Rhetorical structure theory: looking back and moving ahead. Discourse Studies, 8(3), 423-459.

Tombros, A. 2002. *The effectiveness of query-based hierarchic clustering of documents for information retrieval.* PhD dissertation, Dept. of Computing Science, University of Glasgow.

Vapnik, V. 1998. *Statistical Learning Theory*. NY. Wiley.

Vrij, A. 2000. *Detecting Lies and Deceit*. NY: Wiley.

Zhong, S. and Ghosh. J., 2004. A Comparative Study of Generative Models for Document Clustering. In *SIAM Int. Conf. Data Mining Workshop on Clustering High Dimensional Data and Its Applications.*

Zhou, L., Burgoon, J. K., Nunamaker, J. F., and Twitchell, D. 2004. Automating Linguistics-Based Cues for Detecting Deception in Text-Based Asynchronous Computer-Mediated Communications. *Group Decision and Negotiation, 13*(1), 81-106.

Appendix A. Sample RST Analysis.

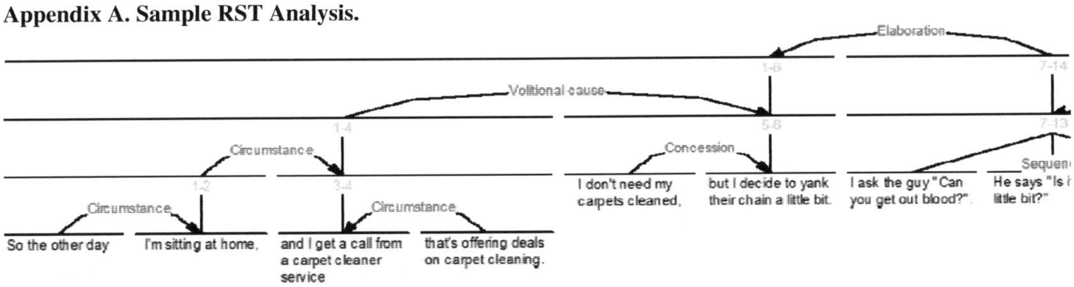

Appendix B1. Distributions of Expected Levels of Deception and Truthfulness in Deceptive Stories.

Legend: ▲ **Expected level of Deception (Judges);** ▬ **Expected Level of Truthfulness (Judges)**

— RST Level of Deception; - - RST Level of Truthfulness (transformed to the interval (0,1) with 0 min)

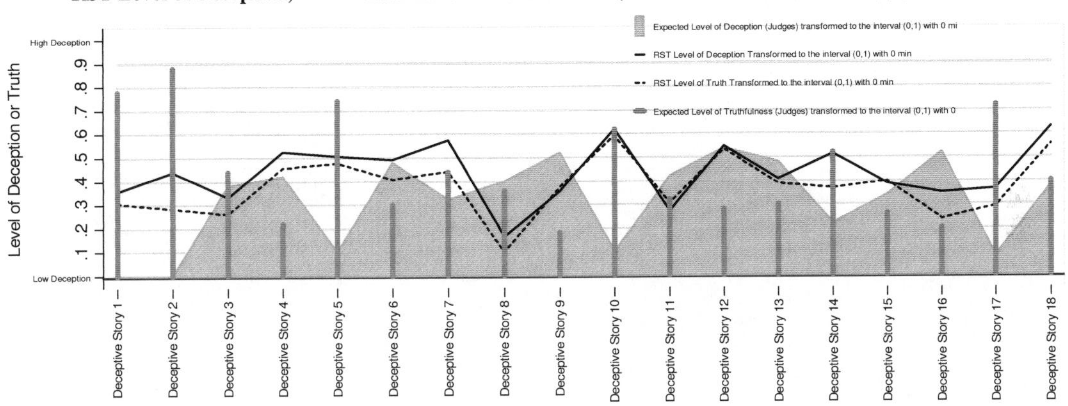

Appendix B2. Distributions of Expected Levels of Deception and Truthfulness in Truthful Stories.

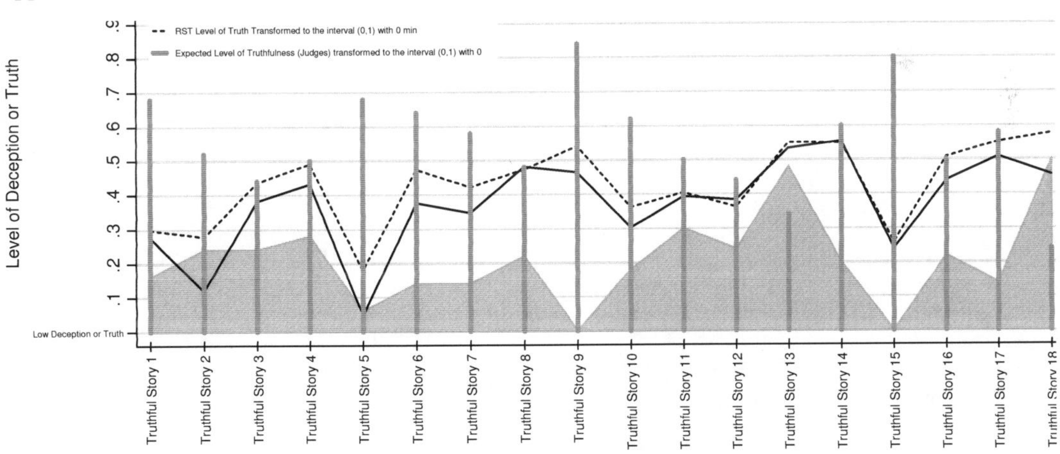

Appendix C. Comparison of the Normalized Frequencies of the RST Relationships in Truthful and Deceptive Stories: Difference in Means Test.

RST relationships appearing in truthful and deceptive stories with **NO** statistically significant differences	RST relationships appearing in the truthful stories with statistically significantly **GREATER** normalized frequencies than the deceptive ones	RST relationships appearing in the truthful stories with statistically significantly **LOWER** normalized frequencies than the deceptive ones
Background, Circumstance, Concession, Condition, Conjunction, Elaboration, Enablement, Interpretation, List, Means, Non-volitional cause, Non-volitional result, Purpose, Restatement, Sequence, Solutionhood, Summary, Unconditional	Antithesis (t=2.3299) Evidence (t=3.7996) Joint (t=1.5961) Volitional cause (t=1.8597) Volitional result (t=1.8960)	Preparation (t= -1.7533) Evaluation (t= -2.0762) Disjunction (t= -1.7850)

Appendices D1 –D4. Distribution of Deception and Truthfulness Levels for Deceptive Stories

D1. Distribution of Deception Level (Judges)

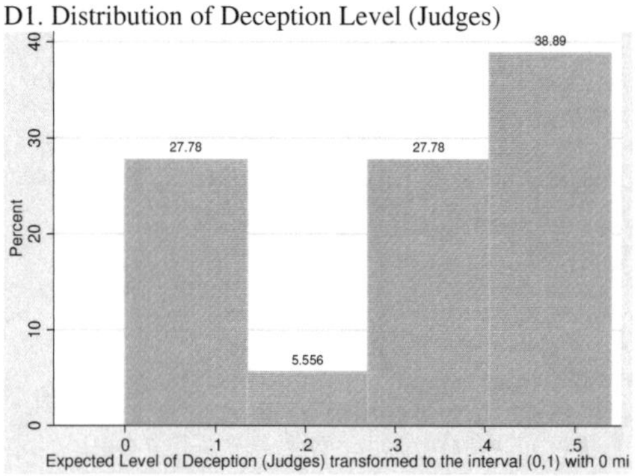

D2. Distribution of Truthfulness Level (Judges)

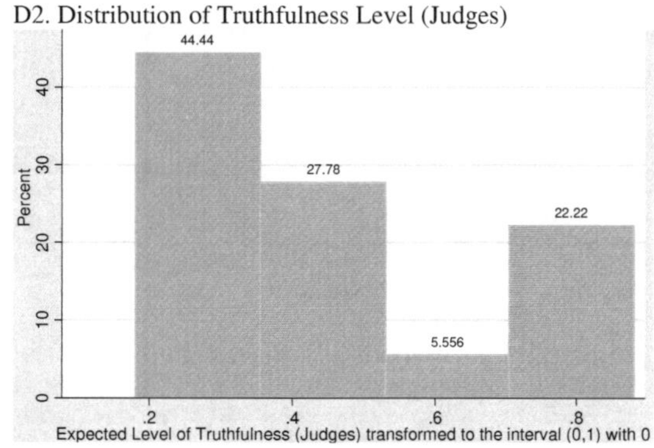

D3. Distribution of Deception Level (RST)

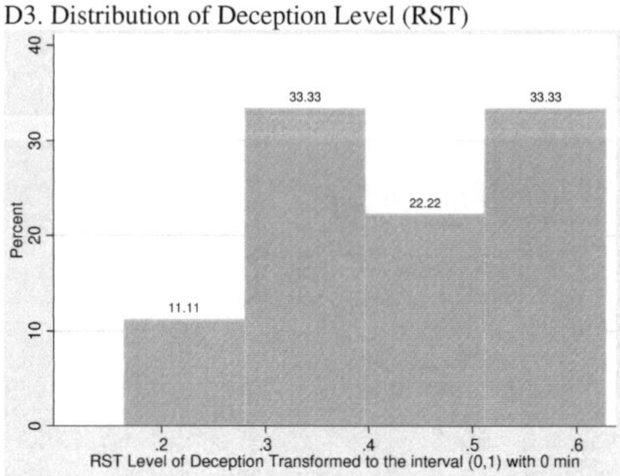

D4. Distribution of Truthfulness Level (RST)

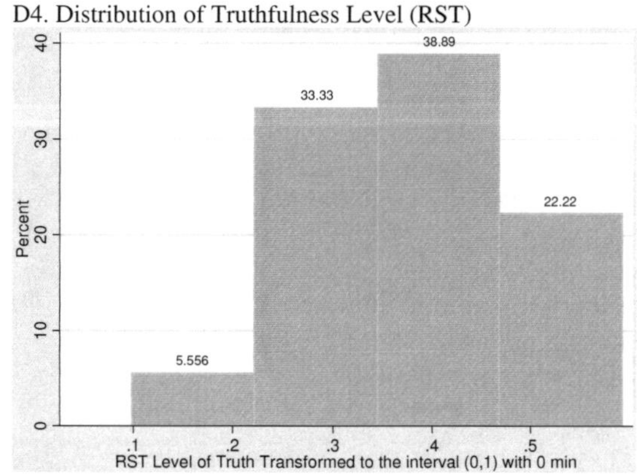

Appendices E1-E4. Distribution of Deception and Truthfulness Levels for True Stories

E1. Distribution of Deception Level (Judges)

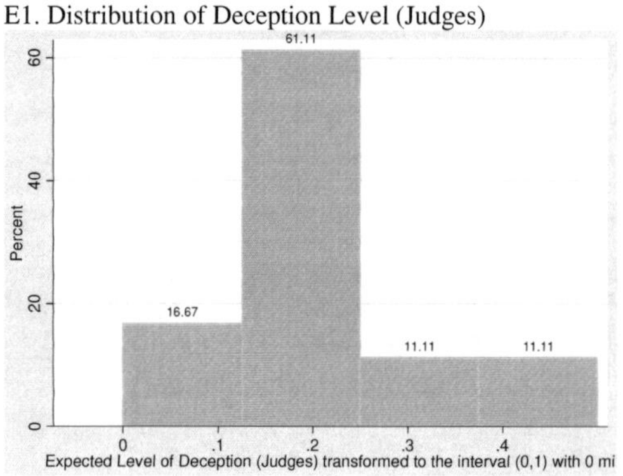

E2. Distribution of Truthfulness Level (Judges)

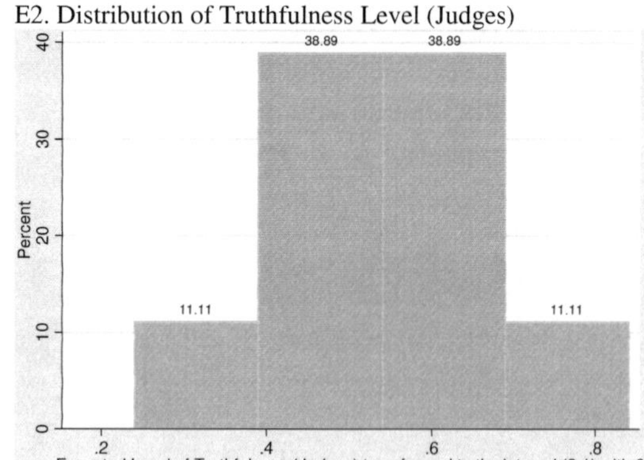

E3. Distribution of Deception Level (RST)

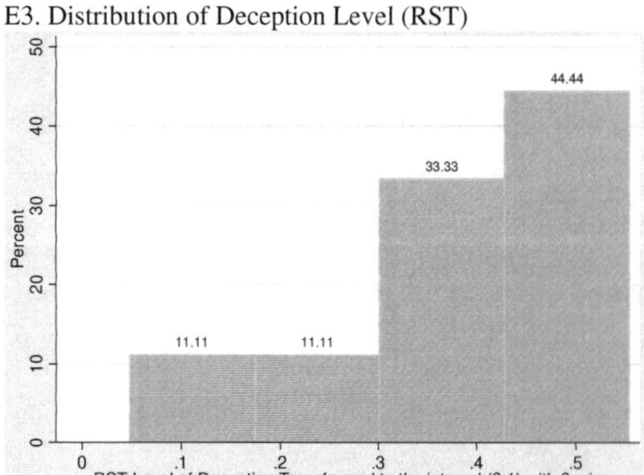

E4. Distribution of Truthfulness Level (RST)

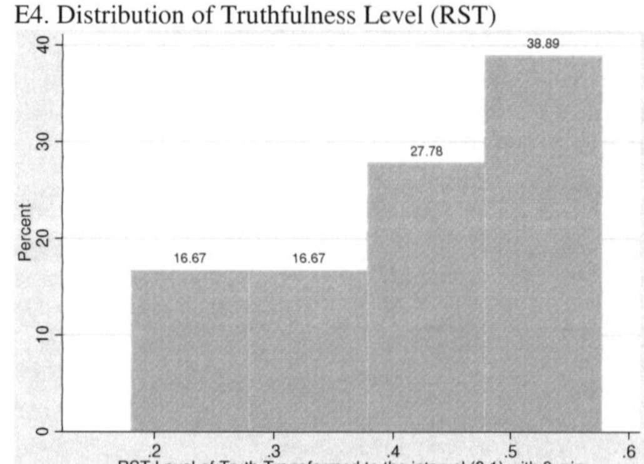

Author Index

Almela, Ángela, 15

Bachenko, Joan, 31
Baxter, Daniel, 48
Blandón-Gitlin, Iris, 1
Bogdanova, Dasha, 86

Cantos, Pascual, 15
Cardie, Claire, 23

Derrick, Douglas, 49
Dinu, Liviu P., 72

Elkins, Aaron, 49

Fitzpatrick, Eileen, 31
Fornaciari, Tommaso, 39

Gariup, Monica, 49
Gillam, Lee, 5
Gokhman, Stephanie, 23

Hancock, Jeff, 23
Hauch, Valerie, 1

Juola, Patrick, 91

Li, Deqing, 63

Masip, Jaume, 1

Niculae, Vlad, 72

Ott, Myle, 23

Poesio, Massimo, 39
Prabhu, Poornima, 23

Rosso, Paolo, 86
Rubin, Victoria L., 97

Santos, Eugene, 63
Solorio, Thamar, 86
Sporer, Siegfried Ludwig, 1, 78
Sulea, Maria-Octavia, 72
Swerts, Marc, 55

Valencia-García, Rafael, 15
Vartapetiance, Anna, 5
Vashchilko, Tatiana, 97